THE CHARACTER OF THE EURIPIDEAN HIPPOLYTOS

Scholars Press
Studies in the Humanities

Suicide	John Donne William A. Clebsch, editor
Tragedy as a Critique of Virtue: The Novel and Ethical Reflection	John D. Barbour
Lyric Apocalypse: Reconstruction in Ancient and Modern Poetry	John W. Erwin
The Unusable Past: America's Puritan Tradition, 1830 to 1930	Jan C. Dawson
The Visual Arts and Christianity in America: The Colonial Period through the Nineteenth Century	John Dillenberger
Chaos to Cosmos: Studies in Biblical Patterns of Creation	Susan Niditch
Melville and the Gods	William Hamilton
The Character of the Euripidean Hippolytos: An Ethno-Psychoanalytical Study	George Devereux

THE CHARACTER OF THE EURIPIDEAN HIPPOLYTOS
An Ethno-Psychoanalytical Study

George Devereux

Scholars Press
Chico, California

THE CHARACTER OF THE EURIPIDEAN HIPPOLYTOS
An Ethno-Psychoanalytical Study

George Devereux

Publication of this book was made possible in part
by a gift to Scholars Press from Barbara S. Boyle
in memory of her grandfather
Frederick W. Shipley, a classicist
and her father
Walter C. Shipley, a psychologist

© 1985
George Devereux

Library of Congress Cataloging in Publication Data

Devereux, George, 1908–
 The character of the Euripidean Hippolytos.

 (Scholars Press studies in the humanities series ; no. 8)
 Bibliography: p.
 Includes index.
 1. Euripides. Hippolytos. 2. Hippolytos (Greek deity)
in literature. 3. Psychoanalysis and literature. 4. Sex in
literature. I. Title. II. Series: Scholars Press studies in the
humanities series ; no. 8.
 PA3973.H7D48 1985   882'.01   85-11779
 ISBN 0-89130-789-3

Printed in the United States of America
on acid-free paper

To
Geoffrey Gorer
in admiration and friendship

CONTENTS

Preamble *ix*
Acknowledgements *xi*
Bibliographic Notice *xi*

Introduction *1*

1. Gender and Fantasy *19*
2. Hippolytos and Theseus *59*
3. Hippolytos' Merits and Phaidra's Love *85*
4. Hippolytos' Diagnosis *115*
5. Epilogue *141*

Appendix I: Seneca *155*
Appendix II: Phaëthon *157*
Index *159*

PREAMBLE

Some years ago a most distinguished psychoanalyst wrote to me as follows about my book *From Anxiety to Method in the Behavorial Sciences* (1967): "It is necessary reading for all analysts, even those who think there is nothing more to analysis than its practice. I know of no other work in our field that is so precise, original, and important in contributing to the essence of analysis, which is not its private practice but its contribution to psychology. It must be better known."

In my reply I mentioned that the book was written between 1935 and 1938. Unfortunately, my talking about it only persuaded my professors that I was a freak. Moreover, for thirty years, no one would so much as look at the MS.

My eminent correspondent answered as follows: "I was fascinated and disturbed by the unhappy history of *From Anxiety to Method*. I am not surprised that you had difficulty in getting it published, for I am sure that had I been a referee many years ago, I would also have been confused and put off by it. I have learned so much from it and so much enjoyed your case illustrations only because of the many years in which others have written enough that we can catch up with what you were saying so long ago. I presume that I would have been, back then, so unsophisticated about countertransference and even more so about its relationship to methodology (whether in psychoanalysis or in the other behavorial sciences) that I would not have tried to read what in those days would have been difficult."

This quotation is the corner-stone of my Preface. All my life my work has been swept at once under the rug, because I was steadily twenty years or more ahead of my time. For brevity's sake, chronological evidence supporting this claim is adduced in a footnote.[1]

---

[1] (1) *Reality and Dream* (New York, 1951) was rapidly remaindered. It was reprinted in 1969 and has long been o.p. It is now available (1982) in French and about to come out in German.

(2) *Psychoanalysis and the Occult* (New York, 1953), an anthology with two long chapters by me (opposed to parapsychology), was soon remaindered, but reprinted in 1970.

(3) *A Study of Abortion* (New York, 1955) was quickly remaindered. It was reprinted, with a new chapter, in 1976.

(4) *Therapeutic Education* (New York), published in 1956 and soon remaindered. It is the only one of my older books not yet reprinted.

(5) *Mohave Ethnopsychiatry* could be published in 1961 only as an uncopyrightable royalty-less *Bulletin of the Bureau of American Ethnology*. There has been since one authorized, augmented reprint (1969) and an unauthorized (commercial) reprint of the (uncopyrightable) first edition, in 1974.

The data given in this footnote speak for themselves: until quite recently I have been talking to the deaf. My career (if it can be called one) matched the late recognition of my work. Not once, since I took my Ph.D. (1935), did I have a position guaranteed for more than one year, nor was I ever fully accepted into the hallowed precincts of Academe. In fact, I taught myself the Greek alphabet at age 55 precisely because I had despaired of ever getting a hearing from the anthropologists. It is characteristic of my lifelong insecurity that in the spring of 1981 (at age 73) it suddenly occurred to me that, for the first time in my life, my future was guaranteed, albeit on the very modest level of old-age Social Security checks. But, at 76, I am still like Thoukydides' Athenians: I will give peace neither to others nor to myself.

I made no concessions nor compromises at a time when I was literally starving. I will make none today when, thanks to old-age Social Security, I know where my next meal will come from.

For the same reason I am not prepared to offer an apology for once more applying psychoanalysis to classical studies. The willfully ignorant, the prejudiced, the intellectually dishonest and plain damn fools deserve no attention. I have written a book I believe in. I am confident that if it is not accepted today, it will, like my earlier books, be accepted twenty or thirty years hence.

For those who are open to new truths, I present my *Hippolytos* as a new paradigm of construction in the study of great literature. A substantial part of the *Introduction* is devoted to the problem of what is and what is not present in a literary masterpiece.

---

(6) *From Anxiety to Method* (Paris and The Hague) was published, after a thirty-year wait, in 1967. It is now translated into German (regular and pocket book), French, Spanish, Italian.

I then published two volumes of my *formerly totally ignored*—i.e., hardly ever cited—theoretical papers in a French revision. The first (1970) is now in its fifth French printing and was translated into English, German, Spanish, Italian. The second (1972) is also available in English, German, Spanish, and Italian.

A collection of essays, *Tragédie et Poésie Grecques*, was published in 1975 (Paris).

Dreams in Greek Tragedy, published both in England (Blackwell: Oxford) and in America (Berkeley: University of California), has been reissued in paperback and has appeared in German.

Baubo, though written in French, first appeared in German (1981); the French edition appeared in 1983, the Spanish in 1984.

Femme et Mythe, 1982. Published in Italian, 1984; German and Japanese rights sold.

ACKNOWLEDGEMENTS

I am indebted to Professor Charles P. Segal of Brown University for a consistently critical reading of this book's penultimate draft and for many post-1962 references. As a result of his suggestions, I rewrote various passages in which, meaning to criticize some of Hippolytos' modern encomiasts,* I *seemed* to condemn—and not just diagnose—that dramatic personage.

I am indebted to the Fritz Thyssen Foundation of Cologne (West Germany) for a grant which enabled me to put this work and also some others in shape for publication.

* E.g., A. J. Festugière, *L'enfant d'Agrigente*, Paris, 1950; id., *Personal Religion Among the Greeks*, Berkeley, CA, 1954.

BIBLIOGRAPHIC NOTICE

At the time this book was first drafted, I knew only the relevant books and papers of E. R. Dodds, H. E. Barnes, H. D. F. Kitto, G. M. A. Grube, D. Grene, I. M. Linforth, E. M. Blaicklock, L. Méridier, and A. J. Festugière. The texts I used were those of Méridier and W. H. Barrett. After reading the penultimate draft, Prof. Charles P. Segal attracted my attention to most of the literature published in the last fifteen years and put photocopies at my disposal. Prof. Hans Herter sent me his paper "Hippolytos und Phaidra," and Prof. Walter Burkert his paper "Greek Tragedy and Sacrificial Ritual." I was glad to discover that a number of papers[1] published since I prepared the first draft confirm many of my earlier conclusions.

[1] A. V. Rankin, "Euripides' Hippolytos: A Psychopathological Hero," *Arethusa* 7: 71-94, 1974; J. Glenn "The Fantasies of Phaidra," *The Classical World* 69: 435-42, 1976; J. J. Smoot, "On a Vase-Painting: A Clearer Picture of Euripides' 'Hippolytos,'" *Comparative Literature Studies* 13: 292-303, 1976 (chiefly on the poor contact between father and son); C. Segal, "Pentheus on the Couch and on the Grid," *Classical World* 72: 129-48, 1978.

INTRODUCTION

The present work is primarily a clinical analysis of Euripides' characterization of his "second" Hippolytos, and of its consequences for the surviving drama that bears his name.

I propose to demonstrate Euripides' psychological acumen in terms of clinical and ethnological experience, systematized by means of classical psychoanalytic theory, which is universally valid, since it always both demands and permits a complementary ethnological analysis.[1]

Though I also seek to increase the reader's understanding of Greek creativity by going to the Greeks, instead of bringing them to us, I do not engage primarily in literary criticism but in pan-human ethnopsychoanalytic research. Mankind is one *precisely because* it can cast Greek, French, or Hottentot shadows, and my concern is not with the shadow but with the substance.

It seems unnecessary to restate here my justification for this approach to Greek tragedy. The reviews of the book in which I originally put it forth[2] showed that the openminded needed no formal justification. But they demonstrated also that the very cogency of my approach drives "the unregenerate, unanalyzed and unanalyzing tribe of classical scholars" (E. R. Dodds) to venomous sarcasm and even to cynical distortions of facts and of statements.

A major difficulty in discussing this play is that its focal problem, sexuality, tends to be discussed in "moral" terms which often causes matters of considerable importance to be overlooked. Thus, the correspondence between the slave's advice to Hippolytos to give Aphrodite her due (88ff.) and the Nurse's warning Phaidra not to provoke Aphrodite by being refractory to her will (473ff.) is mentioned—if at all— only in passing. Hippolytos' repression of his sexual drive and his consequent self-praise increase as the play develops, while Phaidra's suppression (deliberate inhibition) of her sexual urge remains constant in *this* play.[3] When her passion for Hippolytos, revealed by the Nurse, is vehemently rejected by the young

---

[1] G. Devereux, *Ethnopsychoanalysis*, Berkeley, 1978.
[2] G. Devereux, *Dreams in Greek Tragedy*, Oxford and Berkeley, 1976.
[3] In the lost *Hippolytos*, Phaidra's inhibitions were too weak to control her passion: she herself approached Hippolytos.

man, her one thought is to save her good name and to destroy the credibility of Hippolytos, whose angry outburst (612) makes her believe that he would betray her secret to Theseus. This parallelism is crucial, because precisely the latent affinities between the character of Hippolytos and of his antagonist Phaidra make the *Hippolytos* a masterpiece.

Worse still, in the *Hippolytos* sex is seemingly treated in terms of a value system not only historically remote from the modern critic[4] but also inseparable from personal experiences. Hence, one can study objectively only the manner in which the drama handles this problem psychologically, particularly since few critics state their own value-criteria openly.[5]

Tongue in cheek, Winnington-Ingram is an exception to this rule. He defines the problem with the wit, urbanity, and accuracy one has come to expect from him: "I am rather frightened of the subject; it can rouse strong emotions. Those to whom, by reason of temperament or religion, Hippolytus makes a strong appeal may resent an account of him which appears detached and at some points critical. . . . Did Hippolytus die in some degree a martyr to his own idea of himself? I shudder away from this hypothesis."[6]

Inspired by Winnington-Ingram's example, I intended to be as objective as the child in the tale of the *Emperor's New Clothes*: not breaking taboos (thereby indirectly admitting their continued sway) but by ignoring them. I confess myself Empedoklean (Freudian)[7] in my conception of Aphrodite, and Homeric in my reverence for her lovely works. But I can do so only if my concern here is not some (arbitrary) hierarchy of "moral" values. It is psychologically that I must examine the *Hippolytos'* most controversed aspect: sexuality—a topic about which it is almost impossible to be objective.[8] Indeed, like all basic drives, it is not rational[9] and also non-communicable; accounts of the experience of both need and gratification are not self-resonantly perceived.[10]

---

[4] On short range changes of attitude toward sex (Aristophanes to Plato) cf. K. J. Dover, "Eros and Nomos," *Bulletin of the Institute of Classical Studies* 11:31-42, 1964.

[5] Gilbert Norwood (*Greek Tragedy*[4], London, 1953, p. 209) uses prudent parentheses: "Hippolytus errs (in Greek eyes) by his complete aversion from sexual passion." But Jean Racine—a good Hellenist—left well enough alone for, though pious, the poet in him did not hate and despise the very source of life and creativity: his hero is in love with Aricie.

[6] R. P. Winnington-Ingram, in *Euripide, Entretiens Hardt*, vi, Vandoeuvres, 1960, pp. 186-87.

[7] The Empodoklean Aphrodite is Freud's Eros; cf. Emp. *frr.* 71-75, 98, 128, 151 D.-K. The Nurse (359-60) is a pragmatic if somewhat vulgar Empedoklean.

[8] G. Devereux, *From Anxiety to Method*, op. cit., 1967, chap. 9.

[9] H. Hartmann, "On Rational and Irrational Action," in G. Róheim (ed.), *Psychoanalysis and the Social Sciences*, i, New York, 1947.

[10] G. Devereux, *From Anxiety to Method*, op. cit.

Introduction 3

An even greater problem results from the current complacent conviction that we are sexually "liberated," though we have preserved the pathological separation between love and sex, and have simply inverted their valuation.[11] This point is crucial.

In my view *Hippolytos rejects sex because it is inseparable from love*. Like many neurotics on the analytic couch, he can neither love nor bear being loved. It matters, in my opinion, that whereas the Euripidean Hippolytos has many philological encomiasts, not one of them *loves* him the way G. W. F. Hegel loved the "heavenly Antigone."

Euripides himself, who shows affection and compassion not only for Herakles and his friend Theseus, for Andromache and the captive Trojan women, and even for the raving Orestes and his sister Elektra, seems to remain aloof from Hippolytos, perhaps because all that is *valuative* in the treatment of sex ultimately derives from the myth,[12] and the myth called only for a chaste hero—*not* for a pathologically sex phobic one. The Biblical Joseph, quite as much as Bellerophontes, Peleus, and others, loved and married precisely because they were genuinely virtuous. It is from Euripides' *Stheneboia* that we learn that love leads to wisdom, virtue, and poesy, and that stupid women—the kind Hippolytos prefers to wise ones (638ff.)—dishonor their husbands.[13] If, as seems probable, the *first* characterization of the (veiled) Hippolytos (foil to a brazen Phaidra) was derived from the myth,[14] in that play the youth was probably chaste, not sex phobic—a point I will take up again later.

In short, the chitchat about Hippolytos' "chastity" is Orwellian "newspeak,"[15] resembling much modern sexual research in its shortsighted preoccupation with *manifest behavior only*. Chastity—a psychological concept—concerns physical acts only incidentally. Before Plato it denoted mature and disciplined—because loving—*positive* sexual conduct. In E. *Hipp*. 11, Aphrodite—herself *hagne*,[16] as is also Eros (E. *fr*. 269.2)—approvingly calls the venerable Pittheus "chaste."

In short, that Aphrodite—who is hardly chaste—is called *hagne* is of some moment, for Hippolytos claims to be *hagnos* chiefly because of his sexual abstinence. This point matters for, contrary to what is often

---

[11] As a young woman put it: the word "love" is no longer acceptable in terms of the "nouvelle pudeur."
[12] Also intimated by D. Grene, "The Interpretation of the *Hippolytus* of Euripides," *Classical Philology* 34: 45–58, 1939, esp. p. 49.
[13] E. *Sthen. frr.* 672, 663; 662 N² (cf. also, on X. *Cyr.* 3.1.8-10, K. Gaiser, "Griechisches und christliches verzeihen," in W. Kraus et al. [eds.], *Latinität und alte Kirche*, 1977, p. 79).
[14] This hypothesis is plausibly presented by Barrett, op. cit., p. 11. Cf. also his comments on Sophokles' *Phaidra*, ibid.
[15] G. Orwell, *1984*, New York, 1949.
[16] L. Preller and C. Robert, *Griechische Mythologie*, 1.348.2, Berlin.

alleged, the epithet *hagne* is *not* attested for *all* female deities. Hera and Hestia are nowhere so called.[17] Even Hippolytos admits Phaidra's chastity (1034ff.). The Choros even invokes the graces—who favor love and marriage—on the Grace-less Hippolytos' behalf (1140 ff.). Hippolytos' revulsion of incest and adultery is primary in the myth; it is secondary in the drama, which is dominated by his sex-phobia[18] and in which the doubly unlawful nature of the temptation tends to obscure, for the non-clinician, the real nature of Hippolytos' neurosis.

Sexual decency, like cleanliness, is of course "next to godliness." But the sex-phobic Hippolytos is no more "chaste" (sexually decent) than a mysophobic compulsive handwasher is "clean." Both are driven by an irrational dread of (symbolic) dirt.[19] The *rest* of the compulsive handwasher's body is, moreover, often quite as dirty as the sex-phobic's mind.

Euripides gave a new psychological meaning to the myth in devising his second (*crowned*) *Hippolytos*. Euripides—*not* the myth—made sex phobia Hippolytos' last ditch defense against atypical oedipal anxieties.[20] The Nurse's incestuous-adulterous procuring did not mobilize Hippolytos' *nominal* chastity, but his *real* sex phobia. The (recorded) public outcry at Athens against the first *Hippolytos*—which, like the myth—depicted a brazen Phaidra and a truly chaste Hippolytos, inspired Euripides' psychologically penetrating, and therefore necessarily also artistically brilliant, solution of turning a myth of chastity into the tragedy of self-destructive, sex-phobic narcissism. For the psychoanalyst, Hippolytos is silent not because of his oath but because Phaidra's accusation is psychologically true, though "displaced."[21]

This matter is of some importance. Euripides apparently did not rewrite any of his other failed dramas to please the public. In fact, criticism only seems to have made him more persistent in his ways.[22] In this

---

[17] Cf. C. F. H. Bruchmann, *Epitheta Deorum*, Leipzig, 1893.
[18] Grene, op. cit., pp. 46, 49, sensed this; L. H. G. Greenwood, *Aspects of Euripidean Tragedy*, Cambridge, 1953, pp. 46–47, did not.
[19] Religious "cleansing" material is usually "dirty" (Heraclit. *fr.* 5 D.-K.): pig's blood in Greece, cow's urine in India, and (*intentionally disgusting*) emetic concoctions among the Kikuyu. For the legitimacy of this comparison, cf. S. Freud, "Obsessive Actions and Religious Practices," *Standard Edition*, ix, London, 1959. Blaiklock (op. cit., p. 40) misuses the psychoanalytic technical term "sublimation," on which see K. A. Menninger, *Love against Hate*, New York, 1942; G. Róheim, "Sublimation," *Psychoanalytic Quarterly* 12: 338–52, 1943; F. Déri, "On Sublimation," *Psychoanalytic Quarterly* 8: 325–34, 1939.
[20] A *painter* dreamed of intercourse with his stepmother; in reality he quarrelled with his father, Artemid. 4.20. Cf. Hippolytos' reactions to erotic *pictures*, discussed below (verses 1004ff.).
[21] I use "displaced" in its technical sense: a man who inhibits, suppresses, or represses his anger toward his boss may beat his wife or his child or kick his dog.
[22] Had he reacted *exclusively* to criticism, he would probably have done what Romain Rolland's Jean-Christophe did, when his works were booed; he would have contemptuously played "Malbrouk s'en va-t'en guerre," for a public unable to appreciate anything better.

case, however, he apparently wrote a radically new *Hippolytos*—not a "second" (bowdlerized) one, because he had evolved *a new conception* of both Phaidra and Hippolytos. This means that, precisely because his first Hippolytos was presumably sexually decent, his second one had to be something else; and this "something else" could only be a neurotic sex-phobic. I might add that, in my estimation, the tradition[23] suggesting that public outcry induced Euripides to write a "second" Hippolytous also precludes the supposition tht he meant this time to idealize the young man.[24]

Indeed, for a scandalously brazen Phaidra a genuinely "chaste" (sexually decent) Hippolytos is the natural counterfoil. But for a virtuous Phaidra, who refuses to yield to her passion (1034f., etc.), the only proper counterfoil is *not* a *chaste* youth but a *sex-phobic* one. Only in *that* case does the "distance" between the two antagonists remain constant and unbridgeable. There is, however, more to this. It means that Euripides created, with that clearsightedness that either love or hate can inspire, an unpleasant deviant type akin to Shakespeare's Richard III, Milton's Satan, and El Greco's Cardinal Inquisitor—a tragic, because self-destructive, being at once dazzling, *unlikable, and—(for that reason)—pitiable*; alone, because aloof from "imperfect" mankind. Psychoanalysis has done more than religion or ethics, though less than the arts, to show that this is the essence of tragedy. On the simply human level, Hippolytos is unmasked, condemned, but also illuminated by Euripides' compassionate and inflexibly clinical portrayal.

In short, Hippolytos' character has been so consistently appraised in terms of anachronistic value-scales that, be it but to clear away the smoke-screen, I must discuss it purely as a craftsman of psychology, if only as a first step toward the formulating of a truly balanced overall view. One must approach a great work of art armed with all the scientific understanding one can muster so that, in the end, one can commune with the greatness that the human mind attains only when it contemplates its own smallness.

The main culture-linked difficulty of making a non-superficial, non-behavioristic analysis of Hippolytos' personality is the nature of his chief phobia: his negative obsession with sex. This difficulty even certain Hellenists living in our (allegedly) sexually "liberated" world—of which more anon—failed to overcome. Some discuss Hippolytos' "chastity" (sex phobia) as though male virginity had been a Periklean—or mythical—moral value. Worse still, not one critic of the *Hippolytos* known to me

---

[23] Argum. of E. *Hipp.*; inexplicably H. D. F. Kitto, *Greek Tragedy* (paperback ed.), London, 1954, p. 213 (note), casts doubt upon this tradition.
[24] "We know nothing of the poet's treatment of (the first) Hippolytus, save that he was given his traditional chastity" (Barrett, op. cit., p. 11).

troubles to explain just *what* is so admirable about sexual abstinence. This matter will be taken up in due time. My task at this juncture is to explain the anxiety-arousing character of sex and to state my position regarding it.

It cannot be said clearly enough that the *Hippolytos* is about love-and-sex. Eros being indivisible, both terms refer to the same thing as, according to the "double language hypothesis,"[25] "psyche" and "soma" are two ways of talking about the same entity.

Eros being already sublime, it cannot (by abstinence or otherwise) be further sublimated;[26] only aggressivity—when cybernetically controlled by Eros—is sublimable.[27] Surgery is a sublimation of aggressivity, not of Eros: it is a substitute for murder but not for love-making.[28]

That the "moral" value of Hippolytos' dread of sex should still be an issue in an age of ostentatious sexual "liberation" does, however, require comment. I hold that in our world there has only been an affective neutralization of Aphrodite, leading to bored fornication, and a contamination of Eros with aggression, producing perversions. Instead of a liberation of love there is a defensive *de*-sublimation of Eros, laced with a "philosophy" of misogynous eroticism of a type peddled first by the "divine Marquis" (de Sade) and now by militant feminists of either—or no—sex.

The polar opposite of Hippolytos is not Don Juan; the opposite of both is incarnated in Andromache and Hektor.[29]

Now, a key difficulty in appraising any major work of art is its inexhaustibility. That word may mean several things: that one can constantly discover new things in a text; that it is a riddle whose elusive solution one can approximate in *several* ways but never quite pin down, that the work is ambiguous, in Empson's sense;[30] or even that it is polyvalent: that it has several—at times mutually exclusive—*precise meanings*. Last of all, great works of art, like oracles, may not only be regularly misunderstood,[31] but their primary purpose may be to *be* "misunderstood," for oracles substitute to a puzzling but meaningful reality-problem a verbal rebus inherently devoid of sense.

As stated elsewhere,[32] belief in oracles involves the erroneous (implicit) assumption that their utterances are not only meaningful, but have

---

[25] C. K. Ogden and I. A. Richards, *The Meaning of Meaning*^{2}, New York, 1927.
[26] K. A. Menninger, *Love against Hate*, 1942.
[27] Eros + aggressivity + dagger = surgery; aggressivity + scalpel = murder.
[28] G. Devereux, *Tragédie et Poésie Grecques*, 1975 (chap. 1); id., *Dreams in Greek Tragedy*, 1976 (General Introduction).
[29] Hom. *Il.* 6.400–502.
[30] William Empson, *Seven Types of Ambiguity*^{3}, Cleveland, 1964.
[31] O. Fenichel, "The Misapprehended Oracle," *The Collected Papers of O. Fenichel*, vol. 2, New York, 1954.
[32] G. Devereux, *Dreams in Greek Tragedy*, p. 51.

one real meaning only. Yet no oracle has a "real," *inherent* meaning other than that which its client ascribes to it, in accordance with his own subjective needs, fears, and inclinations.[33]

One other a priori possibility is that a *major* work of art may have no meaning *at all*—in the sense in which oracles have none. This possibility is best disregarded.

Modifying slightly my earlier views,[34] I now feel that a great work of art is a kind of Rorschach test, while lesser ones, including folk tales (Linton, personal communication), are more akin to the Thematic Apperception Test. The controversy raging over whether Euripides' *Bakchai* is, or is not, "religious" supports this view.[35]

Of course, a work of art cannot be interpreted any way one pleases, just as there is a limit to what a *non*-psychotic is likely to see in a Rorschach card. What the critic sees in it must, to start with, make sense in terms of his *explicitly* stated (and justified) scientific approach.

I therefore challenge, for example, Festugière's conception of a Hippolytos purer than Ivory Soap,[36] because his appraisal of Hippolytos is based not on a *refutable* system of thought (science, or logic and epistemology), but on an inherently irrefutable "revealed" value system.

By contrast, I explicitly state the criteria on which my appraisal of Hippolytos' personality is based. Moreover, one of my main principles is that no strictly univocal ("objective") vision of a major work of art is possible, for "art" is not an object of perception but one of intertwined, multiple *patterns of meaning*. The same is true of what makes *genus homo* human—for man, more even than major works of art, is inexhaustible. In fact, a work of art is, in a sense, *made* inexhaustible by being subjected to a variety of approaches. The more that diversified (*non*-absurd) interpretations of a work of art are possible, the more certain is its status as a major work of art.

I must now specify just what inferences and constructions may be advanced without unduly "straining" the text while still exploiting what, in terms of clinical psychoanalysis, seems an inescapable conclusion. Lest it be urged that Euripides had not read Freud, I will reply that people

---

[33] Cf. also G. Devereux, "Considérations psychanalytiques sur la Divination, Particulièrement en Grèce," in J. Caquot and M. Leibovici (eds.), *La Divination*, vol. 2, Paris, 1968, pp. 449-71.

[34] Cf. G. Devereux, *Tragédie et Poésie Grecques*, 1975, chaps. 1, 4, and 8.

[35] The comments of E. R. Dodds (*Euripides: Bacchae*[2], Oxford, 1960, p. xlviii, note 3) make it clear that Gilbert Norwood was a fool *neither* when he wrote a first interpretation of that play (G. Norwood, *The Riddle of the Bacchae*, Manchester, 1908) *nor*, decades later, when he published his second thought (G. Norwood, *Essays on Euripidean Drama*, Berkeley, 1954).

[36] A. J. Festugière, *L'Enfant d'Agrigente*, 1950; id., *Personal Religion among the Greek*, 1954.

made slips of the tongue long before Freud explained their causes.

This raises an important question: *What is really in the Play?* Any novel interpretation of a major literary work is rejected by some on the grounds that the critic discusses not, e.g., Aischylos' or Shakespeare's drama but what he read into it. It is my thesis that any interpretation based on a scientific—i.e., refutable[37]—system can offer valid new insights. The following example will show this.

An experienced psychoanalyst told me that he had a dream which he could not interpret: "My dream concerned three fishes in a bowl, named Mark, Matthew and Luke." I asked him at once "How about John?" My startled colleague replied, "Now I understand the dream: it is about someone called John." In terms of the psychoanalytic system of interpretation I had adopted, John was *present* in the dream, precisely because, his *absence* was both *conspicuous* (three out of the four evangelists; fish = Christ) and *explicable*. It sufficed to recognize the *Prägnanz* of the system used in dream.[38]

My basic hypothesis is that Euripides' Hippolytos is a clinically well-described and well-defined *character neurotic*. Any hint of the text which fits this hypothesis may therefore be used as confirmatory material. I specify that the hint may be quite small, for the concise Greek drama cannot elaborate psychology in the manner of a novel.

Summing up, then, in characterizing Hippolytos, Euripides created a system or configuration endowed with *Prägnanz*. Any element fitting that configuration (character neurosis) and perhaps even providing its cloture element is therefore by definition *in* the play.[39]

A few additional remarks are in order concerning material found in the myth but not (explicitly) in the drama.

Elements of the myth that underlies the drama must be treated as part of the drama, even when the dramatist *deliberately* modified them. For the myth plays, with respect to the drama, the role the "day residue," already understood by Aristotle (*Insomn.* 3, 461a14ff.), plays in the dream. One example suffices to prove this:

In myth, Deianeira is warlike and virile. In his *Women of Trachis*

---

[37] Sir Karl Popper is mistaken in claiming that psychoanalysis is not refutable and therefore not scientific.

[38] The omission was a means of negating John's existence—for the unconscious is not capable of *direct* negation (S. Freud, "Negation," *Standard Edition*, xix, 1961.

[39] I note in passing that the so-called Pötzl effect (O. Pötzl, "Experiementell erregte Traumbilder in ihren Bezichungen zum indirekten Sehen," *Zeitschrift für die gesamte Neurologie und Psychiatrie* 37: 278–349, 1917) also supports the views just expressed. For the role of *Prägnanz* and of the cloture element in psychoanalytic interpretation, cf. G. Devereux, "Some Criteria for the Timing of Confrontations and Interpretations," *International Journal of Psycho-Analysis*, 32: 19–24, 1951, reprinted in Paul Louis (ed.), *Psychoanalytic Clinical Interpretation*, New York, 1963.

Sophokles first turned her into a gentle Athenian lady . . . and then canceled his innovation by a *second* one.⁴⁰ In myth, the virile Deianeira hangs herself in a properly feminine manner; in Sophokles she kills herself like a man, with the sword. Psychoanalysis calls this the "return of the repressed."⁴¹

The myth is, thus, a constant presence in the poet's mind and hence also in his drama. For man is a chronoholistic system, whose behavior at any moment (drama) can be understood only in terms of his *entire life history* (myth and earlier dramas).⁴²

Diagnosis versus Name-Calling

The Euripidean Hippolytos has countless encomiasts. His flaws, if mentioned at all, are systematically minimized. To make matters worse, non-psychologists tend to mistake the identification and description of a symptom or pathological character trait for moral blame. This misapprehension is especially common in the case of a character neurotic like Hippolytos, for it is all but impossible to appraise certain of his symptomatic character traits—e.g., his arrogance—in morally neutral terms.

I state once and for all that a psychiatric diagnosis is not a form of name-calling: I have not devoted years of research to finding flaws in a figment of Euripides' imagination. Anyone unable to comprehend this simple fact will not comprehend what this book is about.

I make a major issue of this matter, for one or two readers of earlier drafts of this book seem to have felt that my defining Hippolytos as a character neurotic (etc.) constitutes a moral condemnation or even a kind of slander. Now, a diagnosis is simply the technical designation of certain forms of deviant behavior, exactly as the diagnosis "tuberculosis" designates a deviant state of the body. Yet, not so long ago, "tuberculosis" was a "shameful" illness.

It would be *absurd* to "insult" a figment of Euripides' imagination It is a scientifically valid undertaking to determine the type of deviant character Euripides devised for his personage. The finding that the type of psychological disorder Euripides outlined frequently manifests itself in objectionable behavior is predictable. All psychological disorders are, by definition, "socially negativistic."⁴³

In short, though often objectionable, Euripides' neurotic Hippolytos is no more "bad" than a dog suffering from rabies is "vicious." I conclude

---

⁴⁰ A similar doing-undoing occurs when a second parapraxis "undoes" (rectifies) an earlier lapsus. Cf. G. Devereux, "Orthopraxis," *Psychiatric Quarterly* 42: 726–37, 1968.
⁴¹ G. Devereux, *Tragédie et Poésie Grecques*, 1975, chap. 5.
⁴² F. G. Donnan, "Integral Analysis and the Phenomena of Life (i + ii)," *Acta Biotheoretica* 2: 1–11, 3: 43–50, 1936/1937.
⁴³ G. Devereux, *Basic Problems of Ethnopsychiatry*, Chicago, 1980 (chap. 3).

by noting that, contrary to the belief of some critics, the Greek poet need not "love" the principal personage of his play or novel. Already W. Schmid[44] saw that Euripides could not possibly have been in sympathy with his Hippolytos; nothing further need be said on these matters.

The Clinical Approach

The Clinical Approach is justified by Plato's (*Rmp.* 3.8, p. 396a) and Ps.-Longinos' (*de sublim.* 15.3ff.) references to the excellent representation of abnormality in Greek tragedy. The views of modern dissenters[45] may be safely disregarded, for psychologically sophisticated philological research[46] confirms the views of Ps.-Longinos.

As regards the opponents of psychoanalysis, their footless but vehement aggressivity only confirms the theories they reject and therefore deserves no further consideration.[47]

I propose in particular to show that: (1) Euripides devised a recognizable clinical type; the Hippolytos he described is a complex narcissistic character neurotic (*not*: psychotic), with schizoid, paranoid and phobic traits. (2) The pattern he outlined is both complete and coherent: nothing expectable is missing from it; nothing system-alien is added to it. (3) The deeper processes *inferable* from the text fit the psychoanalytic theory of that disorder.

Since the mythical Hippolytos may never have lived, I study exclusively Euripides' "case report" and conclude that the probability of its coherence and appropriateness being due to chance is, for practical purposes, nil.

I will now highlight my modus operandi by contrasting my symbolic (non-metaphoric) interpretations of two elements of this play with the metaphorical ones of various literary critics. This comparison is (1) of the word λειμών = meadow (verses 74 and 210), and (2) of the horse-frightening bull emerging from the sea.

In this play, λειμών is said to represent the female pubis. The question is the identity of the person to whom this pubis belongs. According

---

[44] *Geschichte der griechischen Literatur*, 1.3, 382, Munich, 1929.
[45] T. von Wilamowitz-Moellendorff, *Die dramatische Technik des Sophokles*, Berlin, 1917; W. Zürcher, *Die Darstellung des Menschen im Drama des Euripides*, Basel, 1947.
[46] S. Bezdechi, "Das psychopathische Substrat der 'Bacchantinnen' Euripides,'" *Archiv für die Geschichte der Medizin* 25: 279-306, 1932; E. R. Dodds, "Euripides the Irrationalist," *Classical Review* 43: 97-104, 1929 (= *The Ancient Idea of Progress*, Oxford, 1973); E. M. Blaiklock, *The Male Characters of Euripides*, Wellington, N.Z., 1952; B. Simon, *Mind and Madness in Ancient Greece*, Ithaca, NY, 1978.
[47] B. M. W. Knox, "Clytemnestra on the Couch," *Times Literary Supplement*, 10 December 1976 (pp. 1534-35); cf. G. Devereux, *Dreams in Greek Tragedy*, ibid., 1 April 1977 (p. 403).

Introduction

to A. V. Rankin[48] at verse 74 this meadow symbolizes Artemis' genitals, though Hippolytos hardly realizes it. At 210f., according to B. M. W. Knox,[49] λειμών necessarily refers to a pubis, for κομήτης λειμών (tufted, grassy) clearly recalls "pubic hair" (Ar. *Lys.* 827). J. Glenn[50] marshals both psychoanalytical and classical evidence in support of the symbolic equations: meadow = pubis, tree = penis. Unfortunately he concluded that verses 210ff. refer to Phaidra's pubis. If so, the metaphor gets out of hand. After drinking from a dewy fountain (i.e., supposedly Hippolytos' semen), Phaidra wants to "rest" (to gain relief), lying *in* or *on* her *own* pubis. Fortunately, the matter can be disposed of simply by recalling that the married Phaidra's pubis would be *depilated*. This means that at verse 74 the untouched grassy meadow can only be the *non*-depilated pubis of the traditionally "virginal" (or unwed) Artemis. As in modern Islam, the Greek virgin's pubis was first depilated just before her wedding: a shaven pubis betokened sexual availability.[51]

No interpretation may read more into this passage than an allusion to female sexuality and perhaps even to some hidden nexus between Artemis' non-depilated and Phaidra's depilated pubis (Glenn, op. cit.). Glenn's view, that Phaidra's wish to drink from a spring represents a desire to fellate Hippolytos, is probably too literal. Psychosexually immature women often experience coitus regressively as a form of vaginal nursing at the penis.[52]

The fact that she wishes to drink from the spring, when the tall trees around her supposedly symbolize Hippolytos' phallos, further complicates matters, and this despite fairly common fantasies of the reciprocal convertibility of vulva and phallus.[53]

The only way out is to hold that, at verse 210 too, the tufted meadow is Artemis' virginal pubis. If so, Phaidra unconsciously fantasizes about coitus with Hippolytos, not only in Artemis' wild woods but (perhaps spitefully) on the very lap of her divine rival. I have documented the occurence of such fantasies in the clinic, in obscene jokes and in erotic literature as well. Sexual "sandwich" or "millstones" fantasies are commonly met with in neurotics; they even determine the

---

[48] "Euripides' Hippolytos, a Psychopathological Hero," *Arethusa* 7: 72-93, 1974.
[49] "The Hippolytus of Euripides," *Yale Classical Studies* 13, 1952 (p. 6). Cf. C. P. Segal "The Tragedy of Hippolytus," *Harvard Studies in Classical Philosophy* 70, 1965.
[50] "The Fantasies of Phaidra: A Psychoanalytic Reading," *Classical World*, 435-42, 1970.
[51] In Ar. *Lys.* 825ff., an old woman boasts that her pubis is still singed clean—thus indicating that she is sexually still active or at least available.
[52] As belief among the Mohave Indians in the case of pregnant women, cf. G. Devereux, "Mohave Paternity," *Samiksa: Journal of the Indian Psycho-Analytic Society* 3: 162-94, 1949. As neurotic fantasy in a woman patient, G. Devereux, "Mumbling," *Journal of the American Psychoanalytic Association* 14: 478-84, 1966.
[53] G. Devereux, *Baubo: Die mythische Vulva*, 1981 = *Baubo, La vulve mythique*, 1983.

layered character of space in Euripidean dreams.[54] I must note, however, that apart from Euripidean dreams (two of which are attributed to female personages), most fantasies in which one millstone is male and the other female are those of male subjects.[55] In female subjects the fantasy often implies a simultaneous penetration of the anus and of the vagina by two men.[56]

In short, if the meadow of verse 210 stands for Artemis' pubis, one must suppose also—and this is unacceptably farfetched—that Phaidra (spitefully?) fantasizes about cohabiting with Hippolytos on the very lap of her divine rival.[57]

In discussing the λειμών problem, I dealt with fantasies imputable to Hippolytos and to Phaidra. Matters are different when we come to the bull from the sea and to Hippolytos' runaway team. Though the fright of the horseman notoriously affects also his horse(s),[58] several authorities hold that the runaway team[59] stands for Hippolytos' sexuality. Another author views the sea as the incarnation of the protagonist's sexual drive.[60] To my mind both these psychological interpretations concern not (the Euripidean) Hippolytos' intrapsychic imagery and symbolization; they concern the poet Euripides' *own* imagery only, and presuppose a nexus between the panic of the horses and the panic (or distress) of their driver.

These two examples suggest—though imperfectly—the *sense* in which this book is chiefly a clinical study of the Hippolytos Euripides had devised, and also clarifying in part the difference between clinical-symbolic and literary-metaphorical interpretative approaches. I also indicated that psychoanalytically fanciful (off the cuff) "interpretations" often have quite absurd implications.

Projection

A novel feature of my analysis is the demonstration that the personages of this tragedy are linked to each other in a manner which has

---

[54] G. Devereux, *Dreams in Greek Tragedy*, Oxford and Berkeley, 1976, chap. 8.
[55] G. Devereux, *Ethnopsychoanalysis*, 1978, chap. 7.
[56] Hearsay tales to the contrary notwithstanding, this is anatomically impossible, unless one of the men is a hip amputee. In beliefs and superstitions which involve double penetration, the male is the devil, who has two penises for just that purpose.
[57] This has an odd—if male—equivalent in reality. The male wildebeest ("gnu"), victorious in his fight for a female, can copulate with her only *in the presence* of his defeated rival.
[58] X. *Eq.* 6.13f., 9.11.
[59] Knox, Segal, Rankin, opp. cit.; J. J. Smoot, "On a Vase Painting, a Clearer View of Euripides' Hippolytus," *Comparative Literature Studies* 13: 292-303, 1976.
[60] R. P. Winnington-Ingram, "Hippolytus, a Study in Causation," in *Euripides*, Fondation Hardt, vi, Vandoeuvres, 1960.

hitherto received little attention. My approach to these linkages is partly derived from the finding that, in analyzing A's interaction with B, one must take into account also A's awareness (or notion) of how B sees him and his accommodation to his conviction that B sees him in that particular way. (The same is, of course, true also of B.)

Expressed more rigorously, the psychoanalytic concepts of transference and countertransference necessarily presuppose that in an interaction, A will function at least partly as a projection of B's fantasies, and vice versa.[61] This differs somewhat from mere role-playing, because the role played is (at times unconsciously) felt to correspond to the Other(s)' fantasy.

I therefore believe that the psychological appreciation of the *Hippolytos* is quite incomplete until the complex network of fantasy projections, identifications and even appersonations[62] which link the various principal personages is carefully analyzed.

In concrete terms, each major personage in the *Hippolytos* can be viewed (also) as a projection of some other major personage's fantasy. This is particularly true of the personalities of Hippolytos and of Phaedra, whose interrelationship—though basically defined by the myth and by the drama's plot—are determined in far-reaching ways by each of the two being also a fantasmatic projection of the other.

I particularly stress that where a mediocre author devises his personages—or takes them over from some earlier source—*singly*, and then simply juxtaposes or opposes them *in action*, each of a great poet's personages is not only the poet's *own creature*, but also the *fantasmatic projected creature* of his other personages. It is this that gives great drama the cohesion and structural "organic" tautness, which mere dramaturgical sophistication cannot begin to approximate.

Though I believe this *analysis* of the *network* linking *literary* personages to be novel, it admittedly owes a slight debt to the "social psychology" of George Herbert Mead,[63] which takes into account both A's awareness (or notion) of how B sees him and his accomodation to his awareness (or notion) that B sees him in a particular way.

---

[61] Helene Deutsch, "Occult Processes Occurring During Psychoanalysis," in G. Devereux (ed.), *Psychoanalysis and the Occult* (New York, 1953, 1970 [chap. 12]), calls this "the complementary role." On the complementary role which natives foist upon the field worker, cf. G. Devereux, *From Anxiety to Method*, Paris and The Hague, 1967. For the subsequently narcissistic child, see now Alice Miller, *Das Drama des begabten Kindes*, Frankfurt am Main, 1979.

[62] O. E. Sperling, "On Appersonation," *International Journal of Psycho-Analysis* 25: 128–32, 1944.

[63] G. H. Mead, *Mind, Self and Society*, Chicago, 1934.

Hippolytos and the Traditional Tragic Hero

In Greek tragedy, most psychologically perturbed individuals have "symptom-neuroses."[64] Hippolytos' psychopathology is, however, of a different type. Except for his sex-phobia (and whatever else is directly related to it) he is practically symptom-free, though the over-all structure of his personality is deeply disturbed; he is, in essence, a narcissistic character neurotic. That disorder is fairly common in persons who had the type of infancy and childhood,[65] which the myth of the bastard Hippolytos makes probable. In early childhood such persons were not loved for their own sakes—for what they *were*—but only for their *adult*-gratifying performances, for what they obediently *did*. Hippolytos clearly grew up to be a model *child*, developing an "as if" personality, a "spurious self."[66]

Now, since the "good child" behavior of a chronologically adult individual is often particularly exasperating to those who, in childhood, had directly or indirectly exacted it from the subject, the perennial "model child" can neurotically turn his formerly rewarded "goodness" into a permanent source of irritation to those who made him into what he now is.[67] Hippolytos' numerous aggrieved references to his forebears, his bastardy, and his early life may therefore be veiled reproaches addressed at his elders—chiefly at Hippolyte and Theseus.

It is of great historical interest that similar character neurotics are found also in other Euripidean plays. Their list includes Dionysos and Pentheus, whose affinities with each other *and* with Hippolytos are well brought out by Segal.[68] The temple boy Ion (like Hippolytos, a rejected bastard); the egotistic Admetos, son of selfish parents; Helene, who claims to have acted under divine (external) compulsion; Medeia in her insanely self-righteous moments; even Iphigeneia, perhaps made cruel by her homicidal sacrifices, as well as the suicidally murderous Elektra, Eteokles, and Polyneikes—all are characterized by the periodic eruption of a (usually self-destructive) narcissism.

It is, in short, striking that Euripides should have put on the stage so many narcissistic character disorders, whose aetiology and dynamics psychoanalysis is just beginning to explore.

---

[64] But I concur with E. M. Blaicklock, *The Male Characters of Euripides*^{2}, Wellington, 1952, that the Euripidean Herakles is an epileptic. B. Simon, *Mind and Madness in Ancient Greece*, Ithaca, NY, 1978, p. 304, n. 21, disagrees.
[65] A. Miller, *Das Drama des begabten Kindes*, Frankfurt am Main, 1979.
[66] W. D. Winnicott, *Collected Papers*, London, 1958; H. Kohut, *The Analysis of the Self*, New York, 1971; M. R. Khan, *The Privacy of the Self*, London, 1974.
[67] This maneuver was particularly obvious in a young adult male, whom I had in psychoanalytic treatment some decades ago; cf. G. Devereux, *Basic Problems of Ethnopsychiatry*, Chicago, 1980, chap. 12.
[68] C. P. Segal, "Pentheus and Hippolytus on the Couch and on the Grid," *Classical World* 72: 138–48, 1978.

Introduction 15

Summing up, Hippolytos is misunderstood if one believes him to be psychotic ("insane") and equally misunderstood if the severity of his narcissistic character disorder is underestimated. Psychologically oriented dramatic criticism must therefore bear in mind that he is similar to the many other narcissistic tragic personages whom Euripides put on the stage.

Post-Scriptum

As noted before, W. Schmid[69] saw that Hippolytos was a type Euripides knew and was interested in, since his Ion is a similar, if softer and more priestly type. But the similarities of Hippolytos with the Euripidean Achilleus also deserve attention (*Iphigeneia in Aulis*).

In the beginning of the scene in which Achilleus meets Klytaimestra (who sees in him Iphigeneia's betrothed) he harps just a little too often on his purity and on his modesty in the presence of women (verses 821f., 830, 834 [touch], 839f.). But, from verses 919 to 931, Achilleus' self-praise is continuous. At verses 940f. he even feels that his body (!) has been soiled: it is no longer pure (ἁγνόν). At verses 958ff. he proclaims that ten thousand (?) girls are eager to wed him. At verse 973f. he (somewhat ambiguously but "modestly") asserts that he is either already a god, in that he is Klytaimestra's and Iphigeneia's savior, or else that if he is no god yet, he will become one.

But, after trying to change the army's mind, the tune is different. From verse 1349 onward one hears mostly the shocking news that he, the great Achilleus, had risked being stoned for his pains. At verse 1358 he is, however, once more decided to defend the women.

But it does not come to the acid test. At verse 1551 Iphigeneia consents to being sacrificed—partly because she feels that Achilleus alone cannot save them. Were he to try, the outcome would be the same for them; worse still, the fight could sully Achilleus, fair name and fame. Verse 1394 oddly echoes Achilleus' claim of being desired by *ten thousand* girls; Iphigeneia asserts that one man is worthier to look at the light—to be alive—than *ten thousand* women.

Her speech earns her the highest praise Achilleus can bestow. He declares that a wife like Iphigeneia would be worthy of him! Since her death would be *his* sorrow, he once more offers to fight for her life. Predictably, Iphigeneia refuses the offer; Helene's actions will already cause too many Greek deaths.

Achilleus declares once more his readiness to fight for her; should she change her mind even at the last moment, he will go armed to the temple, to stand by, just in case.

[69] *Geschichte der griechischen Literatur*, 1961 (1.3 p. 382).

16   Character of the Euripidean Hippolytos

Later, in the Messenger's account, there are other slight echoes of the *Hippolytos*. Iphigeneia asks not to be held fast by any Argive—she promises to hold still (1559ff.) while they cut her throat. The last and principal echo is, however, found in verse 1522: Artemis is called "Queen of the gods" (θεῶν ἄνασσαν).

These findings reveal some affinities between Hippolytos and Achilleus. Both are totally narcissistic: they claim to be better, purer, more admirable than other men. The problems of others matter only insofar as they also effect their name and fame. Last, but not least: only in *Hippolytos* and in *Iphigeneia in Aulis* (1522) is Artemis viewed as supreme amongst the deities. This fact too reveals a deep affinity between the heroes of the two plays.

The "Villain"

Tragedy is hard to imagine without at least one evil—or at least dangerously warped or flawed (*hamartia*)—personage, not necessarily onstage,[70] who—intentionally or unwittingly—is the "cause"[71] of the tragic happening. Of course, matters are never cut and dried, for great tragic poets dramatize neither fairy-tale virtue nor penny-novelette villainy. Hence, for some, the villain of the *Agamemnon* is (paradoxically) not Klytaimestra but Agamemnon—a view incompatible with Greek values, though compatible with the ideology of "modern" feminist literary criticism.[72]

Few Euripidean dramas have easily identifiable "villains";[73] hence one's choice is more difficult in most of Euripides' other plays. Thus, in his *Elektra*, Klytaimestra is a retired murderess, who only tries to forget, while Elektra is a potential terrorist. The *Bakchai* is particularly problematic in this respect. Though she slew her son, Agave is not evil. Kadmos and Teiresias are only small-time hypocrites. The choice between Dionysos and Pentheus is likely to be made in terms of the reader's preconceptions and biases.[74]

In this respect, the *Hippolytos* has certain affinities with the *Bakchai*.

---

[70] In Aischylos' *Prometheus Bound*, the evil principle is represented by the tyrannical Zeus and his "lackeys."
[71] I use "cause" here in the sense of A. W. H. Adkins, *Merit and Responsibility*, Oxford, 1960.
[72] Ph. Vellacott, "Has Good Prevailed?" *Harvard Studies in Classical Philology* 81: 113-22, 1977.
[73] Exceptions: *Andromache* (Menelaos), *The Children of Herakles* (Eurystheus), *Hekabe* (Polymestor), *Herakles* (Lykos), *Ion* (Apollon), *Iphigeneia in Aulis* (possibly Menelaos), *Kyklops* (Polyphemos), *Medeia* (Iason, but perhaps also Medeia), *The Suppliant Woman* (Theban Herald), *The Trojan Women* (Greeks).
[74] For me, the villain is Dionysos who, unlike the Aphrodite of the *Hippolytos*, is not only a force but also a genuine person.

Through no fault of her own, Phaidra's divinely-willed destructive love and her struggle against it drives her out of her mind. True, her letter falsely accuses Hippolytos of rape—but she wrote it because she had every reason to fear that, despite his oath, Hippolytos would denounce her (G12).

The Nurse cannot incarnate evil, for she simply puts people above principles. Aphrodite is an even more impersonal force than is the Zeus of Aischylos' *Prometheus*. Also, Hippolytos notoriously and gratuitously defied the goddess, long *before* the latter decided to retaliate. Artemis, the "subhuman goddess" (Kitto), is even more impersonal than Aphrodite and her decision to avenge Hippolytos' death by slaying Aphrodite's beloved befits a Mafioso.

This leaves only Theseus and Hippolytos to choose from, as tainted by *hamartia*. For our society, that demonstrates its undiminished Pauline sex-hatred precisely by claiming to be "liberated," the heterosexual amorist Theseus is obviously the "flawed" person. That he founded democratic Athens, upheld justice throughout Hellas and remained the symbol of hope for the oppressed predictably means little to those whose sole standard of value is the "purity" of the crotch. Critics therefore (falsely) accuse him of intemperateness as a father, of procedural irregularities as judge, and even of recent (!) adultery. For it is an "embarrassing" fact that Hippolytos can be exalted *only* if Theseus is somehow degraded. Whether the Athenian audience viewed Euripides' Theseus as flawed and then awarded the first prize to an eccentric poet who in an unprecedented manner (allegedly) depicted as foolish and offensive the greatest of Athens' heroes, is another matter, to which some thought *might* be given—but is not!

Summing up: (1) Few Euripidean plays have an unmistakable "villain." (2) In the remaining plays the reader's preconceptions decide which of two personages is the source of evil. (3) In the *Hippolytos*, if one takes fifth-century B.C. Athenian values into account, the flawed personage is Hippolytos, not because he is vicious but because—being a sex-phobic, narcissistic character neurotic—he would provoke tragedies in *any* setting in which he happened to find himself.

The Hippolytos as Futurology

Since I have claimed that Euripides was a perspicacious clinical observer,[75] I must indicate *what* he had observed in this instance. His Hippolytos seems to be based on the observation of a nascent type of misfit, originating in times of severe crisis.[76] He observed the first

---

[75] Cf. E. *fr.* 292 N² (*Bellerophontes*) on the physician's duty to observe.
[76] On Hippolytos as a social type, cf. also D. Grene, op. cit., p. 51, and T. B. L. Webster, *An Introduction to Sophocles*, Oxford, 1936—though their attitude toward this type

"orphics"; the Athenian equivalents of our own assorted postwar freaks—as exhibitionistically asocial as the worst Cynics, only turned upside down.

Though Plato and his circle eventually came to idealize this type, that does not mean that Euripides, too, admired it. All I need to indicate here is that Euripides identified and described this personality type the year Plato was born. The poets ability to notice the first ravages of social dry rot appears to exceed that of philosophers and scientists. They are sensitive to the *direction* of impending social change—not because, as Oscar Wilde claimed, "Life imitates Art," but because, like psychoanalysts uncontaminated by metaphysical pretensions and by a trivial sociologism (or culturalism), they respond to the latent content of messages. It is well to recall here that Freud himself repeatedly conceded that the poets had anticipated many of his discoveries.

Yet, few clinicians realize that many of their patients—and especially the narcissistic character neurotics they analyze—are premature social "mutants." A quarter of a century later many once self-confessedly "sick" patients would be recognized as "group ideals"[77] and their symptoms viewed as tokens of their (ideologically defined) "health," as "sane" reactions to a "sick society."

In a society on the decline, the poets recognize in certain of their character neurotic contemporaries the group-ideals of the future. The futurological analysis of great literary works must therefore be assigned a high priority in social research. The second Euripidean Hippolytos, an "orphic" quasi-Platonist, is also a forerunner of the ashram-dwelling psycho-terrorists of our age.

differs from mine. At any rate oracle mongers, beggar priests, and types like Pereginos and Alexandras of Abonoutychos always existed. I deem it possible that, in his *Clouds*, Aristophanes correctly portrayed the Athenian "lunatic fringe," which *may* have *claimed* to follow Sokrates; even in modern universities such disciples are the bane of any teacher of new ideas. On the "Teddy-boys" of antiquity, cf. Apul. *Met.*, Aug. *Conf.*, Procop. *Hist. Arc.* 7; those mentioned by Prokopios even wore "zoot-suits."

[77] G. Róheim, "Psychoanalysis of Primitive Cultural Types," *International Journal of Psycho-Analysis* 13: 1–224, 1932; cf. W. LaBarre, "Social Cynosure and Social Structure," *Journal of Personality* 14: 169–83, 1946 (also, in idem, *Culture in Context*, Durham, NC, 1980).

1

Gender and Fantasy

The Masculinity of Hippolytos

Hippolytos' masculinity is the first of his character traits that I must examine. The crux of the play being the "chastity" of Hippolytos, his maleness is obviously a key element, for the term "chastity" has no meaning when applied to a sexless amoeba. The problem must be analyzed in terms of gender as well as in terms of sex.[1]

The basic finding is that the masculinity of Hippolytos, horseman and hunter, as such is never questioned. I propose to show, however, that—figuratively speaking—he rides side-saddle: as a horseman, his model is the Amazon, not the charioteer Iolaos; as a hunter, his model is Kallisto, not Meleagros or Herakles.

Psychologically, a male's self-definition has two components: "I have male organs" and "I cohabit with women."[2] In Hippolytos' case, the second component is lacking.[3] This however, is an aside. My main initial concern is not Hippolytos' psychological "maleness," but his socio-cultural "gender" masculinity. The definition of the male gender stereotype varies, of course, from culture to culture. A Hopi Indian may consider the Navaho Indian somewhat non-masculine, because the latter does *not* weave; the Navaho presumably considers the Hopi non-masculine because he *does*.[4] Hence, a boy can become socio-culturally "masculine"

---

[1] R. J. Stoller, *Sex and Gender*, vol. I, New York, 1968.

[2] R. R. Greenson, "On Homosexuality and Gender Identity," *International Journal of Psycho-Analysis* 45: 217–19, 1964.

[3] Festugière (op. cit.) did not strengthen his questionable argument that Hippolytos is very young (supra) by urging that he is in the latency period or at least fixated at that stage. Indeed, many a boy between five and thirteen seeks to "save" his penis by renouncing its functioning (Freud, "Three Contributions," op. cit.). However, most Greeks were *not* fixated in the latency period, but in the early post-pubertal stage; cf. G. Devereux, "Greek Pseudo-Homosexuality," *Symbolae Osloenses*, op. cit. I add that, like many other strict Freudians, I do *not* accept Freud's paleobiological (ice-age) theory of the origins of the latency period: it is due to cultural pressures (G. Devereux, "The Primal Scene and Juvenile Heterosexuality in Mohave Society," in G. B. Wilbur and W. Muensterberger [eds.], *Psychoanalysis and Culture* [Róheim Festschrift], New York, 1951).

[4] My American field data are exactly duplicated by my Reungao Moi (males are weavers) vs. Sedang Moi (males do not weave) field data. On male and female social

only if he models his behavior on that of his father or of some other male member of his own group. If he models it on that of an alien male, his group may not consider him a "real" man.

Now, Hippolytos was not raised by, nor even near, Theseus; when Phaidra, first saw him, he was visiting Athens (24ff.) to participate in Demeter's (Barrett) non-masculine (Segal) mysteries at Eleusis.[5] In fact, what differentiates Hippolytos most from his father are precisely those of his activities which critics interpret as tokens of his masculinity: his hunting and horsemanship. Yet the few incidents in which Theseus has something to do with hunting[6] or with horses may well belong to the later strata of his myth, which seek to make him a second Herakles. In short, the mythical Theseus was a civic-minded leader, a seaman, a vanquisher of bulls, a devotee of (a non-Amazonian) Poseidon, an offender against Artemis, uninterested in books—perhaps even in music—and an unabashed amorist. Hippolytos is ostentatiously a private citizen (1009f.), a landlubber, a victim of the sea-bull,[7] uninterested in Poseidon but an ardent worshipper of Artemis. Theseus mocks him for being a reader of *grimoires*, a lyre player, and a singer (verses 954ff.) and, by implication, for being—or simply pretending to be (verse 968f.)—asexual. I stress that even this list of differences between father and son is not exhaustive.

Hippolytos could, of course, have learned Greek gender masculinity from old Pittheus' behavior;[8] but he apparently failed to do so.

---

stereotypes in general, see M. Mead, *Male and Female*, New York, 1950, on the relative unavailability of the Greek father as a male model, cf. Pl. *La.* init.

[5] This is not anomalous for a bastard. Agamemnon reminds Teukros of his debt to his father Telamon, who raised him in his own place, even though he was only his bastard, in Hom. *Il.* 8.283ff. But Andromache (E. *Andromd.* 224) raised Hektor's bastards and Theano (Hom *Il.* 5.70).

[6] The boar hunt at Kalydon (Apollod. 1.8.2); the sow Phaia of Krommyon (Apollod. *Epit.* 1); perhaps even the bull of Marathon (ibid. 1.5-6).

[7] I cannot consider as proven a hint of R. P. Winnington-Ingram ("Hippolytos: A Study in Causation," *Entretiens Hardt*, vi, Vandoeuvres-Genève, 1961) and an assertion by C. P. Segal ("Solar Imagery and Tragic Heroism in Euripides' *Hippolytos*," in G. W. Bowersock, W. Burkert, and M. C. J. Putnam [eds.], *Arktouros*, 1979) that the sea-bull probably symbolizes Hippolytos' own repressed sexuality. I do not deny the symbolism. I simply find no word in the text to substantiate it. Clinically, it would be more plausible to suppose that the bull symbolizes Hippolytos' unconscious guilt feelings. On the practical level the bull need not symbolize anything in particular (except perhaps Poseidon): what panics the horses by "contagion" is Hippolytos' own perturbed state; cf. elsewhere my comments on Xenophon's relevant remarks. More generally, Poseidon and Artemis do not tend to interact in myth.

[8] Virile men were masculine also in old age, both in reality and in Greek myths. G. Murray (*Five Stages of Greek Religion*, paperback ed., Garden City, NY, 1955, p. 30) exaggerates the discontinuity between maturity and old age. On the general problem, cf. R. Benedict, "Continuities and Discontinuities in Cultural Conditioning," *Psychiatry* 1: 161-67, 1938. The Great Comanche Indian warrior became a peacemaker in old age, but remained masculine: cf. R. Linton, "The Comanche," in A. Kardiner and R. Linton, *The*

Gender and Fantasy   21

I now propose to show that Hippolytos hunted like Kallisto or Taygete and that his horsemanship was Amazonian.

Hunting

Except for Herakles, Greek myth is generally little concerned with male hunters. Some of the most famous mythical hunters were women: Atalante, Prokris, Kyrene and, above all, Artemis' company is (as noted) Hippolytos, who calls himself Artemis' hunter.[9] This is almost as though an Elizabethan gentleman had boasted of being the Queen's only *maid* of honor. Even Hippolytos' devotion to Artemis and her "affection" for him are peculiar for, unlike Athene (A. *Eum.* 737ff.), Artemis is not "for the man" in all matters save only marriage. Also, while Athene means to have male proteges (Odysseus [S. *Ajax*] and Orestes), Artemis' only "male" favorite is Hippolytos. Similarly, though mortal men do not challenge Athene,[10] the Aloadai asaulted Artemis and Agamemnon pretended to surpass her as a hunter.[11] More significant still is the frequency wherewith mortal men "forget" to sacrifice to Artemis—always with dire consequences. In short, Artemis was an archaic deity of women. Though a Greek man's total dedication to her may seem edifying to moderns familiar with the worship of the Holy Virgin, in *Greek* eyes Hippolytos' obsession with Artemis must have seemed prima facie evidence of a lack of (Greek) gender masculinity.

Artemis' huntresses also had to refrain from heterosexual relations, though perhaps not from lesbian ones.[12] Seduced huntresses, like Kallisto or Taygete, were punitively metamorphosed into animals.[13]

On the practical level, the heterosexual abstinance imposed on Artemis' huntresses could, of course, be due to the pregnant woman's

---

Psychological Frontiers of a Society, New York, 1945. The spearblade of an old Masai may be as short as that of a youth, but in Masai society only *men* own spears. I know of only one society (in Abyssinia) which feminizes its old men, by circumcising them and then making them wear women's clothes, cf. A. Jensen, *Im Lande des Gada*, 1936. By contrast, the quasi-masculinization of old women is quite common in primitive society.

[9] If this claim is taken literally it could, at the limit, imply that during the hunt he left his companions, since it is *not* claimed that they, too, hunted with Artemis.

[10] Only a woman, Arachne, does: Verg. *George.* 4.246; Ov. *Met.* 6 passim; Nonn. 18.215.

[11] Aloadai: Pi. *P.* 4.88; Apollod. 1.7.4. Agamemnon: *Kypria* (= Procl. Chrest. 1) E-W. I disregard here Niobe, who challenged Leto rather than her children.

[12] Cf. Kallisto's seduction by Zeus, who assumed the form of Artemis, in Ps.-Eratosth. *Catast.* 1, pp. 50ff. R. Similarly, unwed Sedang girls were permitted lesbian, but forbidden heterosexual, relations (my unpublished field data). Kallisto's son by Zeus commits incest with her; cf. W. Burkert, *Homo Necans* (*RVV* 32), Berlin, 1972. I find the alleged link between hunting and *Eros* specious (M. Detienne, *Dionysos mis à mort*, Paris, 1977).

[13] Even Atalante, who was *not* one of Artemis' huntresses, was turned into a lioness and *thereby* deprived of *further* relations with her lover—who was transformed into a lion—for, in Greek belief, lions mate only with leopards: Callim. *Dian.* 216; Paus. 3.24.2; Apollod. 3.9.2; Hyg. *fab.* 99, Prop. 1.1.10. Another huntress, Prokris, notorious for her promiscuity, died in a hunting accident.

incapacity to pursue wild beasts. But Hippolytos' chastity obviously cannot be justified on such grounds. Yet, I cannot refrain from noting a psychological oddity. Hippolytos' angrily utopian fantasy of an exclusively male parenthood may be at the root of Lucian's (V.H. 1.22) droll tale of male pregnancy (discussed in another work).[14] One could also suppose that, like many primitives, the archaic Greeks, too, tabooed sexual relations before the hunt. But even Burkert's exhaustive treatment of Greek hunting rites fails to demonstrate the existence of such a Greek taboo.[15] Had such a taboo ever existed *for male hunters*, it is exceedingly probable that some account of the promiscuous Herakles' many slayings of wild beasts would at least have hinted at it.

Though I concede that it is risky to argue *ex silentio*, I cannot refrain from pointing out that the Ba-Thonga hunter, who daringly goes out to hunt the particularly dangerous hippopotamus, first commits incest with his daughter in the hope that his awesome trespass will make him as terrible as the beast he intends to hunt.[16]

Since I might just as well be hung for a sheep as for a lamb, I add that, given the role of coitus in certain Greek rites, some of them actually involved a "sexualization" of death in all its forms.[17] Also, given the fact that E. *Hipp*. (1ff.) considers coitus as a rite to which Aphrodite is entitled, I suspect that the hunter's sexual abstinence—if indeed it existed—would have been not simply a renunciation (likely to increase his vigor and even more his aggressivity) but also a *mandatory ritual sacrilege*—like Orestes' theft of Taurian Artemis' cult statue (E. *IT*), or like the consequences of a Dodonan priestess' prophecy that the Thebans would be victorious only if they first committed sacrilege. That prophecy caused the Theban delegates to commit the required sacrilege forthwith, by throwing the prophetess Myrtilla into a cauldron of hot water.[18]

Be that as it may, the apparently vegetarian Hippolytos (952ff.) did *not* behave like a normal male hunter: his chastity seems patterned on that of Artemis' "chaste" (= lesbian) huntresses. The notion that Theseus would call a hypothetically non-vegetarian hunter a "vegetarian" for the purpose of insulting him seems pointless to me, the barb of that insult being far from clear.

---

[14] G. Devereux, *Femme et Mythe*, Paris, 1982.
[15] W. Burkert, *Homo Necans*, Berlin, 1972, pp. 72ff.
[16] H. Junod: *The Life of a South African Tribe*[2], 2 vols., London, 1927.
[17] Burkert, op. cit., p. 73. On necrophilia, and also on death as a marriage to Hades (for women) or to Persephone (for men), cf. G. Devereux, "Greek Pseudo-Homosexuality," op. cit., p. 86.
[18] Herakleides of Pontos, apud. Zenodotos 2.84. Discussed in A. B. Cook, *Zeus*, ii, Cambridge, 1925, p. 214.

Since the passage concerning his vegetarianism is held to be puzzling,[19] I propose to show that there is nothing mysterious about verses 952ff.

At verses 108ff. it is stated that the hunters' meal is ready. This, to my mind, proves that the meal does not include the game the hunters had just brought home. This supposition is natural; freshly killed game, especially if hotly pursued before being killed, is tough and not very palatable. Except for the inner organs, venison must be "hung" for several days to soften it and so improve its texture. There is ancient evidence that the Greeks ate first even the innards of freshly slain *domestic* animals (Hom. *Od.* 20.257).[20]

But even though I hold this interpretation to be sound, I do not believe it to be either decisive or complete. I hold that verses 952ff. should be read in the light of Euripides, *The Cretans*, fr. 472 N^2, in which the initiates' omophagous practices (verses 12f.) contrast—in a seemingly equally "absurd" manner—with their abstention from meat-eating (verses 18f.). Yet the two practices are *not* incompatible, for it has been known for nearly a century[21] that in the totemic feast the faithful eat precisely that which is *normally* taboo for them—their own totemic animal. This argument is the more convincing, as wild animals, and especially Artemis' own deer, were regularly sacrificed to her,[22] even if, as in Iphigeneia's case, the "deer" was impersonated by a girl (which is precisely what the traditional Iphigeneia myth inverts euphemistically: a deer is substituted for the girl).

I know of no case in which Artemis required a *male* hunter to be chaste, though, as noted before, she punished those of her own female hunting companions who allowed themselves to be deflowered. It is of great interest that the *only* huntress *not* punished for her heterosexuality was Apollo's mistress, the *solitary* huntress Kyrene. And it seems evident that, in her case, Apollo was quite as much a substitute for his sister Artemis as the warlike girl Deianeira[23] was, in Herakles' eyes, a substitute for her brother Meleagros, whom she closely resembled.[24]

---

[19] Burkert, op. cit., p. 73.0; Barrett, op. cit., ad loc.
[20] Another possible practical assumption may be that, like Herakles, the hunter Hippolytos was chiefly a slayer of dangerous beasts: he would no more have eaten wolves killed during the hunt than Herakles would have eaten the Nemeian lion. One may also think of the modern fox-hunting, "The unspeakable pursuing the uneatable." I admit that this solution has a major flaw: Artemis clearly hunted deer and other edible game animals, which means that Hippolytos did too.
[21] W. R. Smith, *Lectures on the Religion of the Semites*, New York, 1889.
[22] M. P. Nilsson, *Griechische Feste*, Leipzig, 1906, esp. pp. 218ff.
[23] Apollod. 1.8.1; sch. A. R. 1.1212; Nonn. *D.* 35.88, discussed in G. Devereux, *Tragédie et Poésie Grecques*, Paris, 1975, chap. 5. For Kyrene, cf. Pi. *P.* 9.5ff.; A. R. 1.500; D. S. 4.81.
[24] B. 33.165. The Greek tendency to "slide" from one person to another, who is a substitute for the former, is discussed, with many examples, in G. Devereux, "Greek Pseudo-Homosexuality," op. cit.

Hippolytos' so-called chastity thus appears once more, and in every respect, as the functional equivalent of the obligatory (heterosexual) chastity of Artemis' hunting companions. Even his "aim-inhibited" (Freud) erotic attachment to Artemis duplicates theirs.[25] In simplest terms, Hippolytos' attraction to Artemis is the equivalent of a schoolgirl's romantic-erotic "crush" on a handsome, tweedy games mistress.

Horsemanship

What is true of Hippolytos the anatomically male "huntress" is true of Hippolytos the horse fancier who, as noted before, figuratively rides side-saddle. The data indicating this are even richer than those which show him to be a "huntress."

(1) A passion for horses should not be confused with equestrian competence or skill. The former is not really mentioned before the end of the fifth century B.C.[26]

(2) Though most mythical Greeks closely connected with horses were men, they did not live with—and by—their horses the way the Amazons supposedly did.

(3) Though Greek *men* of the mythical age could ride horses, they were *not* riders: the *Iliad* (10.513ff.) thinks it necessary to explain how and why Odysseus came to bestride Rhesos' horses.[27] By contrast, many monuments show Amazons riding horses and fighting with Greek infantry. One source even claims that the Amazons rode so well because the width of the female's posterior made their seat on a horse particularly

---

[25] Ps.-Eratosthenes, *Cat.* 1, pp. 50ff. R., cf. supra. There is good clinical evidence that a behaviorally "heterosexual" neurotic male may, concurrently with such "normal" *behavior*, have *lesbian* (*not* paederastic) *fantasies*: G. Devereux, "Loss of Identity, Impairment of Relationships, Reading Disability," *Psychoanalytic Quarterly* 35: 18–39, 1966 (esp. pp. 33–34); id., "La Renonciation a l'Identité, Défense contre l'Anéantissement," *Revue Francaise de Psychanalyse* 31: 101–42, 1967 (esp. pp. 132–33).

[26] It is not mentioned even in Pindaros' racing odes. In the *Iliad* Nestor knows all about horses and admires those of Rhesos, but he is not "horse-crazy," like Pheipippides (Ar. *Nub.*) or Hippolytos. This difference may possibly be due to a fact, well highlighted by F. Schachermeyr (*Poseidon*, Bern, 1950): in pre-Homeric and Homeric times the horse was something awe-inspiring and uncanny; cf. the myths of cannabalistic and murderous horses (G. Devereux: "Les Chevaux Anthropophages, dans les Mythes Grecs," *Revue des Etudes Grecques* 88: 203–5, 1975). This may explain, *in part*, why the Greeks did not geld horses, though they did geld mules (Hes. *Op.* 790f.) (infra). On the lateness of the practice of gelding horses, cf. P.-W. *R.E.* s.v. Pferd. Xenophon's relevant works show that even in the 5th century B.C. Greeks were afraid of their horses. This need not surprise us: though the Plains Indian tribes of North America were magnificent horsemen, a famous 19th century warrior was called "Man (scil.: an enemy) Afraid of his Horse." (These tribes did not see or acquire horses until the 17th century.)

[27] For an unusual Mykenaian figurine of a man straddling a horse, cf. M. S. F. Hood, "A Mycenaean Cavalryman," *British School of Athens* 48: 84–93, 1953. See, on early riders, J. K. Anderson, *Ancient Greek Horsemanship*, Berkeley, 1961, pp. 6ff.

secure.²⁸ Moreover, the Amazons were believed to be devotees of Artemis (= the great Skythian goddess?), though the nearest Artemis Laphria comes to being associated with horses is her harnessing of deer before she heads northward, i.e., toward what was more or less Amazon (= Skythian?) country (see below).

Now, some have suggested that at verses 1130–34 Hippolytos is seen as bestriding a horse. This possibility is discussed by Barrett in his note on the passage. But, as Professor Segal points out to me, the "yoking together" here συζυγίαν strongly militates against the notion, as do 110ff., which speak of his yoking horses.

Yet, oddly enough, there are indications that Aristophanes may have visualized the presumably Euripidean) Hippolytos as occasionally straddling a horse, for when his Agathon presents Phaidra as daydreaming about imitating Hippolytos, she thinks of riding horseback.²⁹

This does not mean that, according to the best Homeric model, Hippolytos was not primarily a driver of chariots, rather than a rider of horses.³⁰ What is, however, interesting is that Aristophanes chose to speak of "riding" (actively copulating) precisely in connection with Phaidra. Though she is, for the comic poet, lechery incarnate (Ar. *Thesm.* 497, 547; *Frogs* 1043), and even though he uses this verb in an obscene sense also in *Wasps* 501, there is something peculiar about this passage. As far as is known, Agathon wrote no *Phaidra* and, being effeminate, is certainly unlikely to "bestride" a woman so as to put himself into the right mood for the depicting of Phaidra's lechery, by a technique Aristophanes imputed to Euripides' Hippolytos (Ar. *Acharn.* 410ff.).

I suggest, in short, that Aristophanes imagined the Euripidean Phaidra as day-dreaming *also* about straddling a horse, because he imagined Hippolytos doing so, from time to time. After all, in Euripides' time Athens had a strong cavalry, while chariots had not been used in combat since the Lelantine war.³¹

---

²⁸ Dict. Cret. *de bell. Troi.* 4.3, discussed in B. Engle, "The Amazons in Ancient Greece," *Psychoanalytic Quarterly* 11: 512–54, 1942 (esp. p. 516). Though Dict. Cret. is late, the tradition may well be ancient. Since the Greeks had no real saddles, they favored cavalry horses whose spines formed a hollow between the horse's back muscles; cf. Anderson, *Ancient Greek Horsemanship*, op. cit. If a speculation be permitted, I venture to suggest that the mythical horse-name Kyllaros may refer to such a "hollow back," rather than to "bowlegs," for no bow-legged horse could be a superb racer.

²⁹ Ar. *Thesm.* 153, κελητίζεις. Though the question is addressed to Agathon, Aristophanes clearly thinks of Euripides, who allegedly donned rags before writing of beggars (AR. *Ach.* 410).

³⁰ Prof. Segal brought to my attention the discussion of the many references to yoking, in K. J. Reckford, "Phaethon, Hippolytus and Aphrodite," *Transactions of the American Philological Association* 103: 405–32, 1972.

³¹ But I doubt that the text Aristophanes knew had γυμνάδας ἵππους at verse 1134, as

One thing is certain: Hippolytos' passion for horses he neither learned nor inherited from his father. Also, his horses were Enetians (231-1131) and, as I indicated elsewhere, Euripides assuredly imagined them as coming not from the Veneti, but from Paphlagonian Enete, which, in some traditions,[32] is Amazon country. For Greeks, his passion for Enetian (= Amazon) horses would automatically suggest a taste "inherited" from the Amazon "royal horsewoman" (307).

(d) Even Hippolytos' "chastity" may be correlated with his Amazon-like passion for horses, for, while hostile to marriage and to men, the Amazons did periodically mate with outsiders so as to perpetuate their "race."[33] (This, be it noted, fits poorly the later notion that every Amazon was a παρθένος, in the modern sense of being a "virgin.")

Now, the horseman Hippolytos' "chastity" recalls the impotency of certain Skythians, which was believed to be caused either by too much horseback riding, or else by the sacrilegious sack of the temple of Aphrodite (Atargatis? Derketo?) at Ascalon.[34] This linking of Hippolytos with impotent Skythians is legitimate, for the written sources describing that defect are roughly contemporary with E. *Hipp.* and it is most probable that word of mouth information about it circulated at an even earlier date. I do *not* suggest, of course, that Euripides *deliberately* represented Hippolytos as an impotent Skythian. I simply assume that, like other well-informed Athenians, he knew of the existence of this ailment in Skythia (= Amazon country) and had heard its two Skythian explanations: excessive horseback riding[35] and sacrilegious behavior toward the goddess of love.

have all MSS. Reiske's emendation γυμνάδος ἵππον is inescapable.

[32] G. Devereux, "The Enetian Horses of Hippolytos," *Antiquité Classique* 33: 375-83, 1964; id., "The Enetian Horses of Alkman's *Partheneion*," *Hermes* 94: 129-34, 1966. I am indebted to Prof. M. Lejeune, for the information that my conclusions were acccepted by A. L. Prosdocimi: "Il nome 'Veneti' nell' Antichità," *Memorie dell'Academia Patavina (Classe di Sc. Mor. Lett. ed Arte)* 78: 549-90, 1965-66. Prof. Lejeune also appears to accept them; in his paper, "Les Inscriptions Vénètes," *Instituto di Glottologia* (Università degli Studi di Trieste), 1965, pp. 185-206, esp. p. 185, n. 1, he mentioned my findings in a note inserted at the last moment. For Enetian horses in Hom. *Il.* 2.852, cf. G. Devereux, "Homer's Wild She-Mules," *Journal of Hellenistic Studies* 85: 29-32, 1965.

[33] Plu. *Thes.* 26, etc.; cf. W. H. Roscher s.v. "Amazonen," in Roscher, *Lexicon*, col. 270. Leipzig, 1884-86.

[34] Riding: Hp. *Aer.* 22; sacrilege: Hdt 1.105; these defective men practiced a divination taught to them by "Aphrodite": Hdt. 4.67.

[35] Some Herodotos scholars mention in this context the frequency of this defect among the 19th century Nogai Tatars. I concede that much *bare-back* riding can probably traumatize and atrophy the testicles—but the Nogai Tatars had saddles with rigid trees and with stirrups, and so do modern Hungarian horse-herders (*Csikós*), whose virility Hungarian folk-belief takes for granted. Classical philology is, at times, not sufficiently concerned with hard facts. For the Zuni Indians, cf. W. A. Hammond, "The Disease of the Scythians (Morbus Feminarum) and certain Analogous Conditions," *American Journal of Neurology and Psychiatry* 1: 339-55, 1882.

Gender and Fantasy

It should also be remembered that the Amazons were said to *lame* their sons. Now, lameness symbolizes impotency, on the basis of the clinically commonplace "foot (leg)" = "penis" symbolic equation.[36] But, on the other hand, a special virility is ascribed to lame men and to leg amputees.[37]

(4) Artemis is admittedly connected wih horses mainly insofar as her Amazon devotees were horsewomen. The one time Artemis rides in a chariot, she harnesses *very large* deer to it and heads northward, i.e., toward Amazon country.[38] This tale turns out to have complex implications if one refuses to be misled by the sub-arctic harnessing of reindeer—and even by the Santa Claus tradition. I begin by noting that the Greeks had no *cervidae* suitable for yoking or for riding.[39] Next, I observe that the Skythian (and Amazon?) Great Goddess probably had authentic affinities with the archaic Artemis—probably in her role of Mistress of Wild Beasts, for she is so represented on a gilt and engraved silver mirror from Kelermes (seventh–sixth century B.C.).[40] But it is also probable that the deer-masks worn by some fine Skythian saddle-horses[41] (all of them geldings) suggests that Artemis' "saddle" or chariot deer were in reality simply horses wearing Skythian deer-masks, but were represented by the artists as real deer. It is striking that, like the Skythians (Hdt. 4.120), the evasive Keryneian hind used nomad cavalry tactics.

What matters here is that, at least as far back as the fifth century B.C., all really good Skythian saddle horses were geldings—as are, to this day, the saddle horses of most steppe nomads. Now, I hold that the gelding of *horses* is derived from that of reindeer, for whereas, as both Greek and modern evidence proves, stallions *can* be tamed, the male reindeer is practically unmanageable.[42] Thus, the gelding of saddle horses strikingly parallels the impotency of some Skythian horsemen.

---

[36] Cf. the "third leg" = "penis" equation, common even in modern slang; also, foot fetishism.

[37] The second half of a modern Romanian women's proverb warns women against being coitized by lame men, presumably because their awkwardness—also manifest in their rhythmical bobbing gait—makes their coital thrusts very violent. Also, during World War II, a distinguished orthopedic surgeon told me that leg amputees were much sought after by women. Compare Mimnermos *fr.* 15D: Amazon women claimed that lame men made lusty bedfellows.

[38] Callim. *h. Dian.* 110ff.; cf. Nonnos 48.301ff.

[39] Artemis does ride a "deer," e.g., on the so-called "Darius vase." But I flatly disbelieve tales of real deer-drawn chariots in one of Artemis' precincts, which O. Gruppe, *Griechische Mythologie*, Munich, 1906 (ii, p. 1276.9) accepts, as does M. P. Nilsson, *Griechische Feste*, Leipzig, 1906, p. 219. Also, not all *cervidae* can be used like reindeer. Thus, the huge elk are not suitable for work. Owing to a peculiarity of their metabolism, elks become badly overheated when made to furnish work: cf. F. Hanvar, *Das Pferd*, Wien, 1955.

[40] T. Talbot-Rice, *The Skythians*[3], New York, 1961, fig. 16 (p. 87).

[41] T. Talbot-Rice, *The Skythians*, op. cit., p. 11.

[42] This information was provided by a noted specialist of the North, Professor Jean Malaurie.

I concede, of course, that Herodotos—who does mention the impotency of some Skythians—does *not* speak of Skythian geldings, though about a century after Herodotos, Xenophon knew of the existence of geldings in the Persion empire[43] and the Skythian geldings in the Pazyryk tombs are contemporary with Herodotos.[44] Moreover, four hundred years after Herodotos, Strabon (7.4.8) still considered the gelding of saddle-horses a striking peculiarity of the Steppe nomads.[45]

Summing up, the "chaste" Amazon-son Hippolytos' horsemanship and his hostility to Aphrodite parallel the two Skythian *explanations* of Skythian impotency: excessive riding and sacrilegious behavior toward the "Aphrodite" of Ascalon. The literary critic can, if he wishes, treat this as a coincidence. The psychoanalyst, who believes in psychic determinism, cannot help seeing a—perhaps "unintended" but nevertheless revealing—nexus between the chaste Hippolytos and the impotent Skythians.

Hippolytos' Sexual Ambiguousness

Hippolytos' sexual ambiguousness, which is a salient aspect of his personality, is reflected by Phaidra's almost untranslatable remark (351):

ὅστις ποθ᾽ οὗτός ἐσθ᾽, ὁ τῆς Ἀμαζόνος.[46]

That one there, whosoever he is—the Amazon's (son).

His name is, moreover, matronymic: Son of Hippolyte.[47] The verse is said to be vague and defines Hippolytos twice. Not two experts translate it alike.[48] But, in my estimate, the verse is vague only because Hippolytos'

---

[43] X. *Cyrop.* 7.5.62.
[44] T. Talbot-Rice, op. cit., p. 71.
[45] I note that Hesiodos (*Op.* 785ff.) gives *no* propitious date for the gelding of horses, though he does give one for the gelding of mules (791). I conclude from this *not simply* that small Hesiodic farmers had no horses, but that the gelding of mules was patterned on the castration of *bulls*, whereas that of steppe horses was modelled upon the castration of *reindeer*. I am not persuaded by J. K. Anderson (*Ancient Greek Horsemanship*, Berkeley, 1961, p. 38) that "fear of infection" stopped the Greeks from gelding their stallions, for the same risk is present also when one castrates mules or bulls. I hold that the Greeks did not geld their horses, though they castrated other domestic animals, because the gelding of horses originated elsewhere than did the castration of mules, etc. I hope to deal with this matter on another occasion.
[46] Comma supplied by Barrett.
[47] In E. *Ba.* Pentheus is chiefly Agave's son—not Echion's.
[48] M. Hadas: "If he is a man—that Amazon's." H. Berguin: "Whoever may be the one to whom the Amazon gave birth." D. Sutherland: "What do you call him—oh, the Amazon's." Prof. Segal suggests to me that the verse does not refer "to what Hippolytos is, but to what Phaidra perceives. Her phrase can refer to Theseus' previous liaison, to the threat to Phaidra's children, to the ambiguous position of Theseus' bastard. . . . In this context it is not necessarily a contemptuous remark." I cannot agree, for I do not see how it can

personality is hard to pigeonhole; its vagueness mirrors Phaidra's doubts. Also, like many other Euripidean passages, it exemplified the poet's skill in "imitating" the speech of persons under great stress. The only problem is whether the doubt concerns the "who" or the "what."

Barrett's suggestion (ad loc.) that Phaidra *pretends* not to know Hippolytos' name, attributes to her the more than Racinean coyness of a Précieuse. His argument would be more convincing if the drama made something of Hippolytos' suggestively matronymic name, highlighting its "appropriateness."[49] This Euripides failed to do, though both Hippolytos' passion for horses and the manner of his death would have made etymologizing possible.[50] Phaidra's "doubt" must therefore concern not Hippolytos' social identity—perfectly established by the words "the Amazon's (son)" in verse 351 and, in verse 520, by "Theseus' son"—but his nature.[51] That Hippolytos is the Amazon's son by Theseus is clear to Phaidra; all else about him is in doubt, and it is this "all else" that matters here.

Doubt as to the "what"—as to personal and also sexual identity—is frequent in Greek thought, as it is in most primitive and archaic thought. The boundaries between gods, men and animals and also between men and women are often blurred. Gods can be mistaken for mortals and vice versa. Contrary to what Aias Telamonides says (Hom. *Il.* 13.71ff.): "the gods are not easily discerned by mortals" (Hom. *h. Cer.* 111f.). Conversely, man must be careful not to behave in a godlike manner, nor allow others to treat him like a god,[52] lest his forwardness (*hubris*) arouse the envy of the gods (*phthonos*), bringing *nemesis* down to him. What matters here is that concepts such as *hubris* and *phthonos* presuppose the *possibility* of men being mistaken for gods—well reflected by the type of flattery or even precaution (Hom. *Il.* 6.128ff.) which consists in wondering whether a stranger is a man or a god. In a more general way, the whole of external "reality," *as it is reflected in myth*, forms a continuum largely because the Greeks did not have enough conceptual pigeonholes into which to fit, properly and permanently, every product of their mythopoeic imagination. Thus, Achilleus' horse Xanthos was, despite his half-supernatural origins (Hom. *Il.* 16.149ff.), an animal, even when Hera temporarily give him speech (Hom. *Il.* 19.407ff.). But whether a creature like the Sphinx is divine, human, or

---

refer to a previous liaison; also, as Theseus' bastard, Hippolytos cannot threaten the heritage of Phaidra's children and his status is not really ambiguous. I do agree that the remark refers (also) to what Phaidra sees—but what she sees is precisely what Hippolytos is, in fact: a male Amazon. Cf. the neutral ἀνθρώπων of v. 350 preceeding.
49 In the sense of Sokrates' etymologizing in Pl. *Crat.*
50 A play with names and words occurs in other Euripidean tragedies.
51 F. Chapouthier, in "La Notion du Divin," *Entretiens Hardt*, i, Vandouevres-Genève, 1954 (p. 213), rightly argues that Phaidra is confused by Hippolytos' multiple aspects.
52 A. *Ag.* 929. See also my discussion of Hippolytos' grandiosity.

animal cannot be determined with any degree of certainty: it all depends on the manner in which such a being acts at a particular time.[53]

The fluidity of the boundaries between various kinds of beings, and even things, is strikingly manifest in the sphere of mythical sexuality: anyone and anything, from Zeus to the waters of the river Enipeus, can impregnate a woman; anything, from Aphrodite to a cloud or to the earth, can be impregnated; and human beings readily slide from one type of "partner" to another. The cicada in particular exemplifies sexual indiscriminateness: this insect will cohabit with anything at all.[54]

In short, the nature of Greek thought permits one to ascribe to Phaidra a genuine doubt as to just "what" Hippolytos may be—or, at least, what he can be made out to be. Her doubt cannot imply that she believes him to be a god: as indicated above, she calls him the son of the Amazon or Theseus.[55] It is his *sexual* identity which is (legitimately) in doubt, and this type of uncertainty is traditionally Greek. It suffices to think here of Dionysos' sexual ambiguousness.[56] Even more relevant is Eteokles' general order addressed to "man or woman or whatsoever is in betwixt" (A. *Sept.* 197). That verse 351 pertains to Hippolytos' sexual identity was sensed by both Méridier and Kamerbeek.[57] I must go into detail as regards this matter.

Even the most decent Greek male was expected to have a sexual life and to be available to any socially non-tabooed woman. That is Bellerophontes' predicament in Euripides' (lost) *Stheneboia*. This virtuous, but sexually normal, man refuses to commit adultery with his host's wife. Still, it is of some interest that in Euripides' (lost) *Bellerophontes* (*fr.* 293 N²) someone says (presumably to this hero): "Your glory exalts your pride; you think yourself superior to your fellows." In short, Stheneboia's

---

[53] A. I. Hallowell, "Ojibwa Ontology, Behavior and World View," in S. Diamond (ed.), *Culture and History, Essays in Honor of Paul Radin*, New York, 1960, does point out that the Ojibwa consider certain animals as "persons," but fails to note that this happens only when an animal behaves in an *un*-animal-like (= human) manner.

[54] Plu. *Amat.* 767D; cf. G. Devereux, "Greek Pseudo-Homosexuality," *Symbolae Olsoenses* 42: 69–92, 1967, which lists the full range of sexual partners and analyzes the process of "sliding" in Greek myth and behavior.

[55] Whether Hippolytos is megalomaniac enough to consider himself almost divine need not concern me here; cf. E. *fr.* 293 N² discussed below. Grube, op. cit., p. 177, etc., and Barrett, op. cit., p. 178, rightly stress that his *semnos* equals that of Aphrodite. He wishes he could take revenge on the gods, as though he were their equal: E. *Hipp.* 1415. So do Herakles (E. *HF* 1245) and also Achilleus (Hom. *Il.* 22.20), but they have at least the excuse of having one divine parent and Herakles does end up as a god. For Hippolytos' presumptuous attempt to pattern his behavior on that of Artemis, see the relevant section of this study.

[56] G. Devereux, "Le Fragment d'Eschyle 62 Nauck², Ce qu'y Signifie ΧΛΟΥΝΗΣ." *Revue des Etudes Grecques* 86: 277–84, 1973.

[57] L. Méridier in his ed.: "Celui-là—homme ou non" = J.C. Kamerbeek, "Euripide" in *Entretiens Hardt*, vi, p. 19. Grene's (op. cit., p. 48) "somebody" is implausible.

Gender and Fantasy 31

vanity is hurt only because her personal beauty and her attempts at seduction do not suffice to overcome Bellerophontes' moral scruples.

In *Hippolytos* the situation is far more complex. Phaidra feels herself *personally* depreciated, because Hippolytos will not disregard for her sake the taboo on incestuous adultery. As a *woman*, she feels additionally threatened by the total non-responsiveness of this arrogant sexphobic. In verse 351 Phaidra's sense of *personal* humiliation (comparable to that of Stheneboia) is masked by the resentment of the *woman* toward Hippolytos' imperviousness to—and contempt for—her sex in general. She therefore implies that Hippolytos is either a neuter or, more probably, a latent invert: something "in between" in Aischylos' sense.[58] I add that even the chaste Phaidra might have found it easier to struggle against her love had Hippolytos so much as noticed her.[59] One thing at any rate is obvious to the psychoanalyst: both in the "neuter" and in the invert, aggressivity is fused with and cancels Eros. Biologically, both are useless; psychologically, both are incapable of *mature* love,[60] no matter what Platon may say.

I intend to discuss this matter further in connection with the relationship between Hippolytos and Theseus. Here I note only that, in the light of other aspects of this drama, Phaidra's doubts seem justified. But what matters here is not the *objective* correctness of her hint but its *affective* motivation. In a sense, Phaidra is right for the wrong reasons: the correctness of her *noema* is intuitive; it is not the outcome of a correct *noesis*. Her irritated remark was assuredly motivated by the fury of a woman scorned: a man indifferent to her—and to all women—must be an invert or a neuter (eunuch). Scorn is answered with scorn; both "invert" and "neuter" are Greek terms of contempt.[61] The "second" Phaidra's chastity and her obsession with her *aidos*[62] strengthens his interpretation. Even the most proudly chaste woman glories in the number of suitors she had occasion to reject; her erotic renunciation is compensated for by narcissistic satisfactions. Hence, Hippolytos' indifference not only frustrates Phaidra's sensuality[63] but also wounds her self esteem.

---

58 Even in our culture one soothes one's Ego, bruised by a desired person's indifference, by supposing that the inaccessible love object is a neuter or an invert.
59 For the almost hypnotic seductiveness of the narcissist, see the appropriate section of this study.
60 Devereux, "Greek Pseudo-Homosexuality," op. cit.
61 On contempt for (passive) inverts, cf. Dover, op. cit.; for eunuchs, X. *Cyr.* 7.5.58. The hatred of women for misogynist inverts, who entice men away from them (and, perhaps, even compete with them sexually: Theocr. 2.150), is shown by tales of the slaying of Orpheus by sexually frusrated Thracian women (W. K. C. Guthrie, *Orpheus and Greek Religion*[2], London, 1952, pp. 32f., 49, 54; cf. Phanokles (Kern, *Test.* 77) and Ovid, *Metamorphoses* 10.81–85.
62 Dodds, "The αἰδώς of Phaedra," op. cit.
63 Her sensuality did not evaporate in the course of her Euripidean transformation from

She could probably have struggled more effectively against her own passion had Hippolytos given her a chance to reject him; this is both common sense psychology and a common enough literary theme.[64]

The affective motivation of Phaidra's "doubt" about Hippolytos' masculinity is thus obvious; its objective correctness is shown in another passage. The only question is whether, at verse 351, Euripides *consciously* meant to suggest that Phaidra sensed Hippolytos' latent and oedipally determined inversion. This is, in a sense, a pseudo-problem. One characteristic of the great poet is the total fusion of conscious planning with subliminal insight.

The Primal Scene

As a deterrent to sexuality, the primal scene is closely related to the child's obscene and sadistic conception of parental sexuality. Since we do not know how long the Amazon survived the birth of her son, we may not suppose that Euripides had imagined Hippolytos to have witnessed her love-making with Theseus. Nor could he have witnessed his father's sexual relations with Phaidra, since Hippolytos apparently never lived under the same roof with Phaidra and Theseus. But, significantly, this is *about* to become possible since Theseus is expected to arrive at Troezen very soon.

Fortunately, Hippolytos himself refers to sexual sights: he insists that what little he knows about sex he had learned through hearsay and through *looking* at certain paintings, but denies all voyeurism (1001ff.). Now, many Greek vases—which need not be enumerated here[65]—tell us what *kind* of (fifth century B.C.) pictures Euripides imagined Hippolytos to have seen.

For once one can sympathize with Hippolytos' revulsion: poets and musicians have always caught the spirit of true (loving) passion better than graphic artists did.[66] Here the matter of nuances is of crucial

---

a bold into a chaste woman; it assuredly became richer and more nuanced in the second (surviving) *Hippolytos*.

[64] Chimène, in Corneille, *Le Cid*; Melle de La Mole, in Stendhal, *Le Rouge et le Noir*. Both can resist only when pursued.

[65] Cf. J. Marcadé, *Kalos Eros*, New York, 1965, an easily accessible book for the contrast between Greek and Roman-Etruscan graphic obscenity; cf. F. Bömer's review of J. Marcadé, *Roma-Amor*, Genève, 1962, *Gymnasium* 72: 149-51, 1965, which makes some important points. Cf. a *painter's* dream in Artemid. 4.20.

[66] Painters of our time, constantly in quest of the completely new, could take up the challenge to represent the act of Love in the language and spirit of great poetry or of Berlioz' "Romeo and Juliet." This is something even Rembrandt—in his well-known, though carefully hidden, drawings—failed to do. Whether the erotic drawings of a great English painter—which the impotent esthete Ruskin dared to destroy in a museum (without being sent to prison for it!)—spoke the language of Love, as distinct from that of the brothel, can no longer be determined.

importance. It makes a great deal of psychological difference to the child whether he witnesses *love*-making or mere *fornication*. The Mohave child's capacity to sublimate his repeated experiences of the primal scene can be understood in terms of that tribe's positive approach to *love*-making.[67] The Mohave child's reactions would be very different if he had to witness mere shamefaced fornications, scenes such as Euripides *meant* his Hippolytos to have seen represented on vases. The inference that one's own parents also engage in such practices, in mechanical and obscene acrobatics, does not give the child a both passionate and tender conception of sexuality. Rather does it elicit revulsion, conducive not only to a horror of sexuality but, by extension, also of bodily contact of every kind and to a repression of the obscene pictures one had seen.

This is precisely what one must imagine to have happened in the case of Hippolytos, whose tendency to visual repression is discussed in connection with Artemis whom—significantly—he never once actually *sees*. He only *hears* and *smells* her; and these hallucinations belong to sensory spheres not stimulated by ribald paintings.[68]

Hippolytos' Utopia and Infantile Birth Theories

Children are insatiably curious about the origin of babies and, by extension, about the origin (*arche*) or cause (*aition*) of things in general,[69] even in societies which do not try as hard as ours to conceal from them "the facts of life." Nonetheless, all children react to the real facts with anxiety, and either repress them or replace them with weird theories of their own.[70] The child's need both to know and to deny such

---

[67] The Mohave say: "When a couple makes love, body cohabits with body *and soul with soul*." Also: "You can always tell who made love the night before; they carry themselves *proudly*, and their eyes sparkle." This is to be contrasted with our miserable maxim: "After such pleasures, all beasts are sad," which is, moreover, a coldblooded misquotation. The original (Galen) adds: "*except* men and roosters." Cf. Devereux, "The Primal Scene," op. cit.

[68] To call this Euripidean passage "grinning cynicism" (Grene, op. cit., p. 55) shows how much even a fine scholar can misunderstand a master psychologist's stroke of genius and clinical intuitiveness.

[69] A partial sublimination of this curiosity caused a research chemist to specialize in the study of the chemical problem of "status nascendi": K. Abraham, "Restrictions and Transformations of Scoptophilia, etc.," *Selected Papers on Psychoanalysis*, London, 1927.

[70] Modern parents find that they must repeatedly *re*-enlighten their children; cf. S. Freud, "The Sexual Enlightenment of Children," *Standard Edition*, ix, 1959. New infantile birth theories turn up constantly in psychotherapy with children; cf. A. Grinstein, *Index*, op.cit., s.vv. Fantasies of Children, Birth Myths, etc. Common variants are oral impregnation, anal birth, navel birth, etc., some of which are even culturally implemented: impregnation by food (Australian aborigines), oral impregnation and anal birth (Mohave Indian transvestites [Devereux, see op. cit. in note 83 infra]), impregnation by the ear (E. Jones, "The Madonna's conception through the Ear," *Essays in Applied Psychoanalysis*, ii, London, 1951). The clinical and mythological evidence on this point is nearly inexhaustible.

uncomfortable knowledge explains why he so readily accepts the stork, rosebush, etc.—stories of his overly prudish parents, which, like all lies and bowdlerizations,[71] symbolically reaffirm that which they overtly profess to deny.

Infantile sex-theories are not wholly arbitrary. They result, in part, from a systematic distortion of real facts, exactly in the manner in which, e.g., myths distort correct zoological or biological facts.[72]

Emotionally immature adults, who consciously "know better," unconsciously continue to reject correct knowledge and cling to infantile birth theories, which they voice in moments of crisis, of diminished responsibility or of impaired vigilance.[73]

These observations authorize one to view the emotionally immature Hippolytos' angry wish, that men should be able to buy children in temples (618ff.), as a kind of infantile birth theory, and to correlate it with Greek tradition and belief. The possibility that Hippolytos' outburst may echo actual but rejected Athenian "stork stories" is briefly considered at the end of this section.

Hippolytos does not simply curse women; he outlines (in the form of a wish) a detailed "utopian" program for the functional elimination of women, and of sexuality from the social and demographic process. In *that* sense his program has affinities with the kind of birth stories overly prudish parents tell their children—for example, the story that children are bought in shops. This makes it necessary to discuss the relationship between Hippolytos' "program" and Greek tradition and practice.

The wish to buy children in temples can perhaps be correlated with the male Greek practice of consulting oracles in cases of sterility, as did Hippolytos' grandfather Aigeus and also Xuthos, the ancestor of the Athenians, etc.[74] Sterile *women* seem to have gone to temples for divine healing, rather than for oracles.[75] This problem certainly interested Euripides, since he dealt with it in his *Ion*, in his *Phoenician Women* (13ff:) and, very early, in his *Medeia* (669ff.). Moreover if, as many believe, his *Ion* is a pseudo-myth invented by Euripides, this would, if anything, further prove Euripides' interest in this practice.

Though logically it would be desirable to discuss next the fact that, in some myths, *men* consult oracles on how to get children, for reasons of expository convenience I will analyze first the specification that, in order to enable men not to need women, it should be possible to buy

---

[71] G. Devereux, *Tragédie et Poésie Grecques*, 1975 (chap. 8), gives two examples.
[72] On the systematic distortion of such facts in myths, cf. Cl. Levi-Strauss, *Le Cru et le Cuit*, Paris, 1964, op. cit.; *Le Miel et les Cendres*, Paris, 1970, op. cit., passim.
[73] In the guise of jokes, in anger, under the influence of drugs or of alcohol, in dream, during a psychoanalytic session, etc.
[74] Aigeus: Plu. V. *Thes*. 3.3; Xuthos: E. *Ion*.
[75] Literary and epigraphic evidence in Edelstein and Edelstein: *Asclepius*, op. cit.

children in the temples—for gold, iron or bronze—*by weight* (621) and not in the form of coined money.[76] Thus, the rich could buy fine children, and the poor, children of inferior quality. Now, this utopia may be compatible with the outlook of Homeros and of Theognis,[77] but assuredly not with that of Euripides. This fact would, by itself, suffice to cast doubt on Euripides' alleged idealization of Hippolytos.

In appraising the notion of purchase, one must take into account the economic and psychological equivalence of the object purchased and the price paid for it.[78] Our basic symbolic equation is therefore: child = gold (= iron = bronze = wealth). For Greece, the twofold meaning of τόκος, childbirth and interest (also: increase of the flocks), is basic evidence, especially since in many primitive and archaic societies children represent wealth.[79] However, wealth, and in particular gold, also has another symbolic meaning: gold = excrement.[80] The psychological roots of this equation go back to the so-called anal-retentive stage of psychosexual development. Every observant mother knows that the stubborn three-year-old refuses to part with his "valuable" feces. Suetonius more than hints at the nexus between avarice and constipation. He reports that he notoriously avaricious Vespasian's facial expression was that of a man "straining at his stools" (= constipated) and also that Vespasian was the first to tax public privies—i.e., turning excreta into money.[81]

So far, I have documented two equations: baby = gold and feces = gold. The corollary symbolic equation, baby = feces, is equally easy to substantiate even in a non-clinical context, where it manifests itself primarily in the form of theories of anal birth. The most famous classical example is perhaps St. Augustine's remark: "We are born between urine and feces." There is also the peculiar name (Kopreus) borne by Eurystheus' herald

---

[76] This detail is a token of Euripides' tendency to avoid anachronisms. Coining was unknown in Thesean Athens and there is no mention of coins in Homer. Phaidra's letter is, of course, anachronistic; Euripides was perhaps misled by Homer, *Iliad* 6.168ff.

[77] Thgn. 189ff., and passim.

[78] A Sedang Moi slave, of South Vietnam, may not partake of the flesh of the buffalo for which he was sold. That buffalo represents him; his eating its flesh would amount to autocannibalism.

[79] N. Miller, *The Child in Primitive Society*, London, 1928. In some African tribes a cuckolded husband will kill his wife's adulterine *son*, but not her daughter, who, since she will bring in a bride price, represents wealth (G. Devereux, *A Study of Abortion in Primitive Societies*[2], 1975, p. 188). Miller even cites an African young peoples' song, which states that their parents procreated them *so as to have someone work for them*.

[80] Symbolically alluded to in the folk tale of the goose that laid the golden *egg*. (It is to be noted that, in birds, both the colon and the vagina terminate in the cloaca and that, in the human fetus, the colon and the vagina are separated only at a relatively late stage of development).

[81] Suet. *V. xii Caes., Vesp.* 20; cf. his reply to Titus concerning the tax on public privies ("non olet"), 23. To anal birth fantasies (supra) may be added fantasies of oral birth (Kronos): cf. G. Devereux, *Femme et Mythe*, Paris, 1982.

(E. *Heracl.*). One of the feet of Empousa, a female demon especially dangerous to children, was made of ass-feces.[82] Tales, jokes, and beliefs—and even practices—equating babies with feces also occur among primitives,[83] especially in connection with "male births."

These three equations lend significance to Hippolytos' specifications that the *men* should be able to buy children. Now, in myth it was usually the childless father who went to consult an oracle; in historical times it was the barren woman who went to be *healed*. This difference is of considerable interest. In most primitive and archaic societies there is a marked tendency to blame the woman for the sterility of the marriage. The notion that the man may be the sterile (and/or impotent) spouse is expressed only indirectly: Poseidon proudly tells his mistress Tyro that *all* the embraces of a god are fruitful.[84] This implies that those of the mere man may not be. Whether the mythical practice of sending the husband to consult the oracle reflects some belief of this kind need not concern us here. What matters is that Hippolytos' proposal not only seeks to eliminate woman from the procreative process, but also implies an usurpation of her functions by the men. This Utopia is probably rooted in a well-known clinical and ethnological fact: man's—and especially in the sexually inadequate man's—envy of the woman's "mysterious" procreative capacity.[85] These parallelisms are not farfetched, for the fantasy of the male "mother" is quite explicit in Greek myth. Athena was born from Zeus' skull and Dionysos from his thigh.

At any rate, Hippolytos' utopia appears to have inspired Lucian's (*A True Story* 1.22) tale of a race of men who purchase not infants but phalloi made of such substances as they can afford. What underlies this modification of Hippolytos' Utopia is the clinically well-attested "precious substance = baby = phallos" symbolic equation. Moreover, both Hippolytos' purely male Utopia and Lucian's imaginary male society have some affinities with the purely female society of the mythical Amazons, but also differ from them in important respects. The Amazons insure their survival as a race by occasional random cohabitation with men and in Lucian's tale, adult men impregnate the legs of young boys.

[82] *Et. Magn.* s.v. 'Ονοπόλη (ὸνοκώλη).
[83] The "married" Mohave Indian transvestite drinks a constipating decoction, and calls the scybalum he finally passes a "stillborn baby," mourns it, and may even oblige his "husband" to mourn it (G. Devereux, "Institutionalized Homosexuality of the Mohave Indians," *Human Biology* 9: 498-527, 1937 [= various anthologies]).
[84] Hom. *Od.* 11.248ff.
[85] Best know practice: the *couvade*. Other examples: rebirth of the adolescent at initiation from the males; the subincised Australian male's imitation of the menses; the Mohave transvestite's imitation of the menses and of (anal) childbirth; etc. When the old chief of Tea Ha (a Sedang village of South Vietnam) adopted me, he placed a wad of rice-wine-soaked bamboo shavings on his chest and I had to "nurse" at his breast. Cf. G. Devereux, *Femme et Mythe*, Paris, 1982 (chapters on Kronos and Zeus).

Gender and Fantasy

But Hippolytos' utopia excludes *all* sexual relations—even homosexual ones.

A foreseeable objection to my interpretation of Hippolytos' asexual but self-perpetuating all male utopia as being similar to an *infantile* birth theory is that Hippolytos is, at least chronologically, not a child but an adult. But by clinical standards Hippolytos is, like all neurotics, sexually infantile in that in a manner typical of neurotics, he displaces the functions of the genital level to an earlier, pregenital level (wealth = feces = baby).[86] Psychoanalysis can detect a secret clinging to infantile birth theories even in twentieth-century college graduates. What a neurotic knows objectively is one thing; what he unconsciously believes is something else again.

This point is so important, and so little known to the non-clinician, that it seems necessary to quote a relevant clinical incident in some detail.

A college graduate, in his early thirties, suffered from an economically incapacitating, because time-consuming, handwashing compulsion. His generalized mysophobia had begun as a simple syphilophobia, which gradually expanded to include a dread of all dirt and germs, and especially of spinal meningitis, poliomyelitis, and rabies.[87] His dread of germs was mobilized even by *words* designating these illnesses: he often spent *one hour* washing and disinfecting his hands, on finding in his newspaper the *word* poliomyelitis.[88]

One day he spoke endlessly and pointlessly of his grandmother's hens, but carefully omitted any reference to eggs. When I asked him, "Where do the eggs come out?" his index finger pointed to his navel one second *before* his lips could form an answer. I immediately asked, "And where do children come out?" Once more his index pointed to his navel. At this point the patient—a fairly intelligent college graduate—became completely confused. He stammered and rambled, was unable to finish his sentences, and oscillated back and forth between what he "knew" and what he believed: "I know they say that children come out . . . but it is too horrible . . . they *must* come out through the navel . . . they say . . . but it is disgusting. If *that* is where children come out, it would mean that women are *more powerful* than men[89]—but men also have navels—." He rambled on in this manner for some time. After a while he said that he took great pride in passing large stools. "Once, during a

---

[86] On this characteristic tendency of neurotics, cf. Devereux, *Basic Problems*, op. cit., chap. 2.
[87] I note, as a curious detail, that all three of these diseases affect the *nervous* system, as does tertiary (neuro-)*syphilis*.
[88] Hippolytos' feeling of soilure, because his ears had heard immodest words, is discussed further on.
[89] His mother was overbearing; his father gentle.

picnic, I spied on a girl passing her stools. They were enormous—larger than mine ever were. When I saw that, I was ready to go up to her, shake hands with her and admit that, of the two of us, *she* was the better *man!*"

The following implications of this clinical vignette are relevant here:

(1) The dread of dirt (syphilophobia) and compulsive "purity."
(2) Dirty and dangerous germ = the word designating that germ.
(3) Childbirth is an exploit, implying great powers.
(4) Lest men should seem inferior, children must be born from an organ (navel, anus) which *both* sexes possess.
(5) Feces = child = penis.[90]

Since this case history speaks for itself, I can turn to other foreseeable objections to my view that Hippolytos' utopia is, in the last resort, a veiled infantile birth theory.

Some may allege that Hippolytos does not "really" harbor such beliefs, that his fantasy is simply a product of his anger. But it stands to reason that:

(1) Not even drugs (let alone anger) can bring out something not already present in the drugged (or angry) subject.[91]
(2) There is a re-emergence of suppressed attitudes and beliefs in affective states of great intensity.[92]

It could also be objected that Theophrastos (*Char.* 20.7) ridiculed the ill-bred person who discussed in public how his own mother was brought to bed with him. But, since Theophrastos ridiculed only misconducts commonly met with, it is evident that the Greeks, too, were interested in the question "Where did I come from?"—an interest attested by Aischylos (*Choe.* 543).

In short, Hippolytos' outburst must be one treated as a manifestation of an unconsciously held infantile birth theory, one whose mainsprings are fairly easy to discern.

I have shown (supra) that Hippolytos identified with his Amazon mother and professed to be sorry for her—disregarding that all Amazons

---

[90] The feces = (anal) penis and the child = (female) penis fantasy equations are so commonplace in clinical practice that one comes across them in almost every psychoanalysis. The enormous literature on this subject may be located by consulting the proper entries in the volumes of A. Grinstein, *An Index of Psychoanalytic Writings* (3d series), New York, 1956-75.
[91] C. Baudelaire, *Les Paradis Artificiels*, Paris, 1860.
[92] While intoxicated and angry, a southern-born American woman, who actively championed black causes, spoke of her black charwoman in a language studded with racist injuries. A brilliant but alcoholic young scientist, all of whose friends were Jews, expressed violent antisemitic feelings when a very young Jewish girl refused to keep her date with him because he was dead drunk when he called at her parents' house.

perpetuated their race by *casual* cohabitations and, worse still, crippled their bastard sons.[93]

Yet, though he idealizes his mother and hates his father Theseus, nowhere in the drama does he associate his bastardy directed with Theseus. In fact, at verses 1082f., he *seems* to link his mother, rather than his father, with his being a bastard. This surprising nuance makes more understandable than ever his proposal that *men* should get children from the temples (and, presumably, raise them, as Theseus did *not* raise him).

Now, had Hippolytos felt an unambivalent tenderness toward his deceased mother, he would probably have advocated a (female) parthenogenesis—similar to Hera's giving birth to Hephaistos[94]—instead of wishing that men could buy children and then raise them (as Pittheus had raised him and his father as well?). One other thing is quite clear. Hippolytos' utopia is a strictly patriarchal one, and seeks to avoid the birth of bastards in a patriarchal society *only*. This fits the finding that his whole outburst is violently misogynous: it simply transfers his *unconscious* hatred and contempt for his "sluttish" mother to womankind as a whole, in a manner typical of the Mediterranean culture area but modified to fit a bastard's special problems.[95]

Athenian Stork-Tale Equivalents

Since children everywhere evolve farfetched birth theories, and since their parents often cater to that need, such theories must have existed also in Athens. Though it is unlikely that we will ever learn their exact natures, the importance of certain atypical and imaginary forms of reproduction mentioned in many myths shows that even adult Greeks unconsciously harbored residues of infantile birth fantasies.

At any rate, even though Hippolytos' utopia of an all-male asexual reproduction fits a number of Greek fantasies, beliefs, and practices fairly well, I doubt that his story of infants purchased or obtained in temples was a *common* nursery explanation of childbirth in Athens. Had it been a common one, Euripides' audience would probably have burst out laughing, as it may have laughed at the naiveté of Xuthos (E. *Ion*), who readily accepted as his own Kreusa's bastard son by Apollo (whom that god's oracle had foisted on him). At the same time Hippolytos' utopian project is just infantile enought to highlight this sex-phobic's immaturity. It must therefore have—in spirit, if not in the letter—enough

---

[93] Cod. Athen. 1083, *Paroem.* ap. Kugéas, *Sitzungsberichte der Bayrischen Akademie*, Munich, 1910 (4, p. 15) = Mimn. *fr.* 15D.

[94] Hes. *Th.* 927; Apollod. 1.3.5; cf. G. Devereux, *Femme et Mythe*, op. cit.

[95] Bertrand Russell once told me that, for Mediterranean man, all women are sluts, though his mother is a saint. But this maxim does not take into account the special outlook of the bastard.

latent affinities with some standard nursery story to permit Euripides to make Hippolytos' project reverberate in the unconscious of his public. In short, even if some lost Greek nursery tale was the ultimate "root" of Hippolytos' plan, his utopia could only be a highly stylized and modified version of that "original." Short of the miraculous discovery of a private diary less distorted by secondary elaboration than Aelius Aristeides' *Sacred Discourses*, we will never know just how faithful this "copy" is to the nursery tale original, nor the manner in which it "stylized" (distorted) the tale that had inspired it. One can, at most, suppose that this Utopia preserved the *latent* content of the nursery tale, the way Pindaros' version of the feast of Tantalos preserved exclusively the *effective* content (erotized anxiety) of the tale of divine anthropophagy which it professed to obliterate.[96] In other words, it is possible—but no more than possible—that certain irrretrievably lost Athenian nursery explanations of birth were in some manner connected with the excretory process—with the widespread fecal baby fantasy.

Any inference going beyond this point would be speculative in proportion to its pretended precision.

Addendum: Anal Birth

The interpretation of Hippolytos' asexual utopia as an expression of anal birth fantasies is substantiated by the fact that, centuries later, foundlings were denoted by a term recalling their being recuperated from dung hills (κοπρίαρτος). The practice of exposing *unwanted* children on dungheaps and even in rubbish dumps exists to this day. As for miscarried or aborted small embryos, they are often flushed down the toilet. It suffices to recall in conclusion that the rejection of bastards is a common mythological theme, and is also underlined by Agamemnon's reminding Teukros of the debt he owes his father Telamon, who raised him in his palace even though he was a bastard (Hom. *Il.* 8.283ff).

The Phantasmatic Virginal Mother

The phantasmatic virginal mother, whose ultimate expression—parthenogenesis—has haunted men's imagination since the dawn of time, sharply contrasts with the realistic conception of the mother as the father's sexual partner. Hence when a playmate tells a child the facts of life the usual, and at times violent, reaction is: "Maybe *your* mother does; mine doesn't!" This denial nearly always has an obsessive, reality-alien character.

Parental sexuality upsets even primitive children, living in huts or

[96] G. Devereux, *Tragédie et Poésie Grecques*, op. cit., chap. 8.

Gender and Fantasy

tents that provide no privacy.[97] The initial trauma is real, though non-interference with childish curiosity can lead to its sublimation[98] in the form of creative intellectual curiosity.

Such sexual knowledge is especially upsetting for the bastard whose social handicaps are due precisely to his (unmarried) mother's "misconduct." Sibling-rivalry with his father's socially privileged legitimate children (1455) further stimulates the bastard's sensitiveness, as does his hatred of his father's lawful wife. One is also constantly reminded of Hippolytos' bastardy,[99] which he deplores and finds hard to bear (1082 ff.), even though he professes to be reconciled to being a private person; he does not seek to usurp the throne destined for Phaidra's legitimate children (1010ff.). Nonetheless, in a passage that puzzles some commentators, he attributes his misfortunes to "crime-stained parents, of forebears came evils that press me" (1378; cf. Barrett, ad loc.). This passage strikingly parallels Phaidra's lament about her own sexually depraved female kin (338ff.): her general statement, that "knowing evil (sex) of one's father and mother makes even a brave man into a slave" (424f.),[100] explains who Hippolytos' "crime-stained parents, forebears" really are. Equally pointed is his outburst against deities worshipped at night (106).[101] His social inferiority, caused by his bastardy, is one of the principal motives of his blind hatred of sexuality. Such reactions are common not only among bastards but also among legitimate children born to socially or racially disparate parents.[102]

Since some illegitimate children hate sex blindly, the both mythical (St. Gregory) and real practice of dedicating bastards to monastic chastity probably meets their neurotic needs more than halfway.

The underprivileged are also particularly prone to compensate for their handicap by claiming supernatural powers or trying to "shine" in

---

[97] G. Devereux, "The Primal Scene and Juvenile Heterosexuality in Mohave Society," in G. B. Wilbur and W. Muensterberger (eds.), *Psychoanalysis and Culture* (Róheim Festschrift), New York, 1951.
[98] The Yuman Indians believe that precociously intelligent children have observed parental coitus. G. Róheim, "Psycho-Analysis of Primitive Cultural Types," *International Journal of Psycho-Analysis* 13: 1–204, 1932 (p. 195).
[99] Nurse: 309; Theseus: 962; Hippolytos: 1082, etc. Professor Segal notes that many modern critics underplay Hippolytos' bastardy.
[100] Cf. also E. *Bellerophontes*, fr. 298 N².
[101] Cf. the outburst of Pentheus (E. *Ba.* 485ff.), who actually spies on his mother and aunt, whom, like the rest of the Mainades, he *rightly* suspects of illicit sexual behavior; G. Devereux, "Trance and Orgasm in Euripides' *Bakchai*," in A. Angoff and D. Barth (eds.), *Parapsychology and Anthropology*, New York, 1974. In general, see Dodds, ad loc., in his ed. of E. *Ba.* Cf. A. *Sept.* 364f. for: nocturnal rite = coitus.
[102] G. Devereux, "Neurotic Downward Identification," *American Imago* 22: 77–95, 1965.

some—socially relatively marginal—way.[103] This explains both Hippolytos' ostentatious "purity"—a quality which many admire in others but seldom desire for themselves[104]—also his staggeringly arrogant conviction that he *alone* is of the elect.

Another peculiar—and, I believe, hitherto largely unnoticed—aspect of Hippolytos' resentment is that the bastard's *conscious* resentment is usually directed at his father and, by extension, at the male sex. Now, though Hipplytos is certainly not tender toward Theseus, his real resentment is directed at women—at his "poor, unhappy mother" (1082ff.). His one explicit expression of pity for his mother concerns, in reality, mainly his own bruised self (1144, cf. 1079-80): he speaks briefly of her futile parturition and then laments the bastard's fate.

All things considered, the moment his mother ceased to be a virgin, she also ceased, *ipso facto*, to be admirable; at best she deserves pity, but nothing more.[105] His unconscious hatred of his "immoral" mother is displaced *to her sex in general*. It is through, and behind, this hatred of sex that his derivative hatred of his father manifests itself. There is also something paradoxical—at least for reasonable minds—in the fact that a *vegetarian* "orphic" (952ff.) bookworm should be an ardent hunter. This is basically incompatible with "orphic" behavior.[106]

Verse 645 provides a rough explanation of this paradox. After stating that he hates intelligent women (Phaidra?) and prefers stupid ones (barbarian Amazons?), Hippolytos argues that women should consort only with *silent wild beasts*. That, of course, is precisely what Artemis does and what his Amazon mother formerly did. However, women also associate with men and, in the child's neurotic vision of parental coitus, father is a silent, nocturnal beast or ogre, i.e., precisely the kind of silent beast or aggressor one finds in all three Euripidean dreams.[107] Hippolytos' hunting—like that of countless neurotics—thus also has an aggressive oedipal significance.[108]

---

[103] Illuminating discussion, with special reference to younger sons in Tanala (Madagascar) society, by R. Linton, "The Tanala of Madagascar," in A. Kardiner and R. Linton, *The Individual and his Society*, New York, 1939, pp. 270ff.
[104] Cf. St. Augustine's famous prayer: "Oh Lord, make me chaste, *but not yet.*"
[105] Hippolytos' irrationality is strongly highlighted by the fact that Hippolyte, the captive, had no choice in the matter.
[106] W. K. C. Guthrie, *Orpheus and Greek Religion*², London, 1952; I. M. Linforth, *The Arts of Orpheus*, Berkeley, 1941. Omophagous (?) vegetarians: E. *The Cretans, fr.* 472 N². Prof. M. Detienne also attracted my attention to Pythagorean warriors. These are odd combinations, that fit well the basic illogicality of supernaturalism (see Chap. 4).
[107] G. Devereux, *Dreams in Greek Tragedy.* op. cit., chap. 8.
[108] K. A. Menninger, "Totemic Aspects of Contemporary Attitudes toward Animals," in Wilbur and Muensterberger (eds.), op. cit.; J. C. Flugel, "Some Psychological Aspects of the Fox-Hunting Rite," *International Journal of Psycho-Analysis* 12: 483-91, 1931. For a conscious gunning down of a neighbor's ducks, as a substitute for killing one's parents, cf. G. Devereux, "Schizophrenia vs. Neurosis," *Psychiatric Quarterly* 34: 710-21, 1960.

Hippolytos' almost conscious wish to kill his father is revealed with dazzling skill. Challenging Theseus, he says: "had *you* tried to seduce *my* wife (mother?), I would kill you" (1041ff.). This peculiar and insolent counter-challenge[109] hurled at Theseus, who had shown a momentary desire to kill Hippolytos only at verse 895f., speaks for itself. For anyone able to *feel* the reality of oedipal son-father rivalries, no further evidence is needed.

In short, Hippolytos is haunted by the discrepancy between the mythical wild virgin his mother was *before* she met Theseus and the (imaginary) "trollop" she became afterwards *in his eyes*. By identifying himself with the virginal Amazon, he tries to restore the *status quo ante* in his own person. The "scandal" never happened, since in the virginal Hippolytos the sexless Amazon mother lives again, to give "calumny" the lie. This is how the neurotic mind operates and its defensive maneuver seems adequate until subjected to real stress. At that point it becomes painfully evident that the *status quo ante* cannot be restored, or the slate wiped clean, until Hippolytos himself—the living, tangible proof of his mother's "sluttishness"—*ceases to exist*. This is commonplace suicidal reasoning.

By means of his clumsy, arrogant, unconciliatory "defense," and especially through his devious attempt to provoke Theseus into killing him personally,[110] Hippolytos prepares the ground for his own destruction. This much Euripides must have sensed, since the notion of "accidentally on purpose" self-contrived deaths haunts all of Greek tragedy.[111] This may even mean that, psychologically, the fatal *taraxippos* (horse-panicker) is not so much Poseidon's bull as Hippolytos own panic, which infects also his horses. Xenophon, being an expert, realized that the horseman's own panic can affect his horses—usually with fatal results.[112] Whether Euripides actually had this in mind, I do not profess to know. I simply recall that he was probably rich enough to have served in the cavalry.

Artemis

As late Greek myth defined her, and as Hippolytos imagined her, Artemis closely resembles the imago of the "virginal" mother, provided

---

[109] Pasiphaë similarly provokes Minos, E. *The Cretans*, 33f. (Page, *Greek Literary Papyri*, Cambridge, USA, 1942; Loeb Library, p. 76). On wife = mother cf. G. Devereux, *Ethnopsychoanalysis*, 1978 (chap. 7).
[110] Cf. Sokrates' provocative second speech (Pl. *Apol.* 38d, seemingly denied in 37 init.), alos the behavior of Indian captives at the stake.
[111] Unconscious-purposive complex maneuvers leading to one's death are well documented and analyzed in K. A. Menninger, *Man Against Himself*, New York, 1938. I have reservations only regarding the reality of the "death instinct," for reasons partly set forth in O. Fenichel, "A Critique of the Death Instinct," in *The Collected Papers of O. Fenichel*, New York, 1953 (vol. 1, pp. 363ff.).
[112] There are hints about the need for the *rider* to be self-controlled, in X. *Eq.* 3.9, 3.12, 6.13f., 9.2, 9.9, 9.11, 10.2, and perhaps also in Simon = X. *Eq.* 11.6

that one does not allow elegant Hellenistic statuary to overshadow her archaic traits. Basically ferocious, Artemis sends her scourges in retaliation for even slight offenses, especially if they challenge her virago-like masculinity. Thus, in one version, Iphigeneia's tragedy is caused by Agamemnon's boast that, as a hunter, he is a match for Artemis.[113] Her close connection with Hekate, regardless of how it is conceived, also makes her suspect. Even more disturbing is her role as a producer and healer of insanity,[114] for only someone who can cause insanity can also cure it: doesn't one pray to mad berserker Ares for peace of mind (Hom. *h. Ares.*)?

Being the deity of the Wild, who threatens to encroach on cultivated fields and to endanger the livestock, her cult is largely conciliatory, corresponding to what gangsters call "protection money." Artemis' "good" aspects represent only the euphemistic denial of her bad one; she is no more truly helpful than the Erinyes are really Eumenides.[115] It is, I repeat, only an euphemism; it is prudent to harp on the clemency of a tyrant if one wishes to stay alive. Of course, the same may be said also of many other deities and of supposedly benign utopias as well.[116]

Man's *conception* of the deity (or of Utopia) is inextricably interwoven with the child's image of its parents.[117] Adults behave toward the child in such a manner that the latter evolves—and *rightly* evolves—an image of the adult which corresponds to the text-book behavior of the psychopathic personality.[118]

That Hippolytos' *private* Artemis is not the "real" Artemis does not

---

[113] Procl. *Chrest.* 1 (= *Kypria*). He violates her grove (S. *El* 563ff.).
[114] O. Gruppe, *Griechische Mythologie und Religionsgeschichte*, Munich, 1906 (2.1273; n. 4) citing *inter alia*: Pherec. *FHG* 1.94.97; E. *Hipp.* 142; E. *Hel.* 570; S. *Aias* 172; Orph. *h.*, 36.5, A. 910.
[115] G. Devereux, *Dreams in Greek Tragedy*, op. cit., chap. 4.
[116] Where the *conception* of the deity is indisputably good, diabolism is not far away. For the idea of total goodness so disturbs man that he resorts to theological (or ideological) prestidigitation: the kindly deity's (or ideology's) human high priests become ravening monsters. The Inquisition was a form of diabolism, as was (and is) every secret police serving a "good" utopianism. Man, the ambivalent animal, remained unreconciled to the absolute goodness impacted to Jesus and therefore found ways which profess to implement that total goodness through sheer evil. In 1956 some communist Hungarian refugees felt that the communist régime had betrayed "ideal" communism—as, in the opinion of many Christians, the Inquisition betrayed the "real" teachings of Jesus. Yet, such "betrayals" are inevitable, for they are rooted in Man's insuperable ambivalence.
[117] Pl. *Lgg.* 931 A; Plu. *frr.* 46,89. Sandb. Cf. S. Freud "The Future of an Illusion," *Standard Edition*, xxi, 1961.
[118] G. Devereux, "Charismatic Leadership and Crisis," in W. Muensterberger (ed.), *Psychoanalysis and the Social Sciences*, vol. iv, New York, 1955; *Basic Problems*, id., op. cit., chap. 4. No theology known to me was able to avoid the reef of patterning the deity on the all too human parent. Psychopathy defined: Sir D. K. Henderson, *Psychopathic Personality*, Oxford, 1952.

seem to be obvious to everyone. What obscures the "heretical" nature of Hippolytos' conceptions is the absence of the notion of heresy in classical Greek thought. It is, hence, necessary to stress that Hippolytos' Artemis is not the Artemis of other Greeks—at least not on the surface. Yet, underneath, she is the same,[119] since Hippolytos' idealized Artemis represents a systematic denial of the real one, for lies, denials, and bowdlerizations modify only the externals of a story but preserve its basic structure (Lévi-Strauss) and latent affective content (supra note). The real Artemis is very much present behind her "lovely" façade, extolled, e.g., by Méridier.[120]

The data bearing on this point are copious. Artemis herself does not claim that she is pre-eminent among the gods; Hippolytos does it for her, and Aphrodite rightly resents it (16). Had Artemis the proper respect for Zeus, she would have made Hippolytos give up his exalted conception of her preeminence. But she does not do so, because Hippolytos' conception of her importance visibly supports her own conceit.

The infantile sources of Hippolytos' notions are obvious: for the very small child the parents are ideally perfect and superior to all other beings.[121] The discovery that their parents are neither omnipotent nor perfect is therefore always a blow to children. Some never quite get over it, and others never accept the inevitability of this discovery, spending their lives questing for a perfect substitute parental imago. The extent to which one accepts the imperfections of one's parents is therefore a good empirical measure of one's emotional maturity.

There are good reasons why Hippolytos never attained this maturity. The bastard's bruised Ego needs rehabilitation by a "superior"; the neglected child hungers to become the "elect" of a deity.[122] The human parents' "non-favorite" child becomes the *only* favorite of a "superior" mother substitute. Thus, Hippolytos incessantly boasts of being the *one* person permitted to associate with Artemis. This is the clinically familiar fantasy of having mother all to oneself. Artemis concurs (1338): she prefers Hippolytos to all other mortals. One can sympathize with her; the number of mythical men who—because they did not really feel like it—"forgot" to sacrifice to her suggests that, unlike Athene, Artemis did not have many sincerely dedicated devotees. One cannot but suppose that the agricultural Greek was simply too busy with his farm and/or with his civic duties to have much time to roam the wilds in her company.[123]

---

[119] Kitto, op. cit., p. 217, saw this; he calls her a "subhuman goddess."
[120] Kitto (op. cit., p. 217, note) rightly objects to this distortion.
[121] Proverbially: "My Dad can lick your Dad." The feeling that the parents are psychopaths develops later.
[122] Conquerors are often originally underprivileged persons, experiencing the need to be "mother's heroes" (G. Devereux, "La Psychanalyse et l'Histoire," Annales 20: 18–44, 1965).
[123] I must insist on this point. Modern urban man has weird notions about the "backward" peasant's or jungle-dweller's familiarity with the forest. Both are afraid of it. This is

This brings me to the (implicit) basis of Hippolytos' assertion of Artemis' preeminence, which seems to please that goddess so much. I refer to Artemis' connection (identity?) with another Lady of the Wilds—with the Mountain Mother, or the Great Mother of the Gods— and note the "paradox" that the virginal (?) Artemis should have been equated with a kind of super-mother, represented as polymastic or as multiscrotal (no nipples; cf. H. P. Duerr, *Sedna*, Frankfurt am Main, 1984) in Ephesos and perhaps also in other parts of Asia Minor.

Hippolytos' somewhat monotonous obsession with Artemis' virginity is also a component of the "virgin mother" complex, where "virgin" (παρθένος) is to be understood both in the strict and in the broad sense. For, it is evident that παρθένος did not originally mean *chiefly* a sexually intact girl. It denoted simply a woman *not* living under the authority of a man—and especially of her mate.[124]

But Hippolytos'—or anyone else's—preoccupation with the virginity of Artemis (or of a mere girl) necessarily implies what I must call an obsessive "crotch-mindedness" (for no other word will do). That obsession is present even if, for "decency's" sake, it assumes a poetic guise. In verse 74 Hippolytos waxes lyrical over the purity of Artemis' λειμών "meadow" (= pubis).[125]

---

as true of modern Transsylvanian tree-fellers as of the agricultural Sedang Moi, who are not true-blue men of the jungle: they stick, whenever possible, to their villages, their paths and their fields, dreading the jungle which surrounds them on all sides. A Sedang Moi boasted that, unlike others, he drew his livelihood from the jungle (G. Devereux, "Auto-Caractérisations de Quatre Sedang," in J. Poirier and F. Raveau, eds., *L'Autre et l'Ailleurs*, Paris, 1976 [memorial volume, in honor of Professor Roger Bastide]). The only people really "at home" in the jungle are oppressed groups, who have no choice in the matter: pygmies and persecuted, backward tribes, such as the Phi Tong Luang. Cf. A. Bernatzik, *The Spirits of the Yellow Leaves* (Pt. II), London, 1958. On the "outdoors" Artemis: U. v. Wilamowitz-Moellendorff, *Der Glaube der Hellenen*³, Basel, 1959, pp. 173–80.

[124] I have proven this point in *Femme et Mythe*, Paris, 1982. Here I note simply that any son born to an unwed girl (Hom. *Il.* 16.180; Pi. *O*.6.31) was called παρθένιος. Any illegitimate child conceived by a Spartan girl while the Spartans were away from home, engaged in the long conquest of Messene, was a Παρθανίας (Arist. *Pol.* 306b29; Str. 6.3.2). Moreover, though in Homeros and in Pindaros the reputed father of a παρθένιος son happens to be a god, the Spartan παρθενίας was simply the bastard of a human father. (I cannot agree with the hypothesis [W. G. Forrest, *A History of Sparta*, London, 1968, p. 60] that this name had a geographic origin.) Cf. W. K. C. Guthrie, *The Greeks and their Gods*², Boston, 1955, pp. 102ff., on the original meaning of that term.

[125] For pubis = meadow: E. *Cycl.* 171. I feel that, in Emp. *fr.* 66 D-K, the "divided meadows of Aphrodite" also concerns the pubic cleft. The basic meaning of λειμών appears to be "any moist, grassy place." "Moist" requires no comment, but "grassy" suggests that *not every* Greek woman depilated her pubis. Cf. French slang: female pubis = "la touffe" = tuft, cluster. The emphasis is on this protuberant tuft of pubic hair, which some children *confuse with* the "female phallos," while others believe that it *conceals* the "female phallos." (For the relevant literature on this common childish fantasy and its discussion, cf. G. Devereux, *Dreams in Greek Tragedy*², op. cit., chap. 9).

Having discussed the significance and pertinence of that word for this play in the general introductory section of this work, I will discuss here only some aspects of what preoccupation with this "meadow" means for Hippolytos—a matter not touched upon in my earlier comments.

Hippolytos stresses that the garland comes from a meadow that has neither been grazed by domestic animals nor touched by iron. Barrett (ad loc., p. 171) rightly notes that these specifications apply to land dedicated to a deity and thinks specifically of Artemis' *temenos* by the Saronic Mere. But he then adds the hypothesis that a votary of the goddess was free to gather in such a place material out of which to make a garland for the goddess herself. Hippolytos certainly feels that his virtues entitle him to such a privilege.

Actually the matter is even more complex. By harping constantly on Artemis' virginity, Hippolytos talks in fact incessantly about her sex organs,[126] whose virginal state he constantly bears in mind.

If a free association be permitted, the constant harping on the virginity of Artemis and on the intactness of her meadow (pubis) remind me of once common American publicity for packaged groceries: "untouched by human hands." Though I had no training in psychoanalysis at that time, I spontaneously correlated this slogan with the—in 1932 still strong—puritanism of Americans. What elicited the associative recall of that all but forgotten publicity slogan is, of course, the fact that in E. *Cycl.* 171, Silenos imagines the pleasure it would give him to touch a female pubis (= meadow, λειμών) with his *hands* (χεροῖν).

Now, since I believe that an Athenian virgin was depilated for the first time on the eve of her marriage, I tentatively conclude that Hippolytos' picking flowers for Artemis—in Artemis' own tabooed meadow—to make a garland for her comes very close to a fantasy of defloration.[127]

---

[126] I once analyzed an almost obsessively puritanical woman who, at one point of her analysis, declared that she felt certain that my impeccable professional ethics guaranteed that I would *not* bring my penis with me into the analytic chamber. Just how I could avoid doing so was never made clear. What matters is that her praise of my professional ethics gave her an excuse for talking a great deal about my ("absent") penis. The presence of her own sex organs in the analytic chamber created no problem, for in her opinion women had no sex organs at all—they only had a void (*béance*).

[127] I am quite aware of the grotesque latent implications of this interpretation: Artemis' garland is made, so to speak, of her own freshly plucked pubic hair. I also realize that this is likely to elicit a scandalized outcry on the part of those who would prefer the poet's mind to be properly pasteurized before it goes to work. I can only say that I have heard, from *only slightly* neurotic analysands, fantasies whose implications were equally grotesque, and assume that in the course of my own *didactic* analysis the latent implications of some of my own fantasies were no less absurd. Those whom this implication of Hippolytos' remarks shock would do well to ascertain that the implications of their own fantasies are, like Ivory Soap, 99.44% pure (and logical).

The expression ἀκήρατον, which refers here chiefly to "purity," occurs in the verse (76) that also specifies that the meadow is untouched by "iron," of which more anon.

I might also add that meadows with deep grass—i.e., not grazed over, at least by sheep, and perhaps not at all—are not only traditional trysting places, but may, like Lerne, even be the proper setting for obscene rites[128] and also for ritually animalistic couplings.[129] Hippolytos' strenuous emphasizing that this meadow is untouched (while in E. *Cycl.* 171, the pubic meadow *is* to be handled manually) is a labored—and laborious—denial of the (at least potential) impurity of these "meadows."[130] The details suggest something of the sort. Hippolytos specifies that even the husbandman's iron does not encroach on that meadow—and the nexus between ploughing and coitus is made painfully obvious, even for the "pure," by the loving union of Demeter and Iasion in a thrice-labored furrow.[131] It is just possible that there once existed a tradition about Theseus' first cohabitation with the captured Hippolyte in a meadow, and that it is this that Hippolytos' frantic insistence (on the meadow's purity) seeks to deny. Like many other bastards, he, too, might find comfort in the belief that his *unconsenting* mother was "raped": she would seem the purer for it.[132]

Hippolytos' definition of his relationship with Artemis is, at any rate, arrogant. Though he insists that he is her *only* companion (84), he returns from the hunt in the company of young men. This fits his admission that he never *saw* Artemis: he only *heard* her voice and *smelled* her heavenly perfume (85–86, 1391), of which more later. Evidently his "companionship" consisted only in doing things which Artemis *presumably* also did, at the same time and place: he hunted as—and where— she did. He is her companion in life and in hunting (1092), he connects with her his hunting, his horsemanship, and his (Apollonian?) singing and playing the lyre (1127–39). He is her hunter and servant (1397) as well as her horseman (1399).

Then, surprisingly, the situation is transposed to another plane: the actions just mentioned imply a relationship with the *person* of Artemis.

---

[128] The Polymnos = Prosymnos rite, connected with what M. P. Nilsson (*Griechische Feste*, Leipzig, 1906, p. 289) calls the nastiest of Greek tales.
[129] A. *PV*; cf. G. Devereux, *Dreams in Greek Tragedy*, op. cit., chap. 2.
[130] A Hellenistic group shows Hippolytos and Artemis enlaced and Eros triumphant (though descriptions and interpretations differ; cf. Gruppe, op. cit., 1.606, n. 2). I simply note that a decadent period often makes explicit what a greater age only implied—and does so with a loss of affectivity and tension.
[131] Hom. *Od.* 5.125ff., Hes. *Th.* 969; cf. G. Devereux, "Greek Pseudo-Homosexuality," op. cit., for an analysis of early and late versions of this myth. Cf. also Paus. 9.37.2.
[132] Cf. A. V. Rankin, "Euripides' Hippolytus: A Psychopathological Hero," *Arethusa* 7: 72–93, 1974, p. 81.

Gender and Fantasy

However, as the play opens, he only crowns her altar on returning from the hunt (73f.). As the play ends, in the midst of his dying account of a *personal* relationship, he once more speaks only of his crowning her *altar—not* her person (1399).

The possible objection that the goddess is the same thing as her cult statue (*agalma*) is trite, true to the point of being almost false. Things are never as obvious in the realm of the irrational, which includes the world of the myth.[133]

It is not known what early and "lost" versions of the Hippolytos myth had to say of Artemis' and Hippolytos' "companionship." By Euripides' time a *concrete* companionship could not longer be imagined. Hence Theseus openly mocks this alleged intimacy (948) and even Hippolytos never pretends to have *seen* the goddess. What he did see—what he did approach—was her altar (and statue?), with piety no doubt but also with a sense of *familiarity*. Modern notions blind us to the unusualness of this behavior by Greek standards.[134] In early Greek thought a deity did at times love a human being—but only the way one loves a pet or an appealing bedfellow. Moreover, those whom a deity loved often lapsed into *hubris* and brought about their own downfall. No pre-Platonic Greek would have considered it normal to love a—or "the"—deity in a medieval sense.[135] In Greek terms, it is at least presumptuous and perhaps even sacrilegious for Hippolytos to profess to "love" Artemis and to "walk with her," as a Christian Saint may "walk with God." If the plural pronoun means what I think it means, it is rank *hubris* for him to exclaim: "*We* are banished" (1092ff.).[136]

---

[133] In Homeros and Hesiodos (supra) it is with the "real" Demeter that Iasion cohabits in mutual love. This was a bit too earthy for latter-day Greeks. In a later version, Iasion only tried to *rape* the goddess (D. H. *ant. rom.* 1.61). One source, perhaps because it is fragmentary (Str. 7, fr. 48), mentions no punishment; in another source (Apollod. *Bibl.* 3.21.1) Iasion is punished. Still other sources say that he assaulted only Demeter's *agalma* and was struck down by a thunderbolt for his sacrilege (Scymn. 685, *GGM* 1.223; Hellan. *fr.* 129 *FHG* 1.63 = sch. AR. 1.916). Some late authors shy away altogether from the cohabitation scene (D.S. 5.77.1). Moreover, Iasion is not only never punished in Hades, but is said to have joined the society of the gods (D.S. 5.49.3). In this instance the deterioration of the myth to a euphemism is painfully obvious, even if one ignores Ovid (*Met.* 9.422ff.) as pseudo-myth. For "empty" statues, cf. M. P. Nilsson, *Greek Piety*, Oxford, 1948, pp. 107ff. (Heraiskos).

[134] A. J. Festugière, *Personal Religion among the Greeks*, Berkeley, 1954, deals largely with post-classical religious experiences.

[135] This is true even of the mortal bedfellows of goddesses. Anchises' lust for Aphrodite turns into fright when he discovers her identity (Hom. *h. Aphr.*). In the *Odyssey*, Kalypso and Kirke are clearly in love with Odysseus, but he is not in love with them. It would be pedantry to multiply examples.

[136] I do not think that *this* particular first person plural is a "generic plural," to be interpreted as Hippolytos' way of speaking of himself. It means: "I and Artemis" (in that order!). Incidentally, the whole problem of lapses into the pseudo-plural in drama needs to be re-examined.

Also, unlike some primitives' "guardian spirits,"[137] or Christian guardian angels, Greek deities did not tag after their devotees on their own; they had to be *transported*, the way Aineias *carried* away with him his household gods.[138] The reverse is also true. A deity may depart (Apollon in E. *Alc.*) and his favorite may not be able to follow his god unless *carried away* by the deity. Hippolytos probably assumed that his banishment involved also the banishment of Artemis. This is theologically gratuitous and psychologically grandiose, for it more than hints at an identification with Artemis.

Even his imitation of Artemis' behavior is presumptuous. The notion that something like an "*Imitatio Christi*" could be pious belongs to a much later age. Those Greeks who imitated divine behavior were considered impious.[139]

Hippolytos' *hubris*, even with respect to the gods, is strongly underscored by his exclamation: "Why cannot mortals harm the gods?" (1415).[140] This passage has been discussed so often by Hellenists—especially well by Barrett (ad loc.)—and so many examples have been cited to show its impiety, that its discussion may be deferred until later.

The view that Hippolytos finds in his (fictitious) companionship with Artemis a compensation for his bastardy implicitly suggests that, psychologically, his *present-day* Artemis—the heavenly (59), the virginal (66, 71)—is a fantasied imago of his mother, who *once* was a virgin. Artemis is (retroactively) substituted to the mother, beginning with the moment the latter became Theseus' mistress. Artemis' divine status, tenacious "virginity," and inaccessibility to all men—for even Hippolytos cannot see her—fit her perfectly for the role she has to play in Hippolytos' fantasy. They also offer solid guarantees that he will not be disappointed a second time. Artemis at least will never cease to be a "virgin;" she will not give him a paternal, or even a fraternal, rival for her love. Being perfectly imaginary, and also perfectly cold, she is necessarily perfectly "safe."

---

[137] R. Benedict, "The Concept of the Guardian Spirit in North America," *American Anthropological Association Memoir*, xxxix, 1923.

[138] Or as the Spartans transported the Dioskouroi to Sicily, to be the allies of the Lokrians (D.S. 8.32.2).

[139] Typically Salmoneus: I am not persuaded that, in imitating Zeus' thunder, he was simply acting as a ritual rain-maker (J. E. Harrison, *Themis*², 1927). This view ignores one of the most crucial aspects of shamanism: the belief of a great many primitive people that the practicing shaman's power eventually runs wild, turns against its owner, and destroys him. Trafficking with the supernatural is never safe. I hold that a hitherto unrecognized difference between "religion" and "magic" is that the religious practitioner's powers do *not* turn against him in the end, while those of the magician do. Cf. E. R. Dodds, *Pagan and Christian in an Age of Anxiety*, Cambridge, G.B., 1965 (on late man = God equations).

[140] Hom. *Il.* 22.15ff.; cf. Pl. *Rmp.* 391a.

Gender and Fantasy

Artemis' sorrow over Hippolytos' death has been needlessly exaggerated and even sentimentalized, though one cannot expect a goddess to lament like an Aischylean mourner.[141] Euripides records only that Artemis approved of Hippolytos (1296ff.), that he was dutiful and pious (1307ff.) that she preferred him to all mortals (1331ff.) and that his death saddened her (1338). But when the chips are down, when Hippolytos is on the point of dying, the goddess leaves him at once, lest his death defile her.

Of course, one should not expect a deity to mourn a man deeply and forever. But one somehow expects more from Artemis than a simple *denial* that the death of a good man could please a deity—even though putting things negatively is a typically Greek idiom. I must insist that a few *other* Greek deities did, at times, feel racking grief over a man. Much to Platon's (*Rmp.* 388cff.) disgust, Zeus feels anguish over Sarpedon's fate (Hom. *Il.* 16.432ff., 644ff.). In fact, he can pity even Achilleus' grieving horses (Hom. *Il.* 17.443ff.). Apollon rescues Sarpedon's corpse (Hom. *Il.* 16.666ff.). Also, in E. *Alc.*, he is, I feel, in less of a hurry to leave his doomed favorite, Admetos. (This point carries special weight, since Euripides did *not* like Apollon.) In Hom. *Il.* 23.184ff. Aphrodite protects Hektor's corpse and anoints it. One thinks also of another warlike virgin, Athene, grieving, on a celebrated bas-relief, for the fallen defenders of her city. By comparison, Artemis shows little sadness indeed over the death of the mortal she "loved best."

Also, despite Hippolytos' alleged orphism, Artemis does not imply that her devotee will, after death, enjoy a privileged fate—quite the contrary, in fact (1416ff.)—nor does she hint that he might be resurrected by Asklepios, though that tradition is probably of a fairly venerable antiquity.[142] Hippolytos is "paid off" and dismissed with a reference to the Troizenian cult to be established (see below). Artemis is no *mater dolorosa*, nor is the death scene a *pietà*. This is the principal disadvantage of love for a phantom: though safe, it is, in the end, also unrewarding.

Since speculation so designated is legitimate, I am entitled to indicate that there may be a profound psychological truth in the Greek belief that, at death, even the most intimate relationship between a mortal and an Olympian deity comes to an end. This state of affairs reflects a dim and almost unconscious awareness that the Olympians are the creations of man's imagination—of his need to idealize and to make commitments. With death, both this capacity and this need cease, and

---

[141] J. de Romilly, *La Crainte et l'Angoisse dans le Théâtre d' Eschyle*, Paris, 1958 (on laments).
[142] Data in Barrett, op. cit., p. 5, n. 6; cf. E. J. and L. Edelstein, *Asclepius* (1945), *Testt.* 72, 73, etc. It would, of course, be unreasonable to expect references to Hippolytos = Virbius. On the whole, Fr. Schiller's "Der Mohr hat seine Schuldigkeit getan; der Mohr kann gehn" describes Artemis' attitude quite well.

with it vanish the gods which the living created. Death breaks all connections between the Olympians and the dead: theologically because the gods are soiled by contact with the dead, and psychologically because the gods are no longer even imagined. Even less are they invested with affect ("cathected"). They cease to be *present* reality for the (completely) dead, who pass under the jurisdiction of different gods—of "another Zeus" who is suitable for what the dead are. In the surviving accounts of existence in Hades—from the Homeric *Nekyia* to Lucian— the dead hardly ever refer to the Olympians, for they are no longer involved with them.[143] Even the justice demanded by the offended dead is given to them not so much by the Olympians or by Dike as by the Erinyes, who are at the opposite pole from the Olympians, and their disputes are settled by Rhadamonthys.

Closely articulated with this observation is another peculiarity, which I first mentioned in a purely psychiatric book.[144] The shadows in Hades—most conspicuously that of Achilleus in the *Nekyia*—are in a state of mourning depression. Though the living may think of the dead as those whom they have lost, the shadows in Hades react as though *they themselves* had sustained a loss: they are *mourners*, having, in the most literal sense of the word, lost *themselves*. Only the living can restore them *to themselves*, as Odysseus does by giving them blood to drink. The care and feeding of the dead is a weird chapter of human folly.

A further discussion of this finding, and of its bearing upon the Greeks' outlook on life, is beyond the scope of this study, though it is one of the features of Greek thought which most deeply illuminates Greek concepts of life, death, and the deities.

I am indebted to Prof. Segal for pointing out to me that in one passage (161ff.) the Choros speaks well of Artemis, who is a helper of women about to give birth and is even able to ease the psychic troubles

---

[143] In the Homeric *Nekyia* (*Odyssey* 11) not one ghost refers to the Olympians in the *present* tense. Even the ghostly Double of Herakles (whose divine "real self," married to Hebe, feasts with the gods, 11.602ff.) mentions the Olympians only in connection with his *past*—with his genealogy (11.620) and his first descent to Hades (11.626). The only partly ghost-like (10.493) Teiresias does mention Poseidon (11.102) and Helios (11.109), but *only* in connection with the prophecy he gave *to Odysseus*. Elpenor, not yet buried and therefore *not yet a true ghost*, mentions Kirke (11.62). Antiope's boast (11.261) clearly concerns her adventrures while still alive. The other references to the Olympians either do not concern the dead (Odysseus is repeatedly addressed as "sprung from Zeus"), are *necessitated* by Odysseus' direct *questions* (Artemis: 11.198; Poseidon: 11.406), are genealogical (Persephone, daughter of Zeus: 11.217), or concern the speaker's life on earth (11.436; cf. also Herakles, supra). All other, and quite numerous, references to the Olympians are clearly part of Odysseus' *tale* of his visit to the deceased, and serve to identify the ghosts he saw in Hades. This shows that ghosts have no on-going relationship whatever with any non-chthonian deity. The evidence is conclusive.

[144] G. Devereux, *Therapeutic Education*, New York, 1956, p. 268, n. 0.

Gender and Fantasy 53

of pregnant and parturient women. But, as I pointed out previously, a deity—and even a shaman—who can cure a physical or psychological disorder can also cause it: madness sent by Artemis is not an unusual disorder.[145] Above all, no one in this tragedy, not even the Choros who suggests that Artemis might help Phaidra, shares Hippolytos' exalted and, above all, exclusive obsession with Artemis.

The Relationship Between Artemis and Phaidra

The relationship between Artemis and Phaidra has, to my knowledge, never been closely examined, though such a scrutiny is necessary for an understanding of the *Hippolytos*.

The Choros, which first connects Phaidra's plight with Artemis, inquires (145) whether she had perchance offended Diktynna, the Cretan Artemis barely differentiable from the Mountain Mother,[146] perhaps because Artemis was a prime causer of insanity (S. *Aj.* 172 etc.). It also invokes Artemis (166ff.) as midwife, i.e., again in a role she performed in Cretan belief. Finally the Choros swears by Artemis (713) not to reveal Phaidra's secret to anyone. This invocation is natural: women did swear by Artemis, while men—Hippolytos included—did not. What matters here is that even though this oath, like that of Hippolytos, pertains to illicit sexuality, it is taken by (chaste) Artemis.

The most important passages concern, however, Phaidra's fantasies of hunting and of driving horses—of wandering around in the mountains and meadows which are haunted also by Hippolytos *and Artemis*. Phaidra's fantasy is, in some respect, unusual. While the wish to escape is a recurrent theme of Greek tragedy, what matters here is not the "away *from*" element but the "movement *toward*" a type of world which, unlike Mykenaian huntresses, well-bred Athenian—and perhaps Cretan—ladies carefully avoided.[147] They did not ride horses, nor even, like goddesses, chariots—except as passengers.[148] Since I cannot even find mentions of picnics in the classical age, the sole "outdoors" activity of ladies of Euripides' time seems to have been confined to the Dionysiac *oreibasia*. In short, the world of mountains, meadows, hunting, and

---

[145] S. *Aias* 172; E. *Hipp.* 142, *Hel.* 570; Paus. 3.16.9; Apollod. *Ep.* 2.2; Orph. *h.* 36.5; Orph. *A.* 910, etc.
[146] R. F. Willetts, *Cretan Cults and Festivals*, London, 1962, pp. 179ff., 272ff. For Eileithyia, pp. 168ff.
[147] On Artemis and the outdoors, cf. U. von Wilamowitz-Moellendorff, *Der Glaube der Hellenen*³, 1955, 1.175; on the importance of Phaidra's illness, cf. Dodds, "The αἰδώς of Phaedra," op. cit., p. 102.
[148] J. K. Anderson, *Ancient Greek Horsemanship*, Berkeley, 1961, passim. For a love-sick Malay girl's longing for the (dangerous) jungle, Sir H. Clifford, *The Further Side of Silence*, Garden City, NY, 1922 ed., pp. 367-68. Some Spartan ladies owned racing teams, but did not drive them themselves.

horses was the world of men on the one hand and, on the other, of possessed Maenads, virgin Amazons, and "tweedy games mistresses," like Artemis' hunting companions. A few mythical huntresses (Prokris, Atalante) always excepted, Greek women were not interested in hunting. At the most, they cooked the game brought home by their men.

There was, however, at least one *oreibasia* precedent in Phaidra's family: the myth of Ariadne *may* imply that she became a Mainad on Naxos. These data highlight a basic contrast between Artemis' virginal companions and the sexual Mainads.[149] Artemis killed Ariadne for having surrendered her virginity.[150] Yet both types of women—not to mention mad ones, like Io and the daughters of Proitos—wandered about in the wilds, like wild beasts:[151] Kyrene fought a lion with her bare hands, the Mainads attacked and tore apart large wild beasts, also cattle, with their bare hands, and Agave believed that she killed a lion in this manner.[152]

What, then, is the meaning of Phaidra's fantasy, which so scandalizes her faithful Nurse (212)? It cannot reflect only an identification with Hippolytos.[153] Rather it involves also the wish to substitute herself for the one, Artemis, who—if we are to believe Hippolytos—does roam the meadows in his company and is a substitute for Hippolytos' Amazon mother. This substitution facilitates in turn Phaidra's identification with Artemis, and, through her, with Hippolyte (= Antiope), since she is not only Hippolytos' stepmother but also a successor of, and a substitute for, Hippolyte, and of her more remote predecessor Ariadne as well.[154] In fact, incestuous impulses are often permitted to express themselves—with social approval and in an only slightly disguised manner—by the

---

[149] As may be deduced from this remark, I am rather in sympathy with Pentheus' view that the ecstasy of the Mainads is basically sexual, though not perhaps in the straightforward manner imagined by Pentheus. That the Mainadic seizure was a hysterical attack has been amply proven by Bezdechi, op. cit., and by Dodds, *The Greeks*, op. cit., Appendix I. That the hysterical seizure is a coitus-equivalent is shown, e.g., by the *arc-de-cercle* in *grande hystérie* seizures, which also occurs at the climactic moment of intercourse. The hysterical seizure (or trance) may even be the only sexual safety valve available to frigid women. See in general G. Devereux, "Trance and Orgasm in Euripides' *Bakchai*," in A. Angoff and D. Barth (eds.) *Parapsychology and Anthropology*, New York, 1974 (pp. 36–50).
[150] Stoll ap. Roscher, *Lexikon*, s.v. Ariadne, col. 541.
[151] R. Eisler, *Man Into Wolf*, New York, 1951.
[152] Kyrene: Pi. *P* 9.26ff. For Agave, see E. *Ba*. 1173; she emphatically stresses that she did *not* catch the lion in a net. This evokes a rationalizing pun, equating nets and arms, in connection with the tradition that Herakles killed the Nemean lion with his hands (net): E. *HF* 153f. Cf. the E. *Ba*. 292-f. pun.
[153] On latent psychological similarities between Phaidra and Hippolytos, cf. Dodds, "The αἰδώς of Phaedra," op. cit., passim.
[154] Such psychological identifications, based on approximately identical kinship relationships (mother = stepmother) are facilitated by the fact that the unconscious is not an anthropological expert on kinship; cf. G. Devereux, *Ethnopsychoanalysis*, 1978, chap. 7.

Gender and Fantasy

substitution of a "step" or "in-law" kin for a blood-kin.[155]

Phaidra spontaneously connects her love for Hippolytos with an "inherited" propensity for choosing abnormal persons to love.[156] The sense of this allusion now becomes even clearer. As noted in another section, Hippolytos is attractive to Phaidra precisely *because* he is her (step)-son: a tabooed, incestuous love-object. The harder Phaidra tries to be chaste, the more she identifies herself with Artemis—and through her, with Hippolyte—the more her crypto-incestuousness becomes evident. It contains, of course, a built-in "denial." The Artemis = Hippolyte figure, for whom Phaidra wishes to substitute herself, is an ideally "chaste" one. The incestuous desire is, thus, *seemingly* obliterated by the fantasy of a "pure" hunting companionship. Phaidra apparently believes, or wishes to believe, that were she permitted to associate with Hippolytos *chastely*, as his hunting companion, she could *renounce* her incestuous cravings. This is as good an intrapsychic alibi as the next.[157]

Phaidra's alleged hatred of Hippolytos (962ff.) further proves her attempt to deny, even—indeed, chiefly—to herself, what she really desires. The lady doth protest too much!

One can, moreover, cite a curious and convincing, though indirect, fact in support of the view that (as the Nurse realizes [212]) Phaidra identifies herself both with Hippolytos and with his virginal mother-imago—with the Hippolyte who *once* existed quite as much as with Artemis, who *now* haunts Hippolytos' imagination—the better to implement her

---

[155] A. L. Kroeber, "Stepdaughter Marriage," *American Anthropologist* 40: 562–70, 1940. For marriage (after divorce) to one's former mother-in-law, cf. G. Devereux, "Atypical and Deviant Mohave Marriages," *Samiksa* (*Journal of the Indian Psycho-Analytical Society*) 4: 200–215, 1951. On Phaidra's repressions, cf. Dodds, "The αἰδώς of Phaedra," op. cit., p. 102. Cf. the formally distinct, but psychologically indistinct, Athenian laws forbidding marriage with a uterine half-sibling, but permitting marriage with a paternal half-sibling. The argument that this is a trace of matrilineal reckoning of descent is culturally probably valid, but psychologically irrelevant. Even an adopted sister, with whom one was raised, is *psychologically* a sister: the desire she arouses is incestuous, since the unconscious is no more an expert on genetics than on kinship. Hence, an occasional rich European peasant, who planned to marry his son to his daughter so as to hold the estate together, used to send off his daughter to be raised elsewhere. Azande kings did the same with those of their daughters they eventually planned to marry themselves. This is a bribe to the Superego.

[156] As noted before, I cannot imagine what makes Schmid (op. cit., p. 384, n. 8) say that Euripides is *not* thinking here of Phaidra's familial antecedents. Ovidius (*Her.* 4.51ff.) knew better.

[157] A magnificent répertoire of "chaste" rationalizations, justifying a "pure" companionship, is Stendhal's *Le Rouge et le Noir*, both as regards Mme de Rênal and Melle de la Mole. Other examples will readily come to mind. Man spends much of his time thinking up all the proper excuses for doing exactly as he pleases. His rationalizations only help him to do it *stupidly*.

counter-Oedipal erotic impulses.[158] I refer to the well-documented and generally accepted tradition that the unabashedly sexy Phaidra of the first *Hippolytos* (*Kalyptomenos*) became the chaste Phaidra who, in the second, struggles gallantly against her incestuous erotic impulses. There is a profound psychological truth in this transformation. Even if this were Euripides' only psychological insight, it would suffice to make him a great psychologist. Indeed, it is precisely the fierce—and real—chastity of Phaidra which makes her identification with Artemis-Hippolyte convincing, while highlighting, *at the same time*, the incestuous mainsprings of her attraction to her stepson. The basically "shameless" Phaidra of the first *Hippolytos* could never have identified herself with the virgin huntresses nor longed to roam the meadows. She would have been utterly unaware of Hippolytos' own neurotic needs. She would have dreamed of luring him to her bed in the palace. The idea of joining him, in seeming innocence, in the woods and meadows could not have occurred to her. The chaste second Phaidra is thus, at least in the cultural perspective, bolder than the first, lecherous, one—as "naive" virgins so often are in fact. Phaidra's fantasy of the meadows is thus an anticipation of the pastoral eroticism of innocence (?) in Longos' *Daphnis and Chloë*, in which the boldness of conscious lechery yields pride of place to the perhaps even bolder eroticism of (conscious) "innocence."

A full analysis of this problem would lead me too far away from

---

[158] Parental seductiveness was first highlighted by Freud, though his increasingly "respectable" followers still shy away from this embarassing insight: it is more convenient to blame the child for everything. This timidity is made evident both by the contents of case histories in child psychiatry (G. Devereux, *Basic Problems*, op. cit., chap. 8) and by the scotomatizing of certain obvious implications of the Oidipous myth (G. Devereux, "Why Oedipus Killed Laius," in L. Edmunds and A. Dundes, eds., *Oedipus: A Folklore Casebook*, New York, 1983; also id., "A Counteroedipal Episode in Homer's *Iliad*," *Bulletin of the Philadelphia Association of Psychoanalysis* 4: 90–97, 1955). Any attempt to "rock the boat" by speaking of the shortcomings of parents—which Freud himself took for granted—sends those who give Freud only lip-service into a tailspin, even if, in so doing, they are obliged to adopt developmentally and neurologically fantastic Kleinian views about infant psychology. (M. Klein, *The Psycho-Analysis of Children*, London, 1932, is the relatively tame beginning of a trend which, by now, has degenerated into Grand-Guignol fantasies about the psychic life of the infant.) Any call to reason, any return to Freud's factual objectivity is received with shouts of "heresy" (cf. two out of the three discussions—by Drs. R. Ekstein and A. Coodley—of my "The Cannibalistic Impulses of Parents," *Psychoanalytic Forum* 1: 114–24, 129–30, 1966 [revised version in *Basic Problems*, op. cit., chap. 5]). My paper tamely argued that many parents *have killed and eaten* their children, while children hardly ever *kill* their parents in order to *eat* them; it also stated that the infant cannot be *deliberately anthropophagous*, because it is too young to know the *difference* between human and non-human flesh. The statement of these elementary facts was called "heretical." The encroachments of a "Main Street"—not to say "Park Avenue"—mentality upon psychoanalytic "thought" are fearful and wonderful to behold.

Euripides' *Hippolytos*. I therefore highlight here simply the magnificent psychological imaginativeness—the *sense of pattern* in the realm of the affects—which was Euripides' greatest gift as a student of human nature.

2

Hippolytos and Theseus

Human Relationships

Be they erotic or simply friendly, human relationships are always impaired in neurosis: Hippolytos has no real relationships. He comes on stage in the company of young men, but does not *interact* with them; he leads—they follow. They make up the kind of escort even an illegitimate princeling attracts. They form the one surviving Choros that has absolutely no *function*. In fact, it does not even have the kind of *individuality* that manifests itself in interaction: these young hunters do not interact with anyone. All one can infer is that they are "pure," since otherwise Hippolytos would not associate with them (614, 997, 1018), though they are, no doubt, (implicitly) *less* pure than Hippolytos himself. Like one of my (virginal) patients, he does mention his "friends" now and then, but only to prove that he *has* friends, to whom he claims to be loyal, whether they are present or absent (1000ff.). In reality they are simply apparatus. His one, and only halfway personal, allusion to them (1082f.) has, as is to be expected, Hippolytos' own personality and problems as its focus: "May none of my friends have a bastard's fate!" Thus, even in his show of concern for his friends, he is, as usual, back to his favorite topic: himself.

Significantly, authorities disagree over whether *this* Choros reappears when he is in trouble. Gilbert Murray *makes* it reappear, by assigning to this Choros verses 1104ff. and 1120ff., but his views on this point are not generally accepted.[1] I shall come to this in a moment.

A person as narcissistic and grandiose as Hippolytos, is, by definition, incapable of experiencing friendship "viscerally" and the text confirms this interpretation. Even his "qualities" are resented; Phaidra hates every one of them.[2]

He is the most isolated person in surviving Greek drama; even the

---

[1] W. Schmid, *Geschichte der griechischen Literatur*, 1.3.386, n. 1; cf. Barrett, ad loc., apparatus criticus. Contra: Grube, op. cit., 190.1; Segal (pers. comm.) believes that there was a second Choros.

[2] Schmid, op. cit., 1.3.381, n. 5.

homicidal lunatic Orestes has his Pylades and his sister Elektra; the exiled Oidipous has his Antigone. The hopeless captive Hekabe at least believed Polymestor to be her friend and ally and can, later on, count on Agamemnon's complicity. Pentheus has his city and his grandfather Kadmos. The odious Kreon of S. *Ant.* is wholly committed to his son, wife, and city. Even Philoktetes is needed in the end by someone. Only Hippolytos stands alone; he isolates himself and is isolated from others. Though some praise him (1120ff.), there is no reciprocal, complementary interaction—perhaps not even a homosexual one—between him and his hunting companions. They are not equals. He pipes; they dance. A more shadowy escort—let alone Choros—is hard to find in tragedy. Even his slave is afraid of him.[3] One cannot but contrast the devious and timid way in which his slave works up the courage to offer a timely warning, with the passionate urgency of the Nurse tackling Phaidra. Though she may fear Phaidra's *momentary anger*, she is not afraid of Phaidra as a *person*. Where Hippolytos' slave is accustomed to "walking on eggs" when talking to his master, Phaidra's Nurse is obviously bewildered by her *not* being on a footing of absolute intimacy with her mistress, for the first time in her life.[4]

One cannot even be certain that the slave worries over Hippolytos, for he gives no indication of loving his master the way the Nurse loves "her" Phaidra. Hippolytos' behavior admittedly worries the slave; but does it worry him *for Hippolytos' sake*? It is bad for a slave if his master gets into trouble, especially with a deity. When a god lashes out at a prince, the blow also topples over the prince's court: nearly every Greek Choros makes this point, one way or another.[5]

I do not assert, *ex cathedra*, that the slave does *not* worry over Hippolytos too. I simply believe that he worries mostly about himself, for his utterances do not suggest that he loves his master.

When he is exiled, Hippolytos' close companions (φίλων) follow him as far as the frontier; he himself can ask for nothing more (1138). It has, of course, been suggested—but never proven (supra)—that the Messenger is Hippolytos' slave. Even if this is so, it does not really matter: a slave goes where he is told to go. Hippolytos "friends" certainly did not

---

[3] Cf. E. *Med.* 61, and the remarks of Grube, op. cit., p. 179, n. 4.

[4] Patin, op. cit., i., 52–53, pokes gentle fun at Brumoy's mania for ennobling everyone in sight: for turning, e.g., Phaidra's Nurse into her "confidante." Yet, functionally, Brumoy is right. Status-wise the Nurse is only a (slave?) nurse; functionally she is Phaidra's confidante, though Hippolytos' slave is surely not an "officer."

[5] Xenophon makes the same point with exceptional brutality. He urges that the eunuch makes the best servant, because, being despised by men, the welfare and approval of his master is all that stands between him and a hostile world (X. *Cyrop.* 7.5.62ff.). I note that the totalitarian Platon (*Prot.* 314c) is the only major author who mentions eunuch slaves in classical Athens.

accompany him very far: he left in his chariot and there is no mention of other chariots escorting him. Moreover, being the only victim of the accident, he must have been alone in his chariot. His servants accompany him on foot. This, too, is unusual in Greek drama: most exiles have a companion (supra).

All this does not suggest that Hippolytos was personally greatly beloved, nor would one expect him to be. At home, the princeling had good hunting companions; the exile was abandoned to his fate, except by his servants (1196).

Another detail is even more peculiar: there is no lack of noble epithets in Greek tragedy—even villains rate at times the epithet "blameless."[6] Only Hippolytos rates no noble epithet *before* he gets into trouble, excepting those he so often applies to himself. This is probably without a parallel in Greek tragedy, which is as liberal with "praise names" as any Bantu orator.

Even Phaidra has no praise—*not one word of praise*— for him; for his nobility, beauty, virtue, wisdom—except in contempt (above). She is only obsessively in love—or infatuated—with him. The Nurse does not even waste a routine *xanthos* (blond) on him. At best she calls his Amazon mother a "royal horsewoman" (307). In short, there is a unanimous and thunderous silence about Hippolytos' "virtues." After he is engulfed by tragedy the Choros, the Messenger, and even Theseus do, of course, wax eloquent about this narcissist's *unspecified* merits; previous to that he took care of his own publicity, not being one to hide his lights under a bushel.

How is this sudden change to be interpreted? Is one to see in this unanimous silence, followed by unanimous praise,[7] an illustration of the rule that the non-conformist's merits are despised and ignored (E. *Med.* 214 f.)? Does his death ennoble him, as did Eurystheus', who promised to become Athens' protector despite Alkmene's odious vengeance (E. *Heracl.* 1026)? The explanation is probably much simpler. Some of it is just: "de mortuis." Much of it is necessary, because the tragic character of death must be stressed, *even* in the case of an anything but blameless "hero." Sophokles' Aias is a good parallel: the rebellious, temporarily insane (and therefore grotesque) suicide must be honored in death. Also—fitting Greek conceptions of *dike* (justice)—cognizance must be taken of the fact that Hippolytos was (behaviorally) innocent of the crime imputed to him.[8] His

---

[6] On this epithet, cf. J. E. Harrison, *Prolegomena to the Study of Greek Religion*[3], Cambridge, G.B., 1922, pp. 334ff. Partly contra: A. W. H. Adkins, *Merit and Responsibility*, 1960, p. 81, n. 11 and passim. See now: H. Parry, "Blameless Aegisthus," *Mnemosyne Supplement* 27.

[7] And even then with reservations: the Choros still considers his extreme rigidity unwise; cf. elsewhere. Its sobbing may only be a case of nerves, or, simply, ritual mourning.

[8] On acts as the sole criteria of crime, cf. Adkins, op. cit., passim.

judicially undeserved—though indirectly suicidal—death wipes the slate clean and even calls for a posthumous compensation in the form of a cult. Unappeased heroes, more even than the ordinary dead who harbor grievances, make uncomfortable neighbors.

There remains the Choros' attempt to appease Theseus. Some slight part of all this may be due to discomfort, because an oath (713ff.) prevented *their* telling Theseus the truth. Yet, the Choros seems *less* interested in rehabilitating Hippolytos than in protecting Theseus from the consequences of his hasty and unjust act—from the inevitably tragic implications of being a "cause."[9]

In short, the Choros—though it laments him and even praises him—still shows no *love* for Hippolytos. If its members now attribute to him his previously self-ascribed "noble qualities," they do so mainly because only in this way can they both justify their having kept their oath and persuade Theseus not to behave in a manner ruinous to himself. The Messenger's expression of disbelief in Hippolytos' misbehavior (1249) and the Choros' assertion that he had a good heart are feeble arguments indeed.[10] It is well to recall here that, unlike a Roman *pater familias*, even a king like Theseus could not kill his son (be it only by cursing him) without incurring pollution (*miasma*).

In brief, had anyone really admired Hippolytos, *before* his tragic end, he would have said so sooner; it was shown, however, that before his fatal accident, Hippolytos did not rate even one noble epithet. As for Artemis' last-minute praise of Hippolytos, it is an *ex parte* statement: her own prestige, *amour propre*, and notorious vindictiveness require it. As an objective attestation of Hippolytos' virtues it cannot stand scrutiny.

A further objectionable—and, for a Greek, almost unforgivable—trait of Hippolytos is his lack of in-group solidarity, of civic virtue, and citizenship. Though even the simple citizen, not to speak of a royal bastard, can, by offending the gods, bring calamity on his city (cf. 361), this thought never even crosses Hippolytos' mind. Since he is neither feebleminded nor ignorant—Theseus ridicules his addiction to dusty tomes—his failure to see the possible *public* consequences of his *private* contempt for Aphrodite is a further token of his self-centeredness. In terms of Greek ethics, he therefore stands self-condemned; he is not one of the "lovers" of Athens—or of Troizen—whom Perikles had praised only two years earlier.[11] This is not surprising. Those obsessed with their own salvation always "save" themselves *only*—and almost invariably do

---
[9] On being a "cause," cf. Adkins, op. cit., esp. chap. 6. I feel that the Greeks even dreaded being the "cause" of a lawfully condemned man's death. This may explain why condemned Athenian prisoners had to "commit suicide."
[10] In Athens, an un-racked slave's testimony was worthless.
[11] Th. 2.3.5-46: uncivic citizens are useless (2.40). Hippolytos is the opposite of those whom Perikles praised; in that sense, E. *Hipp*. too is a patriotic play.

so at the expense of their family, kindred and fellow men.[12]

Hippolytos' civic indifference is, moreover, actuated by envy and spite. Were he not a bastard, he would be Theseus' heir. Were he able to accept his exclusion from the succession, he could still be a good citizen. He could be what Teukros is to Aias in the *Iliad* and in Sophokles' *Aias*: the strong right hand and protector of his legitimate brother. Instead, due to his sibling rivalry—expressed in the final petty pinprick he directs at Theseus: "I wish your other children will be as good as I am" (1455)—he so ostentatiously retires from public affairs[13] that he is not even a good citizen.

Hippolytos even turns his lack of civic virtue into a merit. Part of his defense consists in harping on the private character of his life and ambitions and, in so doing, he does not shrink from a barefaced lie. He boldly pretends that he could *not* have usurped the throne by marrying (and *who else* speaks marriage?) Phaidra (1010). Greek versions of Lydian traditions,[14] as well as all of Greek mythology, teach us that this simply is not so, nor is Theseus—whose "obstinate" incredulousness is tendentiously exaggerated by many commentators—fool enough to accept this method of proof. Barrett,[15] surprisingly, finds no nearer parallel than Kallias' case, though there are better examples in myth: Herakles ordered his son Hyllos to marry his prospective "widow" Iole,[16] the "filly of Oichalia," who is pointedly mentioned in *Hippolytos* (545f.) *precisely in connection with Phaidra's anguish*. This was, in fact, one of Herakles' habits: he also made his nephew Iolaos marry his divorced wife, Megara.[17] These precedents are relevant, since the Theseus' myth is in many ways patterned on that of Herakles. An equally close parallel is Phoinix' seduction of his father's concubine, in his father's lifetime.[18]

---

12 G. Devereux, *Basic Problems of Ethnopsychiatry*, 1980, chap. 11.
13 This is unusual. Gaston d'Orléans, brother of Louis XIII, gave so much trouble to the King that Mazarin systematically raised Louis XIV's younger brother to be an ineffectual homosexual.
14 Definitive discussion in H. Herter, "Lydische Adelskämpfe," in O. Wenig, ed., *Wege zur Buchwissenschaft*, Bonn, 1966, esp. pp. 57ff.
15 Barrett, op. cit., p. 12, n. 1, discussing the case of Kallias, who married his mother-in-law (Andoc. 1.124ff.). So did some Hellenistic kings.
16 S. *Trach.* 1221. Herakles specifies that this is *not* an impious act (1245).
17 Apoll. *Bibl.* 2.6.1; D.S. 4.31.1; Plu. *Amat.* 9 p. 754Dff.
18 Hom. *Il.* 9.444ff. Psychoanalytic discussion: G. Devereux, "A Counter-oedipal Episode in Homer's Iliad," *Bulletin of the Philadelphia Association for Psychoanalysis* 4: 90–97, 1955, and id., "The Self-Blinding of Oidipous," *Journal of Hellenic Studies* 93: 36–49, 1973. The excessive honoring of the shamed Phoinix by his kinsmen, which so puzzles some, is good primitive practice. A shamed African, who fled into the bush to kill himself, was brought back by his kinsmen to the village in a triumphant procession (E. E. Evans-Pritchard, *Witchcraft, Oracles and Magic among the Azande*, Oxford, 1937). In parts of Africa the sons automatically inherit (as wives) the father's widows—though not their own mothers

Such incestuous relationships (by proxy) gratify Oedipal impulses, while soothing a bribable Superego.

The royal succession is actually the real crux of the matter. Given Hippolytos' oedipal fixation on his Amazon mother and the extension of this fixation to Artemis (a divine mother imago) it is psychologically inevitable that he should *also* have a—strongly ambivalent—oedipal interest in Phaidra, whom his studied aloofness may have stimulated erotically. What else can explain his *systematic* avoidance of her? After all, she did not pursue him *openly* from the start! Hippolytos' *extreme, blind* violence toward the Nurse is clearly *prima facie* evidence of his panic, elicited by the fact that her proposals needled one of his most deeply repressed impulses, against which his entire existence was one massive defensive maneuver.[19] Hippolytos' awareness that—even though he professes *not* to believe it—a marriage with Phaidra *could* (especially in a society still only emerging from a matrilineal system of succession to the throne)[20] make him replace Theseus on the throne, further enhances the intensity of his conflict and elicits a literally suicidal reaction (silence) when he is confronted with this "objectively" unjust, but unconsciously all too true accusation.

Hippolytos and Theseus

I must begin my discussion with a general point. Several authorities accept as literal truth every one of Hippolytos' favorable statements about himself, but refuse to lend credence to Theseus' (admittedly exasperated) characterizations of his son. My reference to a "vegetarian, orphic bookworm" shocked at least one reader of my MS.

Such critics forget that Theseus, as a judge, does not preside over one of Stalin's purge-tribunals, where Origen could publicly be convicted of promiscuousness and Don Juan of prudishness. Another Euripidean text (*The Cretans, fr.* 472, verses 12ff., verses 18–19, to be discussed in Chapter 4), also links killing with vegetarianism (Hitler too was a vegetarian!). "Orphic" need not mean here more than a mystical tendency (which his privileged affective relationship with Artemis proves to be genuine).[21] As to his being a great reader, this "accusation" is the more striking as Euripides is supposed to have owned an unusually large library—and

---

(H. Junod, *The Life of a South African Tribe*[2], 2 vols., London, 1927). Euripides wrote a *Phoinix, frr.* 804–18 N[2].

[19] An accidental "needling" of a person's nuclear conflict can, even in reality, elicit not simply a panic but even sudden crimes of violence and/or psychotic breaks. It is this that makes "parlor psychoanalysis" so dangerous a game.

[20] G. Devereux, "Socio-Political Functions of the Oedipus Myth in Early Greece," *Psychoanalytic Quarterly* 32: 205–14, 1963; id., *Femme et Mythe*, 1982.

[21] On the lack of love for the gods in the classical age, cf. E. R. Dodds, *The Greeks and the Irrational*, Berkeley, 1951. E. *Hipp.* 1394 does not disprove this.

probably knew that myths do not mention literacy.[22]

All three accusations must therefore have some basis and are clues to Euripides' idea of Hippolytos. To disregard Theseus' views about his son is unjustifiable.

The relationship between son and father in this play cannot be properly appreciated without considering the objective situation that faces Theseus on his return. But, before tackling this matter, I must dispose of echoes of Seneca's *Phaedra* (93ff.) that Theseus' absence was caused by his captivity in Hades, whence he had tried to abduct Helene.

Nothing in the text lends support to this assertion. *Ironically*, he is returning from an oracle, *crowned* (792, 807, 806). The myth of Helene's abduction also fails to substantiate the return from the captivity in Hades. According to one source, Theseus was already fifty-three years old when he abducted the still immature Helene. Plutarchos[23] places that abduction just before Theseus' final banishment from his kingdom.

The other absurd charge, that Phaidra resented Theseus' adulteries, is equally unsupported by the text. To begin with, Theseus is still greatly enamored of his wife, Phaidra; he mourns her passing in words expressing despair (810, 825, 836ff.). Also, as Barrett (ad loc.) well saw, verse 820 implies that Theseus knew of *no fault of his* that could have caused Phaidra to commit suicide. Those ready to take each of Hippolytos' words at face value should be required to accept also Theseus' self appraisal. His words are not those of a man guilty of adultery. The practice of blackening Theseus' character, in order to whitewash Hippolytos' image, clearly disregards that Theseus is depicted as a great and noble hero in *all* Euripidean plays that mention him. Also, the (second) *Hippolytos* would probably not have won a first prize, had it degraded a national hero whose noble character was a souce of great pride to the Athenians.

This matter being clarified, it might be well to recall also that Theseus, though erotically as uninhibited as any ancient hero could be, was noted for his shrewdness and good sense; unlike Herakles and Bellerophontes, he had no psychotic seizures,[24] nor is there any mention of his becoming possessed by Ares—i.e., of becoming occasionally battle-mad, in the Homeric manner.

The situation facing the returning (crowned!) Theseus seems cut-and-dried:

(1) His beloved wife has just hung herself.
(2) She left a letter, accusing her somewhat peculiar stepson of having raped her.

---

[22] The one Homeric allusion to writing (*Il.* 6.168ff.) is connected with trouble for a chaste hero—for Bellerophontes, to whom Euripides devoted at least two tragedies.
[23] *Life of Theseus*, 29.
[24] As have many heroes of the Arthurian cycle, and other epic heroes as well.

(3) The utterances of the Choros are so ambiguous that they *seem* to confirm Phaidra's accusations.[25]
(4) Hippolytos' oath prevents him from revealing the truth.
(5) His defense is not only clumsy but, in some respects, insolent.
  (a) His designation of the Choros in verses 986 and 989 is arrogant ($"οχλος$ = mob).
  (b) In verses 992f. he refers almost contemptuously to his father's accusations.
  (c) At verse 1009, he haughtily depreciates Phaidra's beauty, though he knows how deeply his father was enamoured of her.
  (d) His argument (1010), that he could not have hoped to inherit the kingship by marrying Phaidra is, as Méridier notes, valid in terms of Attic law. But Méridier disregards that the Amazons—and possibly the Cretans—may have had a matrilineal system of succession.
  (e) In verse 1015, his claim that kingship destroys a man's reason is a veiled insult addressed at King Theseus.
  (f) Last but not least, at verse 1086 he threatens the slaves who are about to carry out his father's orders.
(6) His defense abounds, as might be expected, in self praise and in contempt for those he considers inferior to himself.

In short, I concur with Hippolytos' admission that his defense is forensically clumsy (986ff.), though he takes pride even in his inefficiency as a public speaker. He utters the truth in words that persuade those already aware of his innocence—but are assuredly not likely to persuade Theseus, who, having just come home from a voyage, does not know what happened in his absence. I very much doubt that any of Hippolytos' apologists would have believed him, had they been in Theseus' shoes.

This point is consistently ignored, though it is a key element of the tragedy. Had Hippolytos been able to offer a better defense, his father would not have cursed him. Were Theseus a fool, the play would not be a great tragedy but a grinning, gibbering horror-farce. In either case there would have been no tragedy. The play is, however, a tragedy:

(1) Because Hippolytos, though technically innocent, cannot prove his innocence.

(2) Because the man who condemns him is neither a stranger nor a fool, but his own father, misled by appearances so convincing as to preclude any reasonable doubt of Hippolytos' guilt.

Those who see in this confrontation only a purblind Theseus simply destroy the most tragic scene of this great play.

Proceeding from the special to the general, I feel that even though the relationship between Hippolytos and Theseus has given rise to countless moral judgments, it has never been tackled in even approximately

[25] See Méridier's comments on verses 812, 816, 820, on p. 60 (note) of his edition.

authentic psychological terms. The situation has been handled as though it were of cut and dried simplicity: Theseus is dead wrong—the unjustly accused Hippolytos is *therefore* a model son. If the text does not confirm this simplistic and illogical view—which some commentators defend by stretching the evidence to the snapping point—the text is, as I will show in a moment, "improved."

For the time being I note only that the improbability of a *Euripidean* Theseus being odious is as great as that of a Euripidean Odysseus being admirable. This point assuredly deserves to be made before considering the complexities of this father-son relationship.

A self-centered narcissist like Hippolytos cannot love anything or anyone *real*. He is, at best, obsessed by a projection of his own perfection into the empyrean blue: Artemis, being safely unattainable, cannot disarrange the pretty patterns of fantasy by a confrontation with reality.

It is also obvious that Hippolytos refuses to associate with "immoral" persons (995ff.). This means that Hippolytos—who savagely resents his bastardy and the one who made him a bastard—is not the person to forgive his father's former amours, though Theseus is now the faithful husband of the woman who *replaced* the Amazon. All this is in the text—if one but cares to read it attentively.

Hippolytos' exalted conception of himself forces him to *visualize* himself as a good son and he has persuaded some commentators of the reality of his imaginings. Yet, the *only* time he seems to show any affection is when he speaks (914) of Theseus as "more than a friend."[26] Considering the already noted tenuousness of his "friendships," this is little enough. If, on the other hand, Grene is right in suspecting that the relationship between Hippolytos and his friends is at least latently ("platonically") homosexual,[27] his remark acquires curious overtones, particularly since Euripides—witness his *Chrysippos*—was not addicted to homosexuality.[28]

At this point one may expect to hear once more the tired old taboo against inferring Euripides' likes and dislikes from his texts. This taboo is, of course, hardly ever observed even by those who voice it, for it is an impossible taboo. My statement that Euripides was *not* homosexually inclined can be substantiated in several ways.

(1) The Greeks themselves *contrasted* Sophokles' love of boys with

---

[26] Grube, op. cit., 187, n. 1. Admittedly the rest of the scene, as Prof. Segal pointed out to me, makes a more cordial approach impossible.
[27] D. Grene, "The Interpretation of the *Hippolytus*," *Classical Philology* 34: 45-58, 1939 (p. 52).
[28] Tales of his having kissed Agathon are late and unreliable; they may represent—to the modern mind—a scurrilous attempt to make Euripides a "proper" gentleman. Data and discussion in G. Devereux, "Greek Pseudo-Homosexuality," op. cit. But cf., on homosexual regression in old age, M. Hader, "Homosexuality as Part of Our Aging Process," *Psychiatric Quarterly* 40: 515-24, 1966.

Euripides' pursuit of women (*Athenaios* 13.603e).

(2) I am familiar with the problem of Greek homosexuality. I wrote on the subject twice,[29] and Sir Kenneth Dover repeatedly consulted me on this topic while he worked on his epoch-making book, *Greek Homosexuality*, 1978, p. viii (cf. *Homosexualité Grecque*, 1982, p. 9).

(3) I have studied both Mohave Indian[30] and Sedang Moi homosexuality in the field.

(4) As a clinician, I have had homosexuals in treatment.

(5) I know from decades of experience that I readily perceive even subtle clues indicative of homosexual tendencies in men and women alike.

My inability to detect any indication of homosexual tendencies in the surviving writings of Euripides should therefore carry some weight.

It cannot even be argued that Hippolytos deems man's sexuality *less* odious than that of women, for he considers sexuality intolerable *for himself*,[31] though he does identify himself with his ex-virgin mother.

How unwilling most commentators are to face the superficiality of this father/son relationship is best shown by their failure to comment on the fact that *Theseus* shows little nurturant affection for Hippolytos (until it is too late), though this should surely be grist for the mill of Hippolytos' defenders. I will therefore now plead *for* Hippolytos: he did not return his father's love, because there was almost none to be returned.[32] Theseus is disappointed in his unmanly, uncivic, and eccentric son who is utterly unlike himself. The two have only two old and one late trait in common: both are, in a way, illegitimate, and the fathers of both tried to kill them from ignorance; the shrines of both are refuges for fugitive slaves.[33]

I now come to the shallowness of Hippolytos' relationship with his father, as reflected by verses 912f. Before I present my own interpretation of this passage, I wish to caution the reader against viewing it as dogmatic. I concur, in some ways, with Professor Segal's suggestion that

---

[29] G. Devereux, "Pseudo-Homosexualité Grecque," *Ethnopsychiatrica* 2: 221-41, 1979 (= *Symbolae Osloenses* 42: 69-92, 1967. Id., "The Nature of Sappho's Seizure," *Classical Quarterly* 20: 17-31, 1969.

[30] G. Devereux, "Institutionalized Homosexuality of the Mohave Indians," *Human Biology* 9: 498-527, 1937 (repeatedly anthologized).

[31] Since Theseus seems to know Hippolytos inside out (cf. Méridier, p. 20, note), his ridiculing of young men's pretenses to be uninterested in sex, by noting that men can simply "get away" with more than women (a truly Euripidean feminist touch) *may* be pointed. This, however, is too uncertain to be labored (cf. verses 970ff.).

[32] On lack of paternal care in general, cf. Pl. *La.* init.

[33] Plu. *Thes* 26.2; for the fugitive-slave priest of Diana's grove at Nemi, cf. Sir J. G. Frazer, *The Golden Bough*, London, 1890. Hint at Theseus' dubious parentage: verses 1169ff. On the attempt of Aigeus to poison his (unrecognized) son Theseus: Plu. *V. Thes.* 12.2f.

Hippolytos and Theseus

Hippolytos is groping here for contact with his father, but does not know how to go about it: this generates authentic pathos. If the rest of my comments on these verses sound somewhat harsh, this is due less to a lack of compassion for Hippolytos, than to my impatience with those critics who seek to make of him an ideal person, even at the cost of athetising two perfectly authentic and characteristically dramatic verses.

For these two verses have been tampered with even by otherwise exemplary students of this play. Thus, the usually impeccable Barrett relegated them to a footnote, ("justifying" this in his commentary, pp. 338f.).

912 Ἡ γὰρ ποθοῦσα πάντα καρδία κλύειν
913 κἂν τοῖς κακοῖσι λίχνος οὖσ' ἁλίσκεται.

Yet, these incriminated verses manifestly mirror a Greek attitude, as is shown by two facts:

(1) The sympathetic Koryphaios says (173ff.): "My heart burns to learn what has ravaged the queen's body and altered her traits," and

(2) In Sophokles' *Oidipous in Kolonos* (verses 517f.), despite Oidipous' pleas *not* to be questioned, the Choros says: "Seeing, in sooth, that the tale is wide-spread, and in no wise wanes, I am fain, friend, to hear it aright,"

In short, it is odd that verses 912f. should be deemed callous and unseemly, for news—and even idle gossip—spread by word of mouth play an important role in primitive, archaic or, more simply, newspaperless societies. In such societies all members of the in-group feel *entitled* to be told everything, for the fate and actions of one affect all; the Nurse states this in so many words (verses 359ff.). This "curiosity" is a token of solidarity and kinship and not mere eagerness for gossip.[34]

This being said, I now return to the incriminated verses, which Murray did not presume to delete but prettified in his *translation*. The text—in Barrett's translation—says: "For the heart that is fain to hear all is found greedy even amid misfortune"; Murray translates:

"And human hearts in sorrow crave *the more*
For knowledge, *though the knowledge grieve them sore.*"

The italicized words are Murray's, not Euripides'; comment seems superfluous.

Barrett's arguments in favor of the deletion of verses 912f.—which echo in part those of some of his predecessors—run about as follows:

The incriminated verses are held to be a "caricature of gracelessness"

---

[34] When, in the late 1930s, my Mohave Indian friends—who considered me a Mohave—found out that I had *not* let them know that I had been starving, they reproached me for my "unfriendly" silence, which had denied them the opportunity to assist me materially.

even for one as graceless as Hippolytos. (This is a non-psychologist's opinion.) They do not reflect the son's love for his father (Musgrave). (Yet, nothing proves that Hippolytos loves his father; cf. above.) The wording reflects the (hypothetical) interpolator's disapproval. (As well it might; see, however, similar queries in E. *Hipp.* 173ff. and in S. *OC.* 513f., which are not viewed as expressions of the poet's disapproval.) Barrett concludes that: "The lines destroy the pattern of short appeals and expectant pauses." They do! But this is neither the first, nor the last time that Euripides cared less for pattern-making them than for psychological truth.[35] This objection would be more acceptable if the play were by Sophokles. On the dubious value of arithmetical and "pattern" considerations in the editing of texts, Wilamowitz' ironical remarks are still authoritive.[36]

Barrett's last argument is particularly feeble: "They are inconsistent with 911, and so cannot be joined to it by a γάρ." (It depends on whether *Euripides* considered them inconsistent; here, as always, grammar depends on the intention. The particle γάρ thunderously amplifies the contrast between the *outer* show of concern and the *inner*, self-centered indifference—or at least clumsiness—precisely *by* the conjoining of verses 911 and 912-13.)

By contrast, Barrett rightly rejects the old argument that the skipping of of verse 911 of the *Hipp.* in verses 860-65 of the *Christus Patiens* "proves" that verse 911 was not in the *Hippolytos* manuscript used by the author of the *Chr. Pat.*[37] He sensibly points out that verse 911 would not have fit the context in the *Chr. Pat.* (the Virgin addressing the dead Christ). I will add for my part that if a pickpocket steals only my watch, but not my wallet as well, this does not mean that, originally, I had no wallet and bought one only after my pocket was picked.

I now come to a matter of principle: It is always hazardous to emend a text for "psychological" reasons, unless one is very certain that one's reasons are, in fact, psychological, in the scientific sense, and not simply imputations.[38]

This does not mean that Barrett—or Aristarchos—were wrong in doubting the authenticity of certain verses. I simply urge that *these* verses may not be deleted *for psychological reasons*, for they make

---

[35] Zelter rewrote Bach, believing that he improved him. Mendelssohn found contrapuntal "errors" in Bach, and "corrected" them. I do not happen to be a Bach addict, but believe that, Fux' treatise on counterpoint notwithstanding, Bach knew what he was doing.
[36] U. v. Wilamowitz-Moellendorff, *Euripides, Herakles*[4], Hamburg (1959 ed.) 1248ff.
[37] In addition, the quality of the *Hippolytos* MS used by the "author" of the *Christus Patiens* is unknown and its place in the stemma of the *Hippolytos* MSS uncertain.
[38] Aristarchos athetized Hom. *Od.* 23.218-24 for untenable "psychological" reasons; cf. G. Devereux, "Penelope's Character," *Psychoanalytic Quarterly* 26: 378-86, 1957. Their being echoed by E. *Tr.* 929ff. proves their authenticity for the philologist.

excellent psychological sense. Moreover, where the authenticity of some verses is questioned for valid psychological reasons, one must be able to indicate the interpolator's *motivation*.

Why should an actor-interpolator wish to *degrade* Hippolytos at the very moment when he has his hands full trying *not* to make him unbearably odious? In fact, considering most critics' dislike of verses 912-13, it is almost a miracle that they survived the pruning knives of each and every one of Hippolytos' early encomiasts.

It may, of course, be urged that there are also other foolish interpolations in Euripides.[39] But, in each case, the foolish interpolation had a discernible *purpose*; I fail to see, however, the purpose of *this* particular (alleged) foolishness.

Returning to the main problem, verses 912-13 reveal the sleaziness of Hippolytos' (alleged) "loving concern" for his father, and that is what Euripides meant to highlight here. Why should one doubt Hippolytos' "unhealthy" curiosity when, in words which even Blaiklock (p. 46) calls "cynical," he promises to watch with malicious pleasure how Phaidra will face Theseus (661f.)? Hippolytos' conduct toward Theseus is so congruent with his character that it is almost tedious to enumerate the details:

1191: He wishes grief to his father, for doing him an injustice.
1348: "The evil orders of an evil father."
1361: Wrongful acts of father.[40]
1405: Hippolytos mourns "also" his father's misfortunes; obviously he grieves mostly over his own.
1407: He pities his father only after Artemis (1406) tells him that Theseus had been deceived and trapped.
1409: He bewails less his own troubles than his father's *hamartia*; there is much arrogance in this and little compassion.
1435: Artemis must ask him to forgive Theseus.
1442: He agrees to forgive, but only in obedience to Artemis' wishes (cf. 1182: he must "obey" his father's orders).
1445: His request to be held in his father's arms seems, for once, *sentient*. Yet
1448: Theseus must formally ask him to free him from guilt.
1449: Hippolytos grants this request for a formal (purifying) absolution, and is thanked by Theseus (1454).

At this point I must acknowledge a persuasive *caveat* uttered by Professor Segal. He reminds me that even though Artemis had to ask the dying Hippolytos to exonerate his father, the fact that the son was able to utter a pardon had to come "from something in Hippolytos that could obey the Goddess." This supposition is compatible also with the "double

---

[39] D. L. Page, *Actors' Interpolations in Greek Tragedy*, Oxford, 1934.
[40] Barrett (ad loc.) rightly points out that the vocabulary used is one shared by pity and by abuse.

determination" discussed by Dodds and with certain of Lesky's views.[41]

1455: Graceless to the end, Hippolytos reacts to Theseus' thanks with a Parthian pinprick: he "wishes" that Theseus' legitimate children will be as good as he is.

1460: The afflicted Theseus' behavior sharply contrasts with Hippolytos' arrogance. Forgetting his son's eccentricities and haughtily insulting behavior, he finds it in him to exclaim: "What a man!" To my mind this is the one completely foolish thing Theseus says in *any* Euripidean drama.

At this point I, exceptionally, cannot accept Professor Segal's opinion that Theseus' utterance is realistic, partly because the Choros' concluding words, that exalt Hippolytos, are supposedly also realistic. In my view Theseus is chiefly relieved to be freed of pollution—as to the Choros, it gave no striking evidence of psychological sensitiveness in the play. I view their words chiefly as "de mortuis nil, nisi bonum."

Two further points also deserve consideration:

(1) Hippolytos' constant boasting and his speaking of himself and his virtue in the comparative, the superlative, and the absolute implicity insult Theseus—who is obviously *not* "pure"—in every breath. That he is something infinitely more important—that he is real and human, that even his error and rage reflect suffering—is beyond Hippolytos' comprehension.

(2) Hippolytos' unconsciously murderous attitude deserves an especially careful analysis.

When, after an initial outburst of death wishes (887ff., 895) the misled Theseus, showing great self-restraint, only banishes Hippolytos—and not even beyond the Pontos or the Atlas (1053)—the latter insolently replies that, were he in Theseus' place, he would kill him. In saying this, Hippolytos voices the unconsciously murderous oedipal hatred of "mother's avenging hero," which he dares not express openly and therefore projects upon Theseus.[42] Also, Professor Segal has helped me to see that echoes of Theseus' death wishes are perceptible in his first question to the messenger (1164–72).

Psychoanalytically, all this is commonplace: an *inhibited* outward directed aggressivity ricochets and is then redirected at one's own self. It is precisely such a ricocheting aggressivity which eventually destroys Hippolytos, as it destroyed so many other neurotics before and since. Euripides intuitively indicated—though he assuredly had no theory to go by—that Hippolytos' retort reflected his patricidal impulses. I cite in support of my opinion the fact that even primitive shamans know that

---

[41] E. R. Dodds, *The Greeks and the Irrational*, 1951; cf. also A. Lesky, "Göttliche und menschliche Motivation im homerischen Epos," *Sitzungsberichte der Heidelberger Akademie der Wissenschaften, Philosophisch-historische Klasse*, no. 4, 1961.

[42] Cf. Euripides' *Cretans* (*fr.* 11.35ff. P.), in which Pasiphaë provocatively accuses the indignant Minos of murderous and cannibalistic impulses.

impotent anger turns into self-destructiveness.[43]

How hurt Theseus is—and how human his most fierce reactions are even in his error—is best shown by his bitter reaction to the announcement of further bad news about Hippolytos: "Did he rape another man's wife?" (1164). Though he is dead wrong, he is wrong in a human way— in the way of a savagely hurt (but still *sentient*) being—and I hold that it is both psychologically and ethically better to be as feelingly wrong as Theseus is here than to be as coldly right as Hippolytos, the plaster saint, ever fancies himself.

I must stress once again that Hippolytos' aggressivity, arrogance, and insolence are direct results of his anti-sexuality.[44] The charitable and the generous, the wise and the loving, do not hate or despise those less virtuous than themselves. Only the anti-sexual feel that their one "virtue" authorizes them to minimize all other virtues and to hate "sinners" blindly. This is at once commonplace, practical ethics and basic psychoanalytic theory. Even anti-sexuality disguised as promiscuousness is rooted in hatred.[45]

This finding leads up to the last and clinically most certain of my interpretations of Hippolytos' relationship with Theseus. Boy children, hag-ridden by their panicky dread of the erotic-hostile impulses mobilized by their oedipal conflicts, sometimes shy away from their normal ("developmental neurosis")[46] oedipal conflict by restructuring it into a so-called "reverse Oedipus." In such cases the boy identifies himself with his mother and develops latent (passive) homosexual impulses toward the father. This reverse oedipal constellation is one of the most common determinants of both overt and latent homosexuality in men.

Now, Hippolytos is not really a (typically Greek) "man." As shown in another section, his masculinity, so-called, is patterned upon the behavior of the Amazon, with whom he identifies himself. He impersonates—or

---

[43] G. Devereux, *Mohave Ethnopsychiatry*, op. cit., esp. pt. 7, passim.

[44] The younger one imagines Hippolytos to be, the more objectionable his behavior toward his father becomes; this, too, his encomiasts choose to ignore.

[45] *Case*: A fourteen-year-old girl in psychotherapy had been completely promiscuous since the age of eleven. Being filled with hatred, her sexual escapades were simply a means of self-degradation (Devereux, *Basic Problems*, op. cit., chap. 8). At first she refused to cooperate with her therapist, insisting that she was too depraved to deserve help, that it was better to commit murder than to be promiscuous. The day she understood that this was not true, her promiscuousness ceased, since it had not been due to what only laymen call an excessive sexual drive, but to an abnormally intense Oedipus complex and to an almost conscious hatred of her (unconsciously) seductive and hostile (adopted) father. (Devereux, *Therapeutic Education*, op. cit., p. 380, records the tragic sequelae of parental interference with this therapy.) There was as much hatred in this girl's promiscuousness as in Hippolytos' "chastity."

[46] R. Linton, *Culture and Mental Disorders* (ed. by G. Devereux), Springfield, IL, 1956; G. Devereux, *Basic Problems*, op. cit., chap. 15.

rather, appersonates—Hippolyte, his own mother, who was his father's mistress. In the case of a real person, this appersonation would necessarily entail a latent fantasy of oneself as a substitute for, and rival of, the mother *as the father's sex partner*. In Hippolytos' case this appersonation additionally reproaches Theseus also for his "infidelity" to the Amazon,[47] and perhaps also for his neglect of her living replica—her bastard, whom Theseus did not rear in his own palace, as Telamon had reared Teukros in his (Hom. *Il.* 8.283ff.). The relative neglect of his Amazon lover—whom he did not wed—is thus duplicated by Theseus' relative neglect of his Amazon-like son, whom he gave to Pittheus to raise.[48] This, then, is the real root of the *latent* homosexuality which Grene[49] had sensed, but which, not being a clinician, he could neither fully appraise nor really prove. Though it goes without saying that Hippolytos himself is quite unaware of his inclinations, one is struck by his peculiarly worded—and seemingly far-fetched—comment about his friends: "and to consort with friends who essay no wrong, but would think it shame alike to send evil behests to their companions and to requite them with services that are vile" (997ff.; Barrett's translation).[50] I see no possibility of viewing this passage as referring to something else than homosexuality. I must stick to this interpretation of verses 997ff. and the scholia until a more convincing explanation is forthcoming. Barrett's comments seem tangential, save for the reference to the "message" conveyed by the Nurse.

Yet, here, as so often, Barrett quà editor of the text, deserves attention: he shows (ad loc.) that the verse leading up to this passage is "grammatically untidy," because Euripides is groping for a lost thread. In a clinical situation, as in poetic creation, such a groping suggests a sudden and narrowly circumscribed breakthrough of the repressed—heralded, as usual, by hesitant grammar and speech.[51]

Hence, I cannot agree with Barrett that verses 997ff. are simply a further reproach to Phaidra. The text speaks of "evil behests" sent to (male!) *companions* and of "*requiting* them with services that are vile." This can imply only a denial of homosexual practices and of homosexual

---

[47] Since there is no *old* tradition of Theseus' infidelity *to* Phaidra, the allusions in 151–54, 167–70, and 320 can refer only to his previous adventures and to his reputation as an amorist.

[48] On self-confessed paternal inadequacy, cf. Pl. *La.* init.; cf. Devereux, "Greek Pseudo-Homosexuality," op. cit.

[49] Grene, op. cit., p. 52.

[50] On contempt for the passive homosexual in Greece, cf. K. J. Dover: *Greek Homosexuality*, London, 1978; also G. Devereux, "Greek Pseudo-Homosexuality," op. cit. Barrett, ad loc., did not notice the allusion to homosexuality.

[51] A patient, who unconsciously wished his father were dead, once said: "and that would be lucky—(pause)—for him." The *entire* meaning was in the *pause*: the contingency would have been lucky *only* for the father.

prostitution in payment for services rendered.[52] Possibly Hippolytos claims here that he is an ideally homosexual, but behaviorally properly inhibited, young gentleman. By contrast, Theseus is quite "vulgarly" heterosexual.[53] Platon might have praised such a "hero," but Euripides' dislike of fashionable, homosexual athletes is obvious.

Such intrapsychic constellations are found especially in men whose homosexuality masks a desire to be utterly sexless: they enter analysis with the conscious hope that it will turn them *not* into heterosexuals, but into *neuters*.[54] This seems to be also Hippolytos' main ambition in life.

This latent homosexuality is perfectly congruent with Hippolytos' hatred for his father, which persists even after his fatal accident:

1412: Thes. "Would it please Heavens that (this wish) had not come to my lips."
1413: Hipp. "Ah! then you would have *killed me* in your *wrath*."

This supposition is almost, though not quite, gratuitous since—and this is usually overlooked—Theseus asks Poseidon directly and *unconditionally* only once to *kill* Hippolytos (887). Later on, he says only: "*either* Poseidon will send him dead to Hades," *or* he will die slowly in exile (895ff.); still later (1045ff.) Theseus mentions *only* death in exile. The *real* murderousness is *in Hippolytos*. First directed at Theseus, but soon inhibited, it ricochets: he wants Theseus to kill him and, when Theseus fails to "oblige" him, he panics and, in so doing, *contrives* for himself a fatal chariot accident (see elsewhere).

This mixture of homosexual eroticism and aggressivity is clinically commonplace: in perversions, aggressivity is fused wih sexuality—and nowhere more conspicuously than in so-called "anal eroticism" (of which passive homosexuality is one manifestation).[55]

The triad: homosexual attraction to the father, identification with the Amazon mother, and ricocheting hostility to the father, has further

---

[52] It hardly need be recalled that mercenary homosexuality was despised in Greece. For Dionysos' agreeing to prostitute himself for services rendered, cf. Höfer ap. Roscher, *Lex.*, s.v. Polymnos (Prosymnos), cols. 2659-60. The details of that rite suggest that, though reported only by late authors, the tradition is an old one. On mercenary catamites, cf. K. J. Dover, *Greek Homosexuality*, London, 1978.

[53] An upper class, snobbish homosexual, who had *not* read Platon, declared in his analysis that heterosexuality was vulgar; real gentlemen were homosexual. I myself heard a well-known homosexual intellectual use the word "heterosexual" as a gross insult, screaming it at the top of his voice.

[54] One such homosexual gave up the project of entering analysis with me when he learned that he might cease to be homosexual, but would *not* become a neuter. Another such patient I was able to cure.

[55] O. Fenichel, *The Psychoanalytic Theory of Neurosis*, New York, 1946; the essentials of the argument—with Greek examples—are given in Devereux, "Greek Pseudo-Homosexuality," op. cit.

implications for Hippolytos. Even in fantasy he can turn the clock back only to the period when the idealized mother was his father's mistress. As long as Hippolytos himself is alive, his mere existence is a constant reminder of his mother's "fall from grace," not to say "sluttishness." The *status quo ante*—the one which existed before this "disgrace"—can be restored only the day Hippolytos *ceases to exist*, and he *sees to it* that this happens. Chariot (and automobile) "accidents" are made to order for such purposes;[56] Hippolytos is clearly a tragic personage.

My argument may seem complicated, but then so is the human mind. Everyone admits that a computer is complicated and tricky. Why then boggle at the insight that the human mind—which invented it—is also complex?

How much of this did Euripides know consciously? Probably not much. But evidence shows that one's unconscious can solve even objective problems which one's conscious is unable to solve.[57] Aristoteles would hardly have denied that the poet can put himself into an (abnormal) frame of mind and that—as though in a trance (Platon, *Ion*, passim)—he can then reproduce all conscious and unconscious manifestations *compatible* with that particular "frame of mind" (= neurosis, psychosis, character disorder). Did not Sophokles comment that Aischylos *unwittingly* did things right?[58]

It cannot be due to chance that Euripides' data fit psychoanalytic theory and clinical experience perfectly. Hippolytos' personality and behavior are patterned, coherent, and complete. No psychologically false note is struck. Much of this can be plausibly attributed to Euripides' perceptive observation of the first specimens of the young "men" (?) idealized by Platon.[59]

Some of the rest—how much of it no one can confidently say—must have been due to conscious planning. What remains was no doubt taken care of by Euripides' ability to fill-in intuitively—and in what Gestalt psychologists call "a system-adequate manner"—the empty spaces of this framework. That requires neither great genius nor miraculous empathic capacities. Euripides' human mind simply did not repudiate anything

---

[56] Clinical case: during the Hitler regime, a German refugee fantasized killing all Germans and then *himself* as well, so that the last of that "accursed race" would perish. A similar fantasy is found also in, e.g., G. Szántó's Hungarian novel, *The Golden Twig*, Budapest, 1958.

[57] Cf. Devereux, *Dreams in Greek Tragedy*, op. cit., pp. xxii, 163.

[58] Arist. *Poet.* 1455a31; cf. W. D. Ross, *Aristotle* (paperback ed.), London, 1959, p. 278. Sophokles on Aischylos: Athen. 10.428f.; cf. G. Murray, *Aeschylus* (paperback ed.), Oxford, 1951, p. 147.

[59] For the clinician the homosexual atmosphere of Platon's (and Sokrates'?) circle of disciples is unmistakable, as is Platon's contempt for "animalistic" (four-footed beast) (hetero-) sexuality.

human, *without first hearing it*. He observed, heard, and resonated everything with compassion—even, and perhaps especially, where he ended up by condemning it—without ever forgetting what he had understood and felt, while scrutinizing man and man's ways both straight and crooked.[60]

The Procedure

As a King, Theseus sits in judgment over a subject accused of lèse-majesté; as a father he judges his seemingly impious and criminal son. This may shock modern legal sensibilities, but is quite in accordance with the archaic concept of kingship—and of fatherhood as well.

The King is deeply shaken by the loss of his beloved wife (836ff). The father is horrified by the deed imputed to his son. But, though indignant and greatly afflicted, I repeat that he does not talk like any Euripidean madman. Hippolytos—as yet unaware of the crime imputed to him—mildly criticizes his father's general outburst against the absurdities of human existence (924). Theseus' anger is great and his feeling of having been degraded is strong. But he is neither irascible, nor given to violence: Hippolytos himself attests it (1041ff.). The judge is in a state that permits him to judge sanely—the gods permitting. His remark that men are as lecherous as women, though their being men privileges them in this respect, is clearly a lucid man's remark. On the other hand, it cannot be denied that, were Theseus to tolerate the insult to the King and to the father that Hippolytos' (alleged) crime represents, he would lose face—and lesser men than the King of Athens have reacted to the risk of losing face with violence, especially in matters involving sex.[61]

Theseus' Reproaches

Theseus' reproaches—other than the accusation of rape—deserve close scrutiny. Though Méridier[62] rightly says that Theseus knows his son inside out, critics turn a deaf ear to his unfavorable characterization of Hippolytos, calling Theseus irascible or else implying that the grief

---

[60] Nearly everything said about Hippolytos' feelings about Theseus is also applicable to Artemis' behavior toward him; she is, after all, a projection of his personality and therefore, as Kitto says, a "subhuman goddess;" she is unable to empathize with Theseus' spontaneously human ways.
[61] Before World War I, an educated man living in my home town found his wife cohabiting with his Irish setter, whom the enraged man promptly shot and killed. When I heard of this a few years later, I felt that if the man *had* to shoot anyone, he should have shot his wife, rather than the innocent dog. The adults around me did not share this view, which I still hold to be correct.
[62] In his ed., p. 20, note.

and horror he experiences just then have robbed him of capacity to judge his son correctly.

Now, with one exception, every reproach he heaps on his son is intimately linked with one of Hippolytos' *already well attested* traits. It can, at most, be claimed that the negative side of certain of his ways is overemphasized.[63] I take up these traits one by one, in the order in which Theseus mentions them, differentiating between general reproaches addressed at mankind and specific ones addressed at Hippolytos.

General Reproaches

(1) One cannot impart a right mind to people lacking sense (920). It suffices to recall here that Hippolytos' slave tries in vain to make his master behave properly toward Aphrodite (88ff.). Hippolytos misogynistic tirade (616ff.) has shown him to be lacking in commonsense.

(2) It is regrettable that evil is not betrayed by a special kind of voice (928 ff.). Theseus implicitly accuses his son of hypocrisy. This accusation is unfounded, except that, as shown in another section, Hippolytos may *unconsciously* have experienced oedipal wishes toward Phaidra.

Specific Accusations

(1) Theseus ironically calls Hippolytos a "superior person" (948), living in the company of the gods, virtuous and pure in every way (948). Hippolytos repeatedly makes such claims for himself and, in objecting to them, Theseus echoes the views of Aphrodite and the warnings of several other personages.

(2) Orphic. Both Linforth[64] and Barrett (ad loc.) try to prove mainly that Hippolytos was not a "real" orphic. In so doing they disregard Linforth's own thesis that it is far from clear what "real" orphism was (cf. Chapter 4).

In respect to this play, what matters is the Athenian public's "idea" of the orphics. Barrett is overly optimistic in asserting that the public realized that Hippolytos was *not* an orphic. Many must have known only that mysticism (and magic) were essential parts of orphism. Those that knew more than this of orphism would hardly have expected secret matters or the mysteries to be shown or discussed onstage.

One notes at once Hippolytos' complaint over Theseus' failure—just returning crowned from an oracle to utter tragedy—to consult diviners—a profession that Euripides notoriously despised[65] and that Theseus

---

[63] Compare: I am firm, thou art stubborn, he is pigheaded.
[64] I. M. Linforth, *The Arts of Orpheus*, 1941, pp. 50ff.
[65] P. Decharme, *Euripides and the Spirit of his Dramas*, New York, 1909, pp. 64ff.

too holds in little esteem (1058f.). Theseus expresses his contempt for the flight of birds with the same word (χαίρειν) that Hippolytos uses in expressing his contempt for Aphrodite.

There remains the problem of sexual abstinence in orphism. Fehrle, who in this respect follows the example of Dietrich,[66] believed that the Orphics were sexually abstinent; Guthrie[67] mentions orphic misogyny. The evidence provided by the *Hippolytos*[68] is simply set aside by Linforth, as is that of so many other texts antedating Platon. This excessive skepticism seems at times self-serving.

(3) Hypocrisy (955ff.). The charge is unfounded, at least on the conscious level.

(4) As a bastard, Hippolytos does represent a danger (962ff.) to patrilineal dynastic succession. True, the charge seems unfounded in terms of Attic law, which would not have enabled Phaidra to guarantee Hippolytos' succession by marrying him. But Phaidra was a Cretan and Hippolytos the son of an Amazon. The supposition that Hippolytos or Phaidra may have had a Cretan or Amazon type succession in mind is assuredly not proven, but neither is it inherently absurd. After all, Barrett (ad 1010) cites mythical cases in which the defunct husband's property passed to his wife's second husband. Moreover, already at 304ff., the Nurse warns Phaidra that, if she died, the succession of her children to the throne would be endangered by Theseus' bastard—and adds the weighty remark (309f.): "You know Hippolytos!" I cannot imagine that the Nurse names Hippolytos in this manner only in order to indicate *whom* she means. Her statement implies that Hippolytos' (hidden) ambitions are obvious: He is not, like Teukros, a bastard content with being his legitimate half-brother Aias' helper. Also, he has a small personal clique of young men of his own kind.

An overlooked slip of the tongue betrays Hippolytos preconscious ambitions. At 1016 he claims that he only wishes to be the *second* in the City. But we learn both from the Nurse (313f.) and from Phaidra (315) that there are *several* legitimate sons, all of whom would normally take precedence over the bastard Hippolytos. In fact, Hippolytos can be the *second* in the City *only as Theseus' heir apparent*.

Theseus' charge is, thus, compatible with Hippolytos' manifest, observable (310) character;[69] so are the Nurse's suspicions.

(5) A sex-urge (967ff.) is present even in Hippolytos, though a man

---

[66] E. Fehrle, "Die kulitsche Keuschheit im Altertum," *R.V.V.* vi, Giessen, 1910; A. Dieterich, *Abraxas*, Leipzig, 1891.
[67] W. K. C. Guthrie, *Orpheus and Greek Religion*², 1952, pp. 49ff.
[68] O. Kern, *Orphicorum Fragmenta, Test.* 213, Berlin, 1922.
[69] That he is neither civic minded nor an Athenian democrat is shown by his *professed* lack of interest in civic matters and by his preference for membership in an elitist coterie (1017ff.). I shall return to this point later.

can conceal his profligacy more easily than a woman. Also, in a passage which is all too often overlooked, Hippolytos (1367ff.) himself complains that he performed in vain the *painful* duties of piety (virtue) *in the sight of men.*

(6) Charlatan, impostor (1038ff.). The characterization is inaccurate, though Phaidra's (anachronistic) letter makes it seem legitimate.

(7) Arrogance during the trial (1038ff.). The charge is amply justified, as my analysis of the trial procedure will show.

(8) Seducer of women (1068f.). Same remark as for (6).

(9) More addicted to the cult of his self than to filial piety (1081f.). I deem the charge well founded.

The Evidence

The evidence in support of the accusation is very weighty. The written accusation *is* conclusive evidence and would be so viewed by any court of law lacking medical experts, for it is a general judicial principle that people do not trifle at the point of death—hence the value attached to last words and death-bed confessions. For his part, Theseus observes that no one would throw away her precious life from mere vindictiveness (962ff.). Artemis herself admits that Theseus was divinely doomed to be deceived (1335ff., 1406, 1433ff.).

True, both Hippolytos (1055) and Artemis (1321f.) blame Theseus for not waiting for confirmatory evidence. But one can well ask here: What evidence could there be? Artemis, though she forgives Theseus, reproaches him for not investigating the matter further (1321); yet she *twice* concedes that Theseus was doomed to be deceived by divine will (1406, 1433). Both Hippolytos (1055) and Artemis (1321f.) reproach Theseus for not consulting the diviners. Modern critics echo this reproach, though no one has so far proven that diviners played a decisive role in mythical trials or that their responses were believed to be infallible. And, as I noted earlier, Euripides had as little respect for diviners as Theseus has.

Theseus' refusal to believe his son's oath of innocence is, perhaps, a weightier matter—especially since the Koryphaios declares the oath to be legally valid. But, considerations of jurisprudence require one to make haste slowly: the Koryphaios accepts the oath, because he *knows* the real facts—*not* because affirmations of innocence, made under oath, were legally conclusive evidence. The persuasiveness of the evidence militating against Hippolytos is recognized by the accused himself. He even states that, were he in Theseus' shoes, he would kill his son (1042).

Hippolytos also claims that, had he broken his oath to the Nurse, his father would still have disbelieved him (1060ff.). Things are not quite that simple. Had he broken that oath, Theseus could have put the

Nurse—who was, presumably, Phaidra's slave—to the torture in accordance with Athenian practice, and so wrung the truth from her.

There is also the reproach that Theseus refused recourse to verbal proof—i.e., presumably to lawyers' arguments. The reproach is made both by Hippolytos (1055) and, less directly, also by Artemis (1334ff.). One wonders how critics would have reacted to a forensic *agon* between Hippolytos and Phaidra's Nurse.

There remains Hippolytos' regret that the house—an inanimate thing—cannot acquire a voice so as to testify on his behalf (1074f.). One cannot help remembering here that he wished women to associate only with mute beasts (645ff.)—the kind, one presumes, that he himself hunted and killed.

In short, the evidence available at that time seems conclusive. Theseus' conduct of the inquiry into the facts is therefore judicially adequate.

The Third Wish

The Third Wish is, in folklore, invariably silly and wasted. But nothing proves that Euripides was concerned here with the folkloristic motif's pattern. On the other hand, some of the arguments commentators advance to prove that this is the first time Theseus makes use of one of the three wishes granted to him by Poseidon are, to my mind, somewhat finely spun. This, however, is irrelevant for present purposes. What matters is that Theseus cursed his son and Poseidon implemented the curse.[70]

Hippolytos' Silence

Hippolytos' silence is usually appraised either only "morally" or else only practically. Opinion ranges from impatience with his obstinacy to reverence for his fidelity, even to an oath allegedly extorted from him under false pretences. Some hold—with Hippolytos (1062)—that the *uxorious* Theseus[71] would not believe him even if he did break his oath. This does not prevent some of the selfsame commentators from implying also that the "uxorious" Theseus had been currently *unfaithful* to Phaidra, though there is no shred of evidence of any infidelity to Phaidra either in the *Hippolytos*, or in earlier sources: Theseus' philanderings either antedate his marriage, or else postdate Phaidra's death. Other trusting souls (who no doubt believe also everything they read in the *Pravda* or in the *Osservatore*

---

[70] Cf. C. Segal, "Curse and Oath in Euripides' *Hippolytus*," *Ramus* 1: 165-80, 1972, for a detailed discussion.

[71] 810ff.; 817ff.; 836ff.; 860ff. Schmid, op. cit., p. 380.6, recognizes this, yet, incomprehensibly, argues that Theseus was (recently?) in Hades (id., 378.10). Would so "devoted" a husband have *just recently* abducted Helene? The two short references to Hades (836, 1290) do not support that inference.

Romano) are piously indignant because, despite Hippolytos' pleas (1055, 1321ff.), Theseus refuses to consult oracles (1057ff.) or diviners (1321f.). This indignation disregards Euripides' notorious contempt for soothsayers and oracles.[72] In a Sophoklean drama, Hippolytos' demand that the oracles be consulted would have a different meaning and Theseus' refusal to consult them would have to be appraised accordingly. In a Euripidean drama, Hippolytos' request only highlights the inner hollowness of his whole defense. On the mytho-juridical outlandishness of the notion that Greek mythical trials were settled by diviners or oracles, I will have more to say at the proper time.

Hippolytos' silence must be tackled psychologically and, above all, unsentimentally. It leads to his destruction; the drama itself says so. Only Hippolytos (1062)—but not Artemis—assures us that Theseus would not have believed him, even if he had spoken; this is a biased opinion and not even a convincing one at that. Let it not be forgotten that Euripides wrote memorable lines about the value of *real* evidence, in a drama dealing with a very similar problem.[73]

If Hippolytos' silence does lead—as he himself realizes—to his destruction, then the psychologist can only conclude that he remains silent precisely *in order to achieve that end*. The unconscious self-destructiveness of the neurotic need surely not be demonstrated here at length.

I note in this context a curious similarity between Greek tragedy and comedies of error, such as Plautus' *Menaechmi*. In Arnott's opinion, both twins—and the other personages as well—must be almost *incredibly stupid* not to realize that everything that happens points unmistakably at the existence and presence of an identical twin.[74] The tragic equivalent of this monumental imperviousness to the obvious is "heroic" (neurotic) obstinacy and blindness. Talking at cross-purposes in comedy is often mistaken for madness;[75] in tragedy, psychopathology is often not recognized for what it is. In fact, while Old Comedy does not seem to deal with genuine mental illness at all, Greek tragedy deals with little else.[76] I have condemned the

---

[72] There exist, of course a few scattered positive reactions to oracles, or at least to oracular signs that come true. The matter is fairly and conservatively presented by M. P. Nilsson (*Geschichte der griechischen Religion*², 1955, 1.777), who does not consider them proofs of Euripides' vacillation on this matter. Phaidra's letter is, of course, as false as oracles in Euripides are—which is ironical.

[73] E. *Phoinix, frr.* 811, 812, N².

[74] P. D. Arnott, *An Introduction to the Greek Theatre* (paperback ed.), Bloomington, IN, 1963, p. 177.

[75] A point well made in an otherwise psychologically uninformed book: A. O'Brien-Moore, *Madness in Ancient Literature*, Weimar, 1924, pp. 53ff.

[76] A relatively asymptomatic character neurosis is almost as hard to cure as a genuine psychosis. Kitto's (op. cit.) distinction between tragic figure, tragic character, tragic victim is descriptively subtle but, though he handles these concepts with consummate mastery, they are, in the last resort, psychologically unrealistic.

cynicism and lack of reality awareness (bordering on what psychiatry calls "dereism") of the doctrine that adjustment is a valid diagnostic criterion and psychotherapeutic objective often enough not to be suspected of making concession to contemptible pseudo-psychiatric spinelessness, when I say that no sane *ethical* code can justify Hippolytos' silence—least of all when Phaidra is "obviously guilty." Nor can his silence be justified in terms of the private ethics *of Euripides*, who challenged the genuine criminal's traditional right to asylum in temples.[77]

One cannot even explain away his silence by pleading that Hippolytos is so insecure that he must cling, with obsessive rigidity,[78] to his idealized self-image. One does not develop so exalted a self-image, nor does one feel the need to cling to it so frantically, *unless* one must avoid, at all cost, a confrontation with what this façade seeks to conceal: an incestuous oedipal fixation on the Amazon mother, which has spread to the mother-imago Artemis and—as suggested before—may even have begun to involve Phaidra and a reverse oedipal fixation on the father as well. Hippolytos is silent because he is psychologically—though not behaviorally—guilty as charged and (irrational) psychological guilt arouses, by definition, more anxiety than does real guilt.[79]

At one point, as noted, Hippolytos claims only *bodily* purity (1005, cf. perhaps also 1034ff.). But in verse 1006, he admittedly claims to have also a maiden soul. Yet, as Barrett notes (ad loc.), this claim only amplifies the preceding affirmation of his bodily "purity." Putting it bluntly, the sole focus of both claims is: the crotch. Moreover, in interpreting this passage, insufficient attention is paid to a very obvious matter. In Greek, as in all European languages known to me, including Hungarian—which is a Finno-Ugrian language—there is a word for the female virgin; for the male virgin there is at best a word derived from the term for female virgin.[80] This is not surprising, for the model of "sexual virtue" is female virginity.

Excursus

The hypothesis that it is chiefly the existence of the hymen that explains interest in female virginity is ethnologically not entirely verifiable. The Mohave, whose sexual life starts very early, know of the

---

[77] E. *Ion* 1312ff. On inner vs. outer morality, cf. Dodds: "The αἰδώς of Phaedra," op. cit., p. 103.

[78] Defensive rigidity is hinted at in Blaiklock, op. cit., pp. 40–41

[79] It is a commonplace in criminal psychiatry—and was a commonplace twenty years before Freud discovered psychoanalysis—that some major crimes not only try to cover up unconscious guilt-feelings, but are committed *in order to be punished* (R. v. Krafft-Ebing, *Lehrbuch der gerichtlichen Psychopathologie*, Stuttgart, 1875 [note the date!]).

[80] In French, the word *pucelle* is attested already for the 11th century; the term *puceau* appears only in the 16th century and is used mostly in an ironic manner.

hymen and joke freely about defloration.[81] The Sedang, only whose *pre*pubertal sexual life (which includes coitus) is free, seem unaware of defloration and its implications (my field notes). In a number of societies the hymen is deliberately destroyed, sometimes already in infancy.[82]

Last but not least, sometimes the hymen is so unusually elastic that it is occasionally found intact even in prostitutes and in women who had given birth.

Hippolytos' aversion to sexuality is both behavioral and, consciously, also mental. But whereas the Greek virgin desired marriage (including its sexual component: 1140f.) Hippolytos rejects it for himself. In what way such a rejection of the essence and source of life is admirable, I am unable to comprehend, for it is fundamentally akin to what Angyal called bionegativity.[83] In short, many a critic praises Hippolytos for his chastity, but none explains just *what* makes chastity so admirable!

His silence is psychologically a suicidal maneuver and this fits the interpretation that the "real" *taraxippos* is not the bull from the sea, but Hippolytos' own self-destructiveness.

As for the Choros, it is silent for non-psychological, dramatic reasons only, for it can hardly be unconsciously aware of the *psychological* rightness of the accusation. Besides, the membership of the Choros has, since 428 B.C., been increased by the myriads of Hippolytos' subsequent admirers. If one adds that, in Greek tragedy, the Choros is hardly ever a source of *factual* information, being mainly an emotional sounding board, and that (except in his *Bakchai*)[84] Euripides seldom felt at ease with the Choros, what would surprise one would not be the Choros' silence, but its *sober* loquaciousness. The last word on all this was said by Dodds (op. cit., p. 103): Hippolytos gratifies a "repressed impulse under the guise of virtue."

[81] G. Devereux, "The Primal Scene and Juvenile Heterosexuality in Mohave Society," in G. B. Wilbur and Warner Muensterberger, *Psychoanalysis and Culture* (Róheim Festschrift), New York, 1951.
[82] H. Ploss, M. and P. Bartels, *Das Weib*, 11th ed., Berlin, 1927, vol. I, pp. 373ff.
[83] A. Angyal, "The Concept of Bionegativity," *Psychiatry* 1: 303-7, 1938.
[84] G. Murray, *Euripides*[2], London, 1946, chap. 9.

3
Hippolytos' Merits and Phaidra's Love

Preliminaries

In trying to appraise what critics say about Hippolytos' merits, one must contrast:

(1) What Hippolytos says of himself (or is cited as having said about himself) with what others say about him.

(2) What is said of him previous to verse 817 (arrival of Theseus) with what is said of him during the trial (891ff.) and in the Messenger's speech—partly by the Choros which, though knowing him to be innocent, is unfortunately bound to secrecy.

(3) And, finally, what was said before verse 1283 with what Theseus—brain-washed by Artemis, ashamed of his unjust judgment and, above all, afraid of the ritual miasma he had contracted thereby— says of Hippolytos after Artemis appearance on stage (verse 1283–fin).

It will perhaps be argued that the utterances of a goddess carry authority. That much is conceded—but a statement that manifestly does carry authority is not always a *true* statement. Speaking *ex machina* in E. *Ion*, Athena, while telling the truth, uses her authority to minimize Apollon's questionable behavior, including his deceptions. In E. *IT* Athena speaks with authority and thereby obliges Thoas to accept a solution that does not do him justice. Hence, under the circumstances, Artemis, though a goddess, cannot be rated as an unprejudiced character witness; she only uses her authority to make Theseus change his mind. I call this brainwashing.

Hippolytos' Character

It is the conviction of nearly all students of this play that, despite certain flaws, Hippolytos is, on the whole, a thoroughly admirable young man. How this conviction came into being is, in a way, beyond me, for the text gives it no support.

Since the rest of this work deals essentially with the clinical precision of the Euripidean delineation of Hippolytos, I felt it necessary to discuss his character first in terms of the moral values which literary critics usually consider to be basic.

One of Hippolytos' alleged merits is his sexual asceticism. Why abstinence from sex, let alone a sex phobia, should be admirable is not at all clear to me. I will therefore discuss the problem of asceticism, at least briefly, under a separate heading.

The second source of the pro-Hippolytos bias is the fact that he had been unjustly condemned. The unsoundness of that reasoning is implicitly highlighted by a short essay Bertrand Russell published a few years before World War II. Its title, as I recall it, was: "On the Superior Virtue of the Oppressed." The author—not suspect of sympathy with oppressors—simply pointed out that the fact of being oppressed does *not* prove the victim of oppression to be a person of superior virtue. No one denies that Hippolytos was unjustly accused of, and condemned for, rape. But, in terms of Bertrand Russell's argument, this fact does not suffice to turn him into a plaster saint.

I therefore begin by setting forth his foibles, one by one, in terms of commonsense morality. As for the character traits imputed to him by Theseus—or revealed by Hippolytos during his trial—I must, for reasons of expository convenience, discuss them in still another section. These tasks completed, I will be able to turn to the real topic of my book: the neurosis of Hippolytos as depicted by Euripides.

Lack of Insight

Hippolytos approves of all the qualities his slave praises: affability, willingness to listen to good advice, respect for all the gods. He condemns all the flaws his slave criticizes: arrogance, discourtesy, etc. (98ff.). However, he is totally unaware of the fact that he practices none of the virtues he claims he admires and exhibits all the foibles he professes to condemn.

So complete a lack of insight shows that Hippolytos is practically a borderline case.

Hippolytos' Merits

Hippolytos' merits are loudly proclaimed by himself, partly echoed by Artemis, who has a score to settle with Aphrodite, but are unmentioned *by anyone else* until he gets into trouble. At that point pity over his undeserved condemnation leads to assertions of his innocence and even to some praise—but that praise is nowhere near as enthusiastic as that he lavishes on himself. Hippolytos the plaster saint exists only in the imagination of some literary critics.

I propose to set the pattern straight, without turning Hippolytos into a melodrama villain.

The crux of the matter is that compassion for the self-destructive narcissist all too easily turns into an encomium of his alleged virtues.

The first and crucial point to be made is that if Hippolytos or any other dramatic personage is to be studied psychologically, he (or she) must be *imagined* as a real human being. Now, *any* human being deserves compassion, not because all of us are "poor sinners," but because life treats us as if we were just that. Compassion for Hippolytos is mandatory also on artistic grounds. If, reacting to the traditional practice of treating him as a one-dimensional comic strip prig, this magnificent play would be deprived of its tragic dimension and therefore also of much of its artistic scope. This matter is important enough to make the relationship of compassion to both love and hate a focal issue.

Contrary to general opinion, love does not exclude compassion. Awareness of one's lover's—or even of one's dog's—vulnerability and mortality is a basic component of love and tenderness.

The relationship between compassion and hate is less obvious. One can psychoanalyze a patient only if one feels *some* compassion for him—be it but on the score of his illness and (at times) unlikableness. Yet, as Winnicott[1] has shown, one can at times successfully analyze even a patient whom one loathes.[2]

But the compassion one owes to Hippolytos, the human being, does not justify a misrepresentation of the facts. Some claim that *many* were loyal to him. Yet, in actual fact, before his unjust condemnation, even his personal slave dreaded him (89, cf. 100), and only a small band of young gentlemen, addicted to the hunt, were personally involved with him.

The claim that he—as a person—was mourned by the *whole* community must also be nuanced: not the death of Hippolytos but that of an important citizen is a grief to the City (1465f.). As to the Troizenian hair sacrifice, instituted by Artemis, it is no proof of *felt* public sorrow—and this quite apart from the systematically overlooked fact that it commemorates Phaidra's love rather than Hippolytos' "virtue" or death.

This does not mean that his death elicited no regret. The fatal cursing of a son by his father, for a deed he had not committed, is reason enough to elicit public compassion for him. But he was guilty all along also of gross and arrogant impiety toward Aphrodite, which endangered the whole city (99 ff., and even more clearly 359ff.). I admit that had Theseus been aware only of *this* flaw in his son, he would not have asked Poseidon to punish him to the utmost. It is hard to imagine just how a mythical hero would have dealt with his son's impiety. We know how

---

[1] D. W. Winnicott, "Hate in the Counter-Transference," *International Journal of Psycho-Analysis* 30: 69–74, 1949.

[2] I myself did as well as could be expected in treating an odious and boring borderline obsessive. I could not but feel compassion for him for, almost from the day of his birth, his nightmarish mother had poisoned the wellsprings of his being. In his case a predictably interminable psychoanalysis could, at most, prevent a probably irreversable psychotic break.

historical Athens dealt with Sokrates' (alleged) impiety—but *that* can hardly be treated as a clue to what the *mythical* Theseus would have done.[3] I take it for granted that he would *not* have condemned him to death or exile; this much seems probable, since Aphrodite had to *plot* to make him *seem* guilty of a *capital* crime. As to the theater-goer, he assuredly felt—as I do—that the mere fact of being a narcissistic prig does not justify a sentence of death.

That Theseus mourned his son is certain. Since he did utter the fatal curse, he does not try to deny his responsibility, though he *could* have blamed Aphrodite, who had trapped him, quite as angrily as Hippolytos blamed her (1415). There is also much irony in the fact that a notorious amorist like Theseus was deceived into cursing his virginal son for his alleged unchastity—a nuance that seems to have escaped notice.

Yet, even though Theseus felt grief over having unjustly condemned Hippolytos, I believe that he would not have missed his son a great deal or for long. For me, Theseus' formal words of regret are amongst the least moving of this admirable tragedy. One can foresee that Theseus will find it hard to live with the memory of *his own* injustice, and yet doubt that he will experience a severe sense of *loss*. Hippolytos, as a person, was simply not close enough to his father for his death to be experienced as a mutilation of Theseus' ego—as would be the case in true mourning.[4]

Last, but not least, Hippolytos' merits (if any) consist solely of his *unactualized* potentialities. He was doomed by the unfortunate circumstances of his life—as is every neurotic—but he tried at first to make the most of his handicaps (so-called "secondary benefits").

One can suppose that had Rimbaud's childhood been different, he would not have stopped writing poetry at the age of eighteen. Had Eric Satie been less warped, he would have composed works much better than his musical wisecracks. And yet, the actual performances of Rimbaud and Satie permit one to infer the *nature* of their *potential* contributions to civilization. Euripides' play provides no clues to Hippolytos' *unactualized* possibilities. One cannot even say with Gray: "Some mute inglorious Milton, here may rest." Thus, precisely by hoping to be a victor (1016), he admits not having, as yet, won a first prize in the games. He tried to achieve distinction also—or should I say mostly?—as a man of piety and virtue.

Must one suppose that, with a better start in life, he might have

---

[3] There are certain similarities between Hippolytos' arrogant, clumsy, and *provocative* defense, and the defense Platon attributed to Sokrates, whose second speech was provocative enough to cause him to be sentenced *to death* by a majority *greater* than the one that had found him *guilty*.

[4] S. Freud, "Mourning and Melancholia," *Standard Edition*, xiv, 1957.

equaled Herakles as a hunter? That this piety, directed into normal channels, would have matched that of old Pittheus? That he would have been as loyal a friend as Theseus? I do not know, for I am unable to discern in the Euripidean *Hippolytos* an embryonic statesman and lawgiver, a Homeric Hektor, a great poet, or a man of wisdom.

He himself claims only virtues that call for self-restraint. Since, for some reason, these negative virtues still enjoy prestige, I deem it necessary to take (infra) a closer look at the meaning of ascetic practices.

Asceticism

Asceticism, which plays a peculiar role in the history of cultures and religions, is a *do ut des* proposition: by renouncing certain physio-psychological gratification, one obtains culturally valued powers—*though not necessarily for ethical ends*. Ancient Indian asceticism *automatically* earned its practicioner "dividends" in the form of magical powers. Hence, an *evil* demon confidently subjected himself to aeons of asceticism, so as to acquire enough power to dethrone the gods. As to the only one of Thespios' fifty virgin daughters who refused to cohabit with Herakles, she was made by him that perpetually chaste priestess of his own temple (Paus. 9.27.6). Kassandra, who welshed on her promise to let Apollon deflower her, ended up as Agamemnon's concubine and, as such, was murdered by Klytaimestra (A. *Ag.* 1437ff.).

One crucial datum is that, unlike Hippolytos, Bellerophontes, who also refused to yield to a lecherous wife, was *not* a sex phobic.

In myth only goddesses (Athene, Artemis) choose to remain virgins forever. Thetis did not object to *sex*—she objected only to being given in marriage to a mere mortal. Mortal women remained virgins only if they were priestesses obliged to be chaste or if a god tried to force his attentions on them.

I conclude by recalling a well-known but often disregarded fact. A Greek hero would have a cult, *without* having led a virtuous life on earth—and, at times, *despite* a scandalous conduct even after his heroization.[5]

In terms of the sociological scheme I proposed elsewhere, I can assert that a Greek hero was not necessarily either good or bad; he simply had a great "social mass."[6]

Some heroes even had a criminal past. The master thief and perjurer Autolykos (Str. 12.13.11, p. 546), like the burglar and brotherslayer Trophonios (Paus. 9.16.6, etc.), had a dream oracle. Hippolytos heroization is, thus, not the equivalent of a certificate of regular church attendance.

[5] J. E. Harrison, *Prolegomena to the Study of Greek Religion*[2], 1922.
[6] G. Devereux, *Ethnopsychoanalysis*, Berkeley, 1978, chap. 1.

The point is that Hippolytos' "chastity" is nowhere explained in a *rational* way—or at all. He is not even chaste in the hope of getting something tangible in return. His chief *intelligible* reward seems to be the privilege of claiming to be the most chaste of all men. This, however, was not a source of pride to Greek heroes: sexual abstinence except in a ritual context, and for limited periods, was not demanded from *men*. This shows that Hippolytos' "chastity" was an insuperable neurotic phobia, which *he defined as* a virtue entitling him to admiration.

I cannot discuss here the general human tendency to define virtue primarily in terms of the crotch, though I am less convinced now than I was formerly by Freud's argument that defloration is dangerous because it involves the shedding of an affinal relative's blood[7] for the simple reason that, in a great many cultures, the hymen is ruptured very early, without anyone noticing it, for example in the course of infantile masturbation. I never heard a Sedang of South Vietnam refer in any way to *bleeding* at defloration. In fact, the only way of finding out whether a girl had engaged in genuine coitus is to ask: "Has she already killed a pig?" (i.e., to expiate a confessed premarital sexual act).

Male Virginity

All discussions of Hippolytos seem to pre-suppose that pre-Platonic Greece valued male virginity, per se, though the play itself proves the opposite. Male virginity was at most a Semitic (Oriental) value.[8] Hippolytos is the only anti-sexual "male" in Greek myth—and I have shown that verse 351 even casts doubt upon his maleness. Permanent female virginity was only slightly less un-Greek. Aischylos' Danaides claim to resist "only" a forced (and incestuous?) marriage.[9]

Even permanent priestly chastity was fairly rare in Greece. As noted above, Herakles made the only one of Thestios' fifty daughters who refused to be deflowered and impregnated by him his priestess and doomed her to lifelong virginity.[10] The permanent chastity of one male

---

[7] S. Freud, "The Taboo of Virginity," *Standard Edition*, xi, 1957.

[8] M. P. Nilsson, *Geschichte der Griechischen Religion*², i, 90, 94; cf. G. Cumont, *Oriental Religions in Roman Paganism*, New York, 1956, p. 40, p. 222.29. Data on Greek male virginity pertain chiefly to later periods. The scholarship of some studies on this topic (e.g., E. Fehrle, "Die kultische Keuschheit im Altertum," *Religionsgeschichtliche Versuche und Vorarbeiten [RGVV]* xii, etc.) is more impressive than their perceptiveness. Even Blaiklock (op. cit., p. 39) is, for once, simply anachronistic.

[9] This rationalization is feeble enough. Marriage with a paternal cousin would not have shocked an Athenian, who could marry his paternal half-sister; cf. Plu. *Cim.* 4.5f. The fact that Elpinike could then remarry proves that her first ("incestuous") marriage did not degrade her socially; cf. G. Devereux: *Dreams in Greek Tragedy*, Oxford and Berkeley, 1976 (chap. 9).

[10] Paus. 9.27.6. Persian equivalent: Plu. V. *Artax.* 27.3.

priest of a mystery cult was also not spontaneous: he had to be *made* impotent by pharmacological means.[11]

I conclude by noting that Greek myth favors love and sexuality so consistently that anyone who frustrates himself or others—and even his own mares[12]—sexually comes to a bad end, being, like Hippolytos, fairly often destroyed by *horses*. At any rate, in the play itself, besides Hippolytos only Artemis (guardian of *female* virginity) approves of Hippolytos' sex-phobia. This suffices to settle once and for all claims concerning the alleged importance of male virginity in the classical Greek hierarchy of values.

Matters do not change by stressing the cultist aspects of Hippolytos' sex phobia. Not even the most ingenious appeals to "Orphism" can turn Hippolytos into a Periklean "group ideal" or "social cynosure"[13] —not simply because, in normal terms, such cults attract only the lunatic fringe, but because the antiquity of Orphism is itself controversial.[14]

Last but not least, *in myth* Orpheus is either a devoted husband or else a proselytizing homosexual; he is never a "chaste" neuter.

As a matter of fact, even the late Greek's conception of the mythical age was unable to accomodate a sexless Hippolytos. Tradition notwithstanding, a late painting shows Hippolytos and Artemis in a loving embrace, while a Christian source makes him Asklepios' *eromenos*.[15] By

---

[11] Unfortunately the relevant sources are mostly late and/or Christian: Hippol. *haer.* 3.8, p. 162 d.-S.; Jer. *adv. Iovin.* 1.49 p. 320C Vall.; Serv. *V. Aen.* 6.661. Discussion in E. Rohde, *Psyche* (English trans., New York, 1925), p. 231, n. 12. For this effect of hemlock, cf. Ovidius (*Amor.* 3.7.27). The first Greek to *advocate* the castration of men, horses, and dogs was the oligarchal Xenophon (*Cyrop.* 7.5.60ff.). Herodotos' horror of castration is manifest (3.48-49; 3.97; 6.32; 8.105-6). Cf. also Hom. *Od.* 18.85, 116; 21.308: Odysseus' son and his servant are the only mythical heros who actually do (*Od.* 22.474ff.) what Echetos is said to do. Since Echetos ruled on the mainland, might this explain why no palace was found in Ithaca? Cf. G. Devereux, "The Self-Blinding of Oidipous," *Journal of Hellenic Studies* 93: 36-49, 1973. A further case may be Herakles (D. S., 4.10.4).

[12] The tradition that Glaukos' sex-starved mares (Verg. *Georg.* 3.267 and Serv. ad loc.) became maneaters (Probus ad Verg. *Georg.* 3.267) is curiously anthropomorphic: the feeling of being unloved (and/or sex-starved) is one cause of neurotic over-eating.

[13] On these concepts, cf. G. Róheim, "Psycho-Analysis of Primitive Cultural Types," *International Journal of Psycho-Analysis* 13: 1-224, 1932 (esp. pp. 175-99); W. La Barre, "Social Cynosure and Social Structures," *Journal of Personality* 19: 169-83, 1946 = (in) D. G. Haring (ed.), *Personal Character and Cultural Milieu*[2], Syracuse, NY, 1956, pp. 535-46. = (in) W. La Barre, *Culture in Context*, Durham, NC, 1980.

[14] While recognizing the methodological merits of I. M. Linforth's (*The Arts of Orpheus*, 1941) overcautiousness, my views are closer to those of W. K. C. Guthrie (*Orpheus and Greek Religion*[2], 1952) and of L. Moulinier (*Orphée et l'Orphisme*, Paris, 1955). I disagree on fundamental points with V. D. Macchioro (*From Orpheus to Paul*, New York, 1930).

[15] Painting: Preller-Robert, op. cit., 2.747ff. Asklepios: Clem. *hom.* 5.15 = *test.* 83, E. J. and L. Edelstein, *Asclepius*, i, 1945.

Greek standards, these inventions amount to bowdlerization in reverse.[16] What matters here is that the latent (symbolized) content of a bowdlerized myth is the same as the (sometimes manifest) content of the unbowdlerized version: the latent content remains invariant in all transformations of a myth.[17] In the *Hippolytos* the invariant content is an "aim-inhibited" (Freud) unconscious erotic attachment to and identification with a (divine) mother-figure, at once virgin and slutty with overtones of latent homosexuality.

In short, the idealizing of Hippolytos' hatred of love and sex-phobia is not Greek. It was devised largely by his Occidental eulogists who imagine that, in 429/428, Euripides *should* have admired the prototype of a lakonizing, priggish, conceited, horse-crazy, athletic, sex-phobic, virginal, "orphic" dandy who is tempted to break his oath. Since I will deal, in due time, with most of these traits in detail, I mention here only the famous line: "My lips have sworn, my mind has not" (612), which echoes Andromache's contemptuous remark about Menelaos: "There are words on his lips to which his thoughts give the lie" (E. *Androm.* 451–52). This makes Hippolytos a peer of Spartan Menelaos, whom Euripides notoriously despised.[18]

I note in conclusion two points that should be self-evident.

(1) Hippolytos is one of the few do-nothing (unheroic) heroes whom only the *obiter dictum* of Delphi or of a *deus ex machina* could—perhaps as a compensation for injustices suffered—turn into (cult) heroes—no doubt to the great surprise of their former fellow citizens[19] The only socially and religiously noteworthy thing Hippolytos ever did was to die. He concedes that he is socially non-functional; in fact—despite his ambitions—he had not even won a prize at the games (1016ff.) and the Greek simply did not "canonize" people for their piety only.

(2) That his myth is the *aition* of the Troizenian marriage-rite does not

---

[16] By Greek standards (though not by mine), Pindaros (*O.* 1.35ff.) "bowdlerized" Tantalos' cannibal feast into a story of homosexual abduction; cf. G. Devereux, "Why Oedipus Killed Laius," *International Journal of Psycho-Analysis* 34: 132–41, 1953; id., "The Abduction of Hippodameia," *Studi e Materiali* 36: 3–25, 1965. On another bowdlerization by Pindaros, cf. id., "L'Exploitation de l'Ambiguité dans Pindaros *O*.3.27," *Tragédie et Poésie Grecques*, 1975, chap. 8. These articles also discuss, in passing, the psychology of bowdlerization, including "reverse" bowdlerization.

[17] As does the structure of the myth; cf. C. Lévi-Strauss, *Anthropologie Structurale*, Paris, 1958 (esp. pp. 227–55); id., *Mythologiques*, 4 vols., Paris, 1964–71. Cf. G. Devereux, *Ethnopsychoanalysis*, 1978.

[18] Already W. Schmid, *Geschichte der griechischen Literatur*, 1961 (1.3.382.8), pointed out that Euripides *could not* have liked the Hippolytos-type. On his dislike of athletes, ibid., p. 624; cf. E. *fr*. 282 N².

[19] The problem of otiose heroes deserves special study, as does that of Zeus' preposterous son-in-law, Menelaos. Kitto, op. cit., p. 282, rightly observes that nothing matters about Hippolytos, save only his "purity."

prove his "goodness."[20] Once again, contrary to what many commentators imply, that cult commemorates *not* Hippolytos' "chastity" but chiefly Phaidra's love (1429–30): "Kann man denn nicht lesen?" (Wilamowitz).

Arrogant "Purity"

Hippolytos professes to be Purity incarnate (78). He is pure (103), he is sexually intact (1002ff.), he has a maiden soul (1006); adultery is alien to him in thought and deed (1027). He is the most virtuous of all men, may it not displease his father (1100); he surpasses all in virtue (1365) and is the best of men (1242).

Now, even though many societies do not taboo boastfulness, that of Hippolytos increases as the play progresses. He is no longer simply pure and virtuous: he is the *best* of all men. But his virtue is soon revealed to be chiefly a means of degrading others. Now, as pointed out elsewhere, whereas the *absolute* praise Delphi lavished on Lykourgos elicited no resentment, the oracles' statement, *in the superlative*, about Sokrates did not increase the philosopher's popularity. Plutarch's defense of *harmless* self-praise shows that *offensive* self-praise was disapproved in Greek society.[21]

In short, Hippolytos is not only a prig, but also full of self-importance and eager to affirm his superiority over others. His self-centeredness exceeds even that of the Homeric Achilleus.

It is important to observe that others do not share his high opinion of himself *before* catastrophe overtakes him. Only after his chariot accident does Artemis declare him to be a noble soul (1390). Only then does she state that she feels affection for him, while Aphrodite hates his virtue (1402). Artemis also proclaims his purity, virtue, and piety. The Messenger contents himself with affirming Hippolytos' innocence (1250ff). The Nurse's criticism of Phaidra's excessive haughtiness toward Aphrodite (445f., 475f.) applies of course also to Hippolytos; the blame she heaps on Phaidra has many affinities with what the *servitor* tries to tell Hippolytos (88ff.).

The Choros, too, criticizes over-zealousness (785, 1115), and I note that it praises Hippolytos only after his death—and even then *not* for his purity and moral excellence (1115ff.).

The opinion of Theseus cannot be cited here, for his erroneous appraisal of the situation causes him to condemn his son unjustly. I only note that Theseus, too, underscores the arrogance of Hippolytos' virtue (946ff.).

In short, except for Artemis, who is personally involved, Hippolytos'

---

[20] Winnington-Ingram sees irony in the establishing of his cult (op. cit., pp. 191–92).
[21] Plu. *se ipso citra invid. laud.*

ostentatious and arrogant claim to virtue and purity antagonizes everyone in the play.

Piety

Piety, in a polytheistic society, means giving each deity his (or her) due. Yet, as Aphrodite's prologue and many other passages indicate, Hippolytos makes war on Aphrodite (43), is her enemy (49f.), despises her rites (106), and considers her to be of no account (113).

His piety is focused on Artemis to such an extent that he is practically heretical in his monotheism. He believes Artemis to be superior to the other deities, though in ordinary Greek belief she was apparently deemed inferior to all male Olympians and, except for Hestia, also to the female ones. Being a goddess of the Wilds—of the "Draussen"[22]—the agricultural and maritime Greek did not regard her very highly. She can lay claim to supremacy only if she is viewed as a latter-day version of the Great Mountain Mother. It is not by chance that the Choros wonders whether the Cretan Diktynna had driven Phaidra mad (141ff.), and appeals to Artemis "to cure the female distemper" from which Phaidra suffers (161ff.). Like Rhea-Kybele, Artemis can both send madness and heal it.[23]

Aphrodite, whose power even Zeus cannot resist, rightly complains that this haughty (6) but still immature youth has the presumption (18) of claiming to be on a footing of unique intimacy with the goddess whom he proclaims is superior to all others. He claims to be Artemis' sole companion (84)—though he claims, in passing, to be also an austere worshipper of the other deities (1364), Aphrodite (tacitly) excepted. He is Artemis' hunter and *servitor* (1397), her horseman and the guardian of her cult statue (1399). One has the impression that Hippolytos rather imagines that the goddess he worships will find it hard to get along without him. Aristophanes' *Birds* show this to be a Greek conceit.

All this is exceedingly arrogant, and one is not surprised to learn that the only one to approve of Hippolytos' brand of piety is Aphrodite's arch-foe, Artemis. Theseus' questioning of Hippolytos' (polytheistic) piety is justified (948). In affirming his piety toward the gods (1365) Hippolytos clearly ignores his outspoken contempt for Aphrodite.[24]

He does not even shrink from wishing that men were able to hit back at the gods (1415). Another offensive narcissist, Achilles, expresses a similar wish (*Il.* 22.15ff.), the wish to be revenged on a god, that greatly scandalized Platon (*Rmp.* 391a).

---

[22] U. v. Wilamowitz-Moellendorff, *Der Glaube der Hellenen*³, 1959, ii, pp. 173ff.
[23] J. Mattes, *Der Wahnsinn im griechischen Mythos*, Heidelberg, 1970, pp. 42f.
[24] Méridier, ad 1365, states the matter well.

Hippolytos' Merits and Phaidra's Love 95

The conclusions to be drawn are self evident. Hippolytos is not genuinely pious in the Greek sense, even though—animated by vanity, partisanship, and a hatred of Aphrodite—Artemis also attests his piety and undertakes to hit back at Aphrodite on his behalf: she proclaims her intention to slay an (innocent) mortal dear to the goddess of love (1420ff.).

I note as an afterthought that Hippolytos needs Artemis to explain to him that Theseus had been deceived (1400, etc.), though that should by now be evident even to the self-righteous Hippolytos. Artemis must also ask Hippolytos to forgive his father (1435ff.). Pious, Hippolytos may be—spontaneously generous, he is obviously not.

Irascibility

Irascibility toward his social inferiors is one of Hippolytos' unloveliest traits; it is also behavior one would not expect from the son of a hero noted for his kindness to the oppressed (Plu. V. Thes. fin.). Hippolytos' personal slave is clearly afraid of him; he barely dares to offer the advice his master badly needs (88-122). In fact, it is only after Hippolytos has left the scene that the servant dares beseech Aphrodite to forgive his master's arrogance (114ff.). Hippolytos speaks to the Nurse as though she were defilement incarnate (582ff., 601ff.). He threatens the slaves who, obeying Theseus' order, try to seize him (1086f.). He scolds even the slaves who helpfully seek to prop up his broken body (1372ff.).

I submit that this is conduct unbecoming either a hero or a fifth-century Athenian gentleman. No person depicted as admirable in a Euripidean play displays such behavior toward his slaves.

Schadenfreude

The ungenerous Hippolytos will take a malicious pleasure in watching Phaidra having to face Theseus (661). Phaidra herself considers his pride tainted with malice: "To him too my death wil be nefarious, so as to teach him not to pride himself in my misfortunes" (727ff.); "Being linked to my misfortune, he will, in sharing it, get a lesson of moderation" (729-31).

An Inherited Taint

An inherited taint is claimed by Phaidra, whose mother coupled with a bull and whose sister, after becoming Theseus' mistress, made the slaying of her uterine half-brother, the Minotauros, possible.

Theseus suspects (820, 851ff.) that he himself is the victim of some familial sin, for, at 820, he declares himself *personally* innocent of any misdeed. The ancestral sin Theseus has in mind is far from clear, for he has just atoned for the slaying of his cousins, the Pallantids, who had made war on Aigeus and were defeated.

At 1378 Hippolytos sees his tragedy as caused by crime-stained "forebears of old"—a specification which automatically excludes Theseus as the source of a familial curse. Yet, after verse 1100, he turns on Theseus, calling him impious and blaming him for *unspecified* wrongful acts. His language is one common to abuse and to self-pity (Barrett, ad loc.).

I do not profess to know what Euripides had in mind when he made both Theseus and Hippolytos speak of a familial curse caused by the wickedness of some unspecified ancestor. It may have been a routine supposition to make in a difficult situation. One thing only is certain: though at 1378 Hippolytos is not yet reconciled with his father, his reference to "forebears *of old*" clearly shows that even he dares not claim that his father had, through some evil deed, brought a curse upon his own dynasty. This point may well be borne in mind by those who try to blacken Theseus in order to polish up Hippolytos' image.

Hippolytos' "Merit" and Phaidra's Love

Nothing proves better the impossibility of salvaging Hippolytos' merit than Festugière's[25] tendentious last ditch attempt to treat Phaidra's infatuation as a "prix de vertu," attesting by its mere existence Hippolytos' moral excellence. I intend to show that Festugière's views on this matter are biased and at times absurd.

The simplest rebuttal of this view is the fact that tens of millions of Germans were literally in love with Hitler. Does the swooning of hysterical bobby-soxers prove the moral excellence of a crooner? Is the infatuation of "groupie" girls the equivalent of a parson's certificate of regular church attendance? Was Catullus' love for Lesbia a token of her matronly virtue? Is there *any* man who has never been madly infatuated with a bitch, a woman who never adored a cad? Has Freud not called an erotic penchant for degraded partners the most universal of all sexual aberrations?[26]

Leaving general considerations aside, nothing in Euripides' text authorizes one to treat Phaidra's almost insane yearning for Hippolytos as a proof of his merit.

Yet, Festugière (pp. 24ff.) argues that, were Hippolytos without merit, Phaidra would not have fallen in love with him on first sight.

The simplest objection is that *first sight* does not reveal anyone's moral qualities—least of all those of a person with whom one falls in love at once. Love at first sight tells something about the one who so

---

[25] A.-J. Festugière, *Personal Religion among the Greeks* (paperback ed.), 1960, pp. 11ff.
[26] S. Freud, "On the Universal Tendency to Debasement in the Sphere of Love," *Standard Edition*, xi, 1957.

suddenly becomes enamored and nothing about the object of that sudden love. Besides, the slightly shopworn Greek dogma that a handsome body is the reflection of nobility of soul was not shared unconditionally even by Homeros: Nireus, the most handsome of the Greek captains, was a weakling, while the oafish-looking Odysseus possessed great qualities.[27] Even less was it shared by Euripides, some of whose personages deplore that it should be so difficult to tell apart—on the basis of appearance or of voice only—the good from the bad or the speaker of truth from the liar. One of these personages is Theseus, and he voices his misgivings precisely in connection with Hippolytos (925ff.).[28] The fact that, in this particular instance, Hippolytos' (presumably handsome) exterior was *not* misleading (at least insofar as the accusation of rape is concerned) does not weaken my argument: it further shows how little faith Euripides—or his personages—had in the possibility of appraising a person's moral qualities in terms of his physical beauty.

It is also either tendentious or psychologically naive *not* to differentiate between Andromache's love for Hektor (Hom. *Il.* 6.369ff.) (which includes liking, respect, trust, and glorious passion) and a haunting, obsessive, cruelly painful, and irrational infatuation dreaded and yet desired by the Greeks. Phaidra's feelings for Hippolytos have nothing in common with the Homeric and Euripidean Andromache's love, liking, and admiration of Hektor, for Phaidra has *not one* kind word for Hippolytos and it can even be urged that it is *not* love but her pain and shame she discusses most.[29] Worse still, she neither trusts Hippolytos (689ff.) nor does she like his self-ascribed virtues (728ff.). I will return to this point in the concluding portion of this section. Here I add only that the fact that she does *not* praise even his beauty is not significant, for praising the loved one's beauty is largely a masculine habit,[30] at least in the Western world.

The text thus precludes the supposition that Phaidra fell in love with Hippolytos' moral excellence. What caused her to become infatuated with him is, by contrast, not beyond conjecture. For the moment it suffices to note that her infatuation is irrational and Phaidra, who is not psychotic and therefore not lacking in insight, realizes this—though,

[27] Hom. *Il.* 2.671ff., 3.209. Cf. Archilochos *fr.* 93 L.-B. = 60 D = 58 Bgk. Discussion in G. Devereux, "The Kolaxian Horse of Alkman's *Partheneion*," *Classical Quarterly* 15: 176–84, 1965 (esp. p. 179.9). Compare also the contrasting appearances of Sokrates and Alkibiades.
[28] Similar Euripidean passages are cited elsewhere in this study. Barrett, ad loc., cites E. *Med.* 516ff., E. *HF* 655ff., *Skolion*, 889 Page.
[29] Alkestis notoriously has not one word of love for the equally self-centered Admetos, who is the cause of her suffering and death, as Hippolytos is the cause of Phaidra's disaster.
[30] G. Devereux, "The Female Castration Complex," *American Imago* 17: 1–19, 1960.

despite her insight, she is unable to control her impulses.[31] This, in fact, is one of the main causes of her distress.

The next obvious task is to examine Phaidra's qualifications as a character witness, her capacity to make a sensible object choice.

More perceptive than Hippolytos' latter day eulogists, Phaidra views her infatuation not simply as irrational, but as degrading and perverted—as a manifestation of her abnormal sexual heredity, or, if one prefers, of her sexually abnormal familial atmosphere.[32] Though, as regards Ariadne, Phaidra only mentions her (divine, i.e., abnormal) "marriage" to Dionysos (339),[33] she might have noted also that, because of her love for Theseus, Ariadne wrongfully helped him kill the Minotauros. What the Greeks thought of such behavior is glaringly highlighted by the myth of Komaitho, who had betrayed her father to the man she loved and was killed by her lover for her treason.[34]

The psychological appropriateness of Phaidra's allusion to her mother's misconduct is conclusively proven by a hitherto relatively neglected fact. Pasiphaë's predicament is almost a double of that of Phaidra. Poseidon sought to punish Minos by causing the *innocent bystander*, Pasiphaë, to fall in "love" with a bull; Aphrodite seeks to destroy Hippolytos by causing the "innocent" Phaidra to fall in "love" with him. The fundamental significance of such structural doublets is self-evident.

These findings show that Festugière's reasoning leads to extremely peculiar conclusions. If Phaidra's "love" proves Hippolytos' excellence, then one is forced to conclude that Pasiphaë's "love" proves that of the

---

[31] As Laios admits, with equal frankness, his inability to control his impulses (E. *Chrys. fr.* 840 N²). For Helene's insight into the irrationality of her elopement, cf. E. *Tr.* 919f. Countless other Greek examples will readily come to mind.

[32] Schmid (op. cit., p. 384, n. 8) perversely claims that Euripides does not really mean this ("denkt E. nicht ernstlich"). Yet, the familial taint is a commonplace in Greek myth and what Phaidra (424ff.) proclaims—"Even a man of courage is a slave, if he knows of the sins of his mother or father"—applies not only to her children but also to herself, precisely because her utterance is a Euripidean maxim. It matters little in this context whether Euripides had in mind nature or nurture (cf. E. *Tr.* 886), since the reference is not to remote ancestors, but to Phaidra's mother and older sister, who had raised her.

[33] For a discussion of the little-noted fact that, for the Greeks, a marriage between a god and a mortal woman was abnormal and even degrading, cf. Devereux, "Greek Pseudo-Homosexuality," op. cit.

[34] Apollod. 2.4.7; Tzetz. *Lyc.* 932. One wonders whether Theseus deserted Ariadne for similar reasons; after all, the Minotaur was Ariadne's kinsman (E. *Cret.*). It may also explain why, according to one tradition, Ariadne was killed by "chaste" Artemis. The fact that Phaidra views Ariadne's marriage to Dionysos (by becoming a Mainad) rather than her infidelity to the god as *sexually* abnormal behavior, makes it likely that, in E. *Ba.*, Pentheus is *not* wrong in suspecting the Mainads of sexual misconduct; cf. G. Devereux, "Trance and Orgasm in Euripides: *Bakchai*," in A. Angoff and D. Barth (eds.), *Parapsychology and Anthropology*, New York, 1974.

bull! That, however, was not Pasiphaë's opinion: her insistence on the bull's utter unsuitableness as a lover is prima facie evidence of her innocence and of the divine origin of her erotic frenzy.[35] This reasoning cannot be juggled out of sight by means of the threadbare traditional device of treating all Euripidean *agons* as mere forensic displays of sophistic acrobatics, for the compulsive character of all perversions is one of their most striking features.[36] I hold that Phaidra's reasoning, in this perfectly plain passage, echoes, point by point, Pasiphaë's reasoning in Euripides' *Cretans*.

Nor is that all! Paradoxical as this may seem, in terms of Greek ethics and morality Phaidra's passion is even more odious than was that of her mother. This is only to be expected, since in Chinese belief—and now and then also in Greek myth and tragedy—the behavior of a doomed dynasty tends to deteriorate further with each generation. This point is of some importance and requires both detailed documentation and a careful distinction between the first and the second *Hippolytos*. Since, in the first, Phaidra seems to have been a putative widow, Barrett (p. 12.1) wonders whether the Greeks prohibited marriage between a widow and her stepson. Now, though Barrett says that the nearest parallel he could find was Kallias' marriage with his former mother-in-law,[37] there are at least two perfect mythical parallels. In S. *Trach.* 1221ff. Herakles not only makes Hyllos swear that he will marry his quasi-stepmother, Iole, but discusses the lawfulness of his command at length.[38] Moreover, on another occasion, Herakles made his nephew, Iolaos, marry his divorced wife Megara.[39] In the second *Hipp.* the situation is radically different. Since Theseus is known to be alive, the relationship would have been even more incestuous than that of Phoinix with his father's concubine,[40] and it is as such that it must be contrasted with Pasiphaë's zoöphiliac adultery.

Now, both Greek myth and practice conclusively show that incest was deemed more odious than zoöphilia: the former usually culminated

---

[35] E. *Cret.* 4ff. D. L. Page, *Literary Papyri* (Loeb)³, 1950, p. 74.

[36] Devereux, "Greek Pseudo-Homosexuality," op. cit. In many Euripidean passages the "divine" (= external) simply denotes that which clinicians call "ego alien"; cf. Devereux, *Dreams in Greek Tragedy*, op. cit., passim.

[37] Andoc. 1.124f. For primitive examples, cf. G. Devereux, "Atypical and Deviant Mohave Marriages," *Samiksa* 4: 200–215, 1951.

[38] This is one more point Euripides' two *Hippolytos* dramas and S. *Trach.*—whose date is uncertain—have in common.

[39] Apollod. 2.6.1; D.S. 4.31.11; Plu. *Amat.* p. 754E. Whether this is an echo of an obsolete practice—still found in many parts of Africa (H. Junod, *The Life of a South African Tribe*², London, 1927)—or a purely idiosyncratic situation, as in Plu. V. *Dem.* 38 and V. *Artax.* 26.2, I do not profess to know. For dreams about stepmothers: Artemid. 3.26.

[40] Hom. *Il.* 9.449; discussed in G. Devereux, "A Counteroedipal Episode in Homer's Iliad," *Bulletin of the Philadelphia Association for Psychoanalysis* 4: 90–97, 1955.

in a catastrophe; the latter did not,[41] perhaps because it tended to be viewed as a madness, rather than as a sin.[42]

Moreover, one important reason why incest is so systematically condemned is that it represents a kind of *hubris*, for it is an anthropological commonplace that incest is the *normal* form of marriage among the gods. It is, in fact, almost a token of their divine status and it is for *that* reason that incest is forbidden to mortals, or at least to commoners, as is the case in societies (Egypt, Persia[?], Peru, Polynesia, Azande) where royal incest was routine. Indeed, it is natural for the privileged to forbid others to do what they view as a token of their own exalted status (Sen. *Ag.* 271). Though, as a rule, later elaborations of an old myth can shed almost no light on the psychological context of earlier versions, in this particular case one is confronted with human attitudes so basic that I propose to cite, exceptionally, also later interpretations of Phaidra's incestuous desires.

In nearly every known human society the father outranks his son.[43] This implies that adultery with the father's wife is not only oedipal incest, but also extreme presumptuousness (*hubris*). It is therefore of great interest that, in some later accounts, Phaidra represents the incest she desires as something that would make her and Hippolytos glorious, exalted, and, indeed, god-like.[44] It is quite likely that, in this (superficially perplexing) passage, Ovidius drew for inspiration on E. *Hipp.* 409f., in which as Barrett (ad loc.) well saw, Phaidra asserts that adultery and, possibly, sexual disorders in general, originated among the upper classes. This Euripidean passage is generally held to mean that the sexual practices of nobles were simply reprehensible and irresponsible manifestations of idleness and of unbridled power, or, what is much the same, a kind of dissolute fashion of the privileged. But the Ovidius passage just

[41] Data surveyed in Devereux, "Greek Pseudo-Homosexuality," op. cit. Cf. H. Licht, *Sexual Life in Ancient Greece*, London, 1932, pp. 157ff. Modern law also penalizes incest more consistently and more severely than zoöphilia. The problem of the relative "malignancy" of these two deviations does not seem to have been studied by psychiatrists.

[42] This interpretation is not anachronistic. The Mohave Indian explicitly differentiates between "mad" and "bad," precisely in the sphere of sexual misconduct; cf. G. Devereux, *Mohave Ethnopsychiatry*, op. cit., 77ff.; compare also the ancient legal principle: *furiosus satis ipso furore punitur*.

[43] Exceptions exist. In Hawaii, the noble family's "mana" increased in each successive generation, so that the son had more "mana" than his father (R. Linton, personal communication). Napoléon, a self-made man, ironically pretended that his son, whose father was an Emperor, outranked him, whose father had only been a lawyer. The Duke of Saint-Simon's *Mémoirs* are full of quarrels over "precedence" in terms of the relative antiquity of a given family's ducal title, though *within* the family the father outranked his son. Saint-Simon also discussed the problems of etiquette that arose when the younger son of Louis XIV's heir apparent became King of Spain, thus outranking his father, who boasted that he alone could say "The King, my father" *and* "the King, my son."

[44] Ov. *Her.* 4.135ff.

cited—reinforced by Sen. *Ag.* 271—permits one to view the sexual "disorders" of royalty also as formal implementations of their privileged status—sometimes bordering on *hubris* in their usurpation of divine privileges.

This point is so important and also so complex that it deserves further discussion. Royal incest *privileges* are comparable to the *routine* incests of the gods, as the rainmaker's magical acts are comparable to Zeus' causing the rain to fall. In that sense, Harrison[45] was right in saying that Salmoneus was a rainmaking magician whose sympathetic magic involved the (anticipatory) imitation of thunder and lightning. But what is relevant here is not simply that later generations *mistook* his magic for an attempt to vie with Zeus himself, though such a late misunderstanding of ancient rainmaking rites is likely enough. What matters is the particular *twist* this "misunderstanding" gave to Salmoneus' behavior. He was represented *not* as someone capable, by various acts of sympathetic magic, to *induce* Zeus to let the rain fall, but as a man claiming to replace Zeus as an *independent* rain-maker: as someone *causing* rain to fall *through his own powers*, rather than through his ability to *incite* Zeus to cause it to rain. The trigger pretended to be the gunpowder.

This distinction is of the greatest importance. It is closely related to the distinction I made between the *normal* Mohammedan's *cultural belief* in houris, available in Paradise for the sexual pleasure of the defunct faithful, and a hypothetical *insane* Mohammedan's *personal delusion* of having *actually* visited Paradise, cohabiting there with the houris.[46] Similarly, though I believe it very likely that the "showing" during the Eleusinian mysteries involved actual or simulated coitus between "Demeter" and "Iasion"(?), if the woman impersonating Demeter genuinely believed herself to *be* Demeter (both during the rite and afterwards) instead of considering herself only Demeter's understudy—and even that *only* during the "showing"—she would have been guilty of truly sacrilegious *hubris* and would probably have been insane. Indeed, participation in (humanly) unnatural sex-rites is quite likely to disturb the equilibrium of most human beings.[47]

In the same sense, I hold that even if incest, or other sexual deviations from the *routine* human norm, were royal *privileges* and were held to be modelled upon comparable divine privileges, it was not permissible to identify *completely* royal incest with divine incest. Yet that is precisely what Phaidra does in the aforementioned Ovidius passage: she views incest as a means whereby one *accedes* to (and not simply impersonates ritually)

---

[45] J. E. Harrison, *Themis*², Cambridge, G.B., 1927, pp. 79ff.
[46] G. Devereux, *Basic Problems*, op. cit., chap. 1.
[47] I so interpret Io's bouanthropic madness; cf. G. Devereux, *Dreams in Greek Tragedy*, op. cit., chap. 2.

divine status. I deem this self evident, despite the fact that ritually prescribed crimes were part of Greek religious life.[48]

This obliges me to return for a moment to verse 339, in which Phaidra treats Ariadne's *marriage* to Dionysos as a sexual anomaly. The text is clear on this point, though most commentators—cf. Barrett, ad loc.—hold that not Ariadne's *marriage* (to Dionysos) but her *desertion of* the god *for* Theseus was her sin. This view has the advantage of making Ariadne's infidelity comparable to that of Phaidra. But I hold that the text is also meant to say that the cohabitation of a mortal with a deity is an anomaly: a form of sexual *hubris*. I have discussed elsewhere the fact that the human sexual partners of deities invariably fared badly—as did, most of the time, also their half divine children.[49] The same could be said of peasant brides subjected to the *ius primae noctis*, which usually implied a double adultery, of many royal mistresses who ended up in convents, etc.

In short, in Phaidra's outburst against the sexual misconduct of the privileged, one can distinguish two layers of meaning.

(1) The surface meaning condemns sexual disorders in terms of *everyday moral standards*, which affect even those who are entitled, or even obliged, to ignore them. Indeed, given the universality of the Oedipus complex, the obligation to contract incestuous marriages, forbidden to others, is, *of necessity*, a source of anguish to royalty, just as the obligation to decide whether or not to commute a death sentence is a psychological burden for kings and presidents.

(2) On a deeper level, the Euripidean Phaidra refers also to the royal *privilege* of incest (and of disinhibited sexuality), which, as was shown, Ovidius' Phaedra put in the foreground and propounded in a manner which turned the enacting of that privilege into *hubris*, offensive to the gods. That, I feel, is how Ovid understood E. *Hipp.* 409ff. In fact, it is just conceivable that the bold Phaidra of the lost *Veiled Hippolytos* provided an explicit model for the Ovidian passage. I propound this view with some confidence, for, despite his mythological learning and decadent taste for the outlandish, I do *not* feel that Ovid (or any of his contemporaries) was psychologically perceptive enough to put so authentically archaic an argument into Phaedra's "letter to Hippolytus," especially since that argument so closely parallels the *mis*understood rainmaking activities of Salmoneus and so heavily underscores the essence of ritual criminality.

In short, it seems plausible to assume that, both in verses 409ff. and in verse 339, Euripides, knowing full well that royalty once had a right to commit incest and even mated with divinities, deliberately *condemned* such privileged sexual deviations in terms of ordinary human

---

[48] See note elsewhere. Cf. the idol theft in E. *IT*.
[49] G. Devereux, *Dreams in Greek Tragedy*, op. cit., pp. 34, 41, 85; id., *Femme et Mythe*, 1982 (chap 1).

standards, though in his first (*Veiled*) *Hippolytos* his (like Ovidius') bold Phaidra *may* have spoken of the glories of royal incest as a means of acceding to divine status. By contrast, in his *Aiolos*, performed five years after the *Hippolytos*, he no longer appears to have even hinted at royal incest-privileges: Makareus justified his incest with his sister Kanake in a purely subjective manner: "What's shameful if its doer does not think so?" But this provoked such an uproar that Antisthenes at once improvised: "A shame is a shame, though one think so or not."[50]

All this means is that Euripides, though aware that certain sexual disorders were royal privileges, realized that the actual implementation of those privileges was not only incompatible with ordinary ethics, but also tended to arouse anxiety in those who put these privileges into practice, as though they were gods.

It might seem natural to switch at this point from the *cultural* implications of royal incest to its *psychological* implications as a means of self-degradation through sexual misconduct. But reasons of expository convenience oblige me to consider more in detail certain similarities and differences between the sexual aberrations of Phaidra and of Pasiphaë, for that will clarify the role of sexual self-degredation.

Since incest was a royal privilege implying *hubris*, it can be usefully contrasted with Pasiphaë's zoöphilia, which did *not* implement an arrogant privilege[51] and was viewed by Euripides himself as a token of sheer, godsent lunacy.[52]

In terms of Greek *ethics*, Phaidra's incestuous passion is worse than Pasiphaë's zoöphiliac infatuation. At the same time, in terms of Greek *law*, Pasiphaë is more guilty than Phaidra, since (unlike the latter, in the second *Hippolytos*) she yielded to her passion and manifested it in the form of a concrete act.[53] It is also noteworthy that Phaidra dreads mostly that her passion may incite her to commit a deed incompatible with her reputation and self-respect: an act that would degrade her. This makes it necessary to consider next the crucially important problem of sexual self-degradation.

My starting point is that Phaidra's *coup de foudre* occurred at a time when the *only* thing she knew about Hippolytos was that he was her sexually taboo stepson. This suggests that Phaidra's insight into her irrationality, great as it is, is incomplete in one respect.[54] She thinks she

---

[50] Plu. *de aud. poet.* 12, p. 33C. Others attribute the reply to Platon; cf. E. *Aiolos fr.* 19 N².

[51] But there are indications that coitus in an animal disguise may have been a pastoral fertility rite; cf. G. Devereux, *Dreams in Greek Tragedy*, op. cit., chap. 2.

[52] E. *Cretans*, v. 11ff. D. L. Page, *Greek Literary Papyri*³, 1950, p. 74.

[53] On the primacy of the act, cf. A. W. H. Adkins, *Merit and Responsibility*, op. cit., and esp. his discussion of Andokides' *Tetralogies*.

[54] It is a psychiatric commonplace that the neurotic has insight, but that this insight is incomplete, especially as regards his unconscious motivation.

is infatuated with Hippolytos *even though* he is taboo, though it is psychologically much more probable that she was hopelessly smitten with him *precisely because* he was her stepson; because adultery *with him* would destroy her αἰδώς and utterly degrade her. It is this interpretation (already hinted at, supra), that I now propose to document.

One of the most common forms of sexual neuroticism is an uncontrollable propensity for degrading sexual adventures, in the form of a compulsive preference either for "flawed" partners,[55] or else for socially penalized types of relationships. Thus, in clinical practice one constantly comes across girls who are attracted only to married men; non-adulterous relationships simply do not interest them. In considering this matter further, it soon becomes evident that, e.g., even a thoroughly admirable man can be a "degrading" lover for a woman. Had Phaidra been able to cohabit with her *stepson* Hippolytos, morally this would have degraded her *more* than would have an adultery with one of Theseus' subordinates—even if the latter had been inferior to Hippolytos in every respect.[56]

One of the most striking aspects of a neurotic need for self-degradation in a sexual connection is that it occurs mostly amongst the socially prominent: in patriarchal societies it is almost entirely limited to men and to women of high status.[57] This insight goes back at least to Euripides and Sophokles[58] and was echoed afterwards by some Greek and Roman writers, in terms which leave nothing to the imagination.[59]

Now, while the notion that a goddess can become degraded by sexual relations with mortals seems somehow "natural" to the modern mind, it is surprising to note that the notion of degradation intervenes—albeit less overtly—when a mortal woman becomes a god's mistress. This matter cannot be tackled without considering at least in passing sexual relations between mortals and immortals in general, in terms somewhat

---

[55] S. Freud, "On the Universal Tendency to Debasement," op. cit.; R. Laforgue, *Psychopathologie de l'Echec*, Paris, 1944. Preference for lame men: Mimn. (?) *fr.* 15 D.; Lame Hephaistos as husband of Aphrodite and formerly perhaps also of Athene (Erichthonios myth, cf. B. Powell, *Erichthonius and the Three Daughters of Cecrops*, Cornell Studies in Classical Philology, xvii, 1906). Hags: Aristoph. *Ran.* 1193 (Oidipous and Iokaste), psychologically linked with the amorous hags in his *Eccles.* Cf. Pasiphaë and the bull, etc. Also goddesses consorting with mortal men and Omphale with her slave Herakles. Cf. [Petronius] 126 for a particularly telling statement.

[56] A conflict between duty and love can make even love for a worthy man a dishonor for the woman; cf. P. Corneille, *Le Cid*.

[57] G. Devereux, "Neurotic Downward Identification," *American Imago* 22: 77-95, 1965.

[58] Aërope, daughter of King Nauplios, cohabited with a slave: S. *Ajax* 1297ff. and the scholion ad loc. which refers in this connection to Euripides' *Cretan Women*. Already Zeus objected to the amours of goddesses with mortals (Hom. *Od.* 5.118ff.); cf. Hes. *fr.* 204, 98ff.-M-W; cf. *Th.* 967ff.

[59] Cf. also the suspicion that Semele, pregnant by Zeus, had been impregnated by a mere mortal (E. *Ba.*, passim).

different from those in which this matter was briefly discussed above.

The most basic datum is that both male and female deities show a strong—and at times almost exclusive—preference for human lovers; except for Hom. *Od.* 8.266ff. (Ares and Aphrodite), sources of great antiquity hardly ever mention extramarital affairs between major deities.[60] Next in importance is the already noted fact that a goddess is degraded by her cohabitation with a mortal man. Zeus, and perhaps also the other gods, objected to such affairs. This may explain why Aphrodite warned Anchises not to reveal their amours.[61] The human lovers of goddesses are sometimes taxed with *hubris* and almost invariably end badly. This further highlights the degrading nature of the female deities' infatuations.[62]

This, however, is still not the whole story, for the data show that an affair with a deity also degrades the human partner, in the precise sense in which the *ius primae noctis* degraded socially and harmed psychologically the serf's bride. The data bearing on this point are so well known that I will cite only the most striking instance: Marpessa's explanation of why she prefers a human husband to a divine lover.[63] The gods' failure to protect their mortal paramours and bastards (Io, Kreusa, Ion, etc.) is so blatant that men made it a reproach to the gods. Kreusa felt degraded because she had been raped by Apollo (E. *Ion*). Still more striking is that the claims of girls that they are pregnant by a god were often disbelieved. They were suspected of giving birth to bastards fathered by

---

[60] Zeus' Leporello album lists only mortal women, and this despite the fact that, in the *Iliad*, Leto is not Zeus' wife. Extramarital affairs between major deities are reported only by relatively recent authors, partly because they mistook ancient "sacred marriges" for affairs and partly because they appear to have invented new ones. I disregard here the unions mentioned in Hes. *Th.* and the like, since they usually do not distinguish between marital and non-marital unions between deities.

[61] Hom. *h. Ven.* 286ff.

[62] Demeter's lover Iasion is struck by lightning; Tithonos, husband of Eos, becomes senile and paralyzed (cf. Anchises' paralysis); in the bowdlerized myth of Ixion's amours with Hera (= Nephele) Ixion is punished (tied up = paralysis). In the case of Odysseus' amours with Kirke, the danger *seems* to emanate from Kirke herself (Hom. *Od.* 10.296ff.) and this danger is, once more, paralysis and "unmanning" (= impotency). Aphrodite's threat to Anchises provides a bridge between the two risks, though from the psychoanalytic point of view no bridge is needed, since all such risks are rooted in the same complex and form a single continuum. Unfortunately a discussion of the psychoanalytic aspects of the problem would lead one too far afield. As to the fact that it is the seduced *man* who is punished, whereas the seducing goddess escapes scot free, it suffices to recall the Athenian law which permitted a man to kill his wife's lover, but not his unfaithful wife. Further discussion in G. Devereux, "The Self-Blinding of Oedipus," *Journal of Hellenic Studies* 93: 36-49, 1973. Cf. now also G. Devereux, *Femme et Mythe*, Paris, 1982 (chap. 1, "La Divine Maitresse").

[63] Hom. *Il.* 9.534, Apollod. 1.7.8.

ordinary mortals or even by slaves,[64] and were treated accordingly. Some of these motifs have been explained—and many more have only been explained away—by means of inferred rituals. Now, neither an explaining nor an explaining *away* can abolish a fact. Even psychoanalysts, often (and unjustly) accused of seeing symbols only, know that it is unwise not to examine also the manifest content of the dream.[65] In short, whether or not it is possible to explain the ill-treatment of such girls in ritual and symbolic ways, the objective fact is that they were often treated as though they had (*degradingly*) cohabited not with a god but with men of low rank. This is all that matters in the present context.

In E. *Hipp*. the basic datum is manifestly Phaidra's claim that adultery first occurred in *noble* families (407f.). Now, since highborn men always had access to their female slaves and captives, Phaidra's remark can refer only to highborn *women*. I believe, moreover, that, in this passage, "adultery" stands for all kinds of sexual deviations, particularly since only about seventy lines earlier Phaidra had referred to Pasiphaë's zoöphilia and to Ariadne's fatal marriage to Dionysos.[66] It is possible that Phaidra said something of this sort already in the first Hippolytos,[67] and the general idea was subsequently echoed also by Roman poets.[68] Verse 407 must, moreover, be read in the light of verses 383ff., in which one notes a subtle equating of pleasure and of shame. Méridier's (ad loc.)

---

[64] One notes that the motif god = servant is common in Greek myth: Apollon works for Admetos, Aphrodite impersonates one of Helene's serving women, Demeter plays nursemaid to Demophon, Poseidon served Laomedon, etc. King = slave: Rex Nemorensis, Servius Tullius.

[65] Examples of the mistakes one can make if one ignores the manifest content and looks only for unconscious meanings: Devereux, *Basic Problems*, op. cit., chap. 15. Example of a psychotherapy based almost entirely on the examination of the dream narratives: G. Devereux, *Reality and Dream*², 1969.

[66] The only argument that might militate against taking "adultery" as signifying all types of sexual disorders is the word "*thuraious*," which (cf. Barrett, ad loc.) can only mean "outside the *oikos*." But this argument is greatley weakened by the fact that "*thuraious*" occurs in the preceding verse; one notes that Phaidra's reasoning covers more and more ground as she warms up to her subject. The very next passage (condemnation of audacious women) voices a thought Deianeira also expresses (S. *Trach*. 583)—and Deianeira not only killed her husband, but, at least according to Herakles, had also been guilty of other (unspecified) crimes (S. *Trach*. 1127). This allusion, which puzzles commentators, may—but only may—refer to her misadventure with Nessos, since (cf. Adkins, op. cit.) the act was more important in Greek thought than was motivation.

[67] Barrett, op. cit., p. 20, n. 4, on E. *Hipp*. (*Calypt*.) *fr*. 438 N². If so, *fr*. 437 N² too may be part of the same tirade.

[68] Specifically as regards Phaidra: Ov. *rem. am.* 743; Sen. *Phaidra* 204ff. Wealth in these passages clearly stands for high status, since in mythical times only lords were wealthy. The alternative interpretation, that what these poets, and Euripides as well, had in mind was the triad: wealth = luxury = idleness which inevitably leads to immorality, is not exactly anachronistic, though its *complete* development is a post-classical and perhaps even a Christian phenomenon.

claim, that the reference is to "false shame" (*fausse honte*), seems farfetched. What Phaidra refers to is the (far from rare) pleasurable aspect of shame, and this passage, whose translations generally sound awkward, can be translated quite smoothly, once it is viewed as an anticipation of the thought expressed in 407ff. and as reflecting insight into Phaidra's *nostalgie de la boue*.[69]

What is relevant here is that Phaidra is a Cretan princess by birth and Queen of Athens by marriage and comes, moreover, from psychologically unstable stock. She is therefore just the kind of woman who would derive a neurotic pleasure from degrading sexual adventures, which is *precisely* what Euripides, Ovidius, and Seneca say in so many words. Moreover, Phaidra was not the only woman of antiquity to experience such temptations. Some free Athenian ladies apparently cohabited at times with slaves and muleteers.[70] As for the Roman *matrona*, the slave girl Chrysis' speech anticipates, point by point, and most credibly, *all* of Freud's clinical findings.[71] Many a *matrona* delighted in lovers of the lowest status (*et in extrema plebe quaerit quod diligat*) and covered with kisses the marks of the lash on a slave's body. More striking still is that the slave girl contrasts her mistress' penchant with her own preference for men of standing: *she* has no wish to cohabit with a man who, the next day, may be crucified. The fact that a slave girl—an *andrapodon* or *instrumentum vocale*—does not wish to degrade herself further shows how closely this perversion is linked with an exalted status. This is, of course, exactly what Phaidra says and what clinicians know from experience.

Now, an idea may admittedly be present in a culture, and yet occupy in it only a marginal position and have few implications and consequences. I therefore propose to show here that the notion of sexual degradation was deeply rooted in Greek thought.

The cultural nuclearity of a concept can best be proven by showing that a great many *unrelated* facts and ideas are often *forcibly* and

---

[69] Many an obscure passage would seem less obscure, and many a *locus desperatus* less hopelessly corrupt, if commentators credited ancient authors with *genuine* psychological perceptiveness. To take an example almost at random, Pl. *Phdr*. 244dff. would seem less perplexing were it read in terms of the well-known fact that the acquisition of shamanistic and/or mantic powers is in many primitive societies preceded by excruciatingly painful hallucinations and anxiety attacks which do not cease until the sufferer becomes a shaman. (This implies that being a shaman is a "restitutional symptom"; cf. Devereux, *Basic Problems*, op. cit., chap. 1.)

[70] Ar. *Thesm*. 491ff. Pentheus might suspect something of this kind in E. *Ba*., but that is as it may be. Less relevant, because non-Greek, is the ancient Semitic practice obliging every woman, once in her life, to prostitute herself at the temple.

[71] [Petron.] *Sat*. 126 (p. 150 Ernout). A similar view is expressed in regard to Agamemnon's affair with the mad Kassandra by Talthybios (E. *Tr*. 413ff.).

inappropriately correlated with it.[72] Thus, the logically inappropriate *extension* of the notion of sexual degradation can be demonstrated for Greece by showing that it was also applied, or rather, misapplied to *animal* behavior: it was held that a mare had to be *humbled*, by shearing off her mane, before she would accept a jackass, thereby indulging in "adultery."[73] What matters here is not the authentic reluctance of mares to accept jackasses, but its *interpretation* in terms of "humiliation" and "adultery," for these concepts are applicable to human beings only.[74]

I have discussed this matter at length, not because it is likely to seem outlandish to the non-psychiatrist, but because it seemed necessary to show that Euripides' insight into and observation of self-degrading sexual behavior, original as it is, was manifestly made possible by the thought-ways of Greek culture. Otherwise expressed, Euripides' discovery is understandable in terms of the sociology of knowledge (*Wissenssoziologie*). This, in turn, permits one to carry the argument one step further, by showing that one of the key facts (or distinctions) which underlies the psychoanalytic *theory* of this perversion was known to and repeatedly discussed by Plato, and was presumably also known to and discussed by Euripides' contemporary (and friend?) Sokrates. Since I do not impute to Euripides an anticipation of Freud's *theory*, I will not recapitulate it here in its entirety,[75] and will mention only that Freud's theory of this disorder presupposes an incapacity to fuse tenderness ("love of the soul") with sexuality.

Now, Platon distinguished between these two types of affectivity in nearly every passage in which he alludes to love. Broadly speaking, Platon seems to have felt that one should love boys, without engaging in sexual practices with them, and should cohabit with women without

---

[72] Devereux, *Basic Problems*, op. cit., chap. 16.

[73] First reference to the practice: S. Fr. 655 P. The fact that Ailianos (NA 12.16), who also refers to this practice, calls it "adultery" lends support to my view that, in vv. 407f., "adultery" denotes *all* sexual deviations. I must mention here also a curious zoological observation: the most violent recorded sexual attachment of a monkey to his mate was that of a male *Macacus rhesus* to a female *Macacus irus* (= *cynomolgus*). When she was taken from him, he brutally attacked the females *of his own species* that were put in his cage and then savagely wounded and mutilated himself (O. L. Tinklepaugh, "The Self Mutilation of a Male *Macacus rhesus* Monkey," *Journal of Mammalogy* 9: 293–300, 1928).

[74] Cf. a similarly inappropriate imputation of a *sense* of incest to stallions (Arist. HA 9.47f.; Plin. HN 8.156; Varro RR 2.7.9; Ael. NA 4.7) and to male camels (Ael. NA 3.47). This imputation well highlights the importance of the incest taboo in Greek culture. On the use of beliefs about animals, to clarify the meaning of human cultural practices, cf. B. Malinowski, *The Sexual Life of Savages*[3], London, 1932. Logically, this technique is rooted in E. Durkheim's (*Les Formes Elémentaires de la Vie Religieuse*, Paris, 1912) demonstration that man's view of the world is a projection of the structure of his society.

[75] For details cf. S. Freud: "On the Universal Tendency to Debasement, etc.," op. cit.

loving them.⁷⁶ By contrast, Freud views the capacity to fuse love and sexuality as the crux of emotional maturity. It is almost certain that Euripides was aware that his contemporaries made this distinction and drew invidious comparisons between the love of the soul and "mere" sexuality; it is infinitely probable that he did *not* share this outlook.⁷⁷ Whether this helped him to *notice* the kind of behavior referred to in 407ff. is anyone's guess; that it did *not* enable him to anticipate Freud's *theory* is a certainty.

The last argument to be marshalled in favor of the view that one important source of Phaidra's passion for Hippolytos is precisely its quality (= incestuousness and adulterousness) is Phaidra's excessive and indeed obsessive⁷⁸ preocupation with her αἰδώς (self-respect, sense of honor). In simplest terms, in order to derive any (perverted or neurotic) pleasure from one's degradation, one must not only *have* αἰδώς, but must also *overvalue it*. The slave girl Chrysis, who, being only an *instrumentum vocale*, has no αἰδώς, can therefore only *describe* her mistress' outlandish taste for the *canaille, but cannot empathize with it*. For her, it is simply one of the crazy things only the rich and free do.⁷⁹

Some authorities also allege—though I can find no evidence for this in the text—that Phaidra tries to "get even" with Theseus. It has been suggested that her vindictiveness is due to Theseus' amours. One authority, who shall remain unnamed, even asserts that, in this play, Theseus is just returning from Hades, where he had to do penance for his trying to help Peirithoos—whose assistance had enabled him to abduct Helene—to carry off Persephone. This hypothesis is little short of fantastic. The mytho-chronology simply does not fit this interpretation, quite apart from the fact that the text contradicts such a hypothesis. In this play Theseus is Phaidra's much enamoured and apparently faithful husband; he has no adulterous adventures.

If, despite lack of evidence derivable from the text, one insists on imagining that Phaidra wishes to punish Theseus for some sexual trespass, his misconduct must be specifiable. There are, I admit, repeated allusions to Theseus' amorous past in general (151ff., possibly 967ff.;

---

76 This conclusion is inescapable in terms of his recommendation that women whould be held in common (Pl. *Rmp.* bk .5).
77 Had he shared it, he could not have written Andromache's speech (E. *Andr.* 222ff.) about her love for Hektor, parts of which so shock certain critics, who disregard Hom. *Il.* 5.69ff.
78 Dodds, "The αἰδώς of Phaidra," op. cit.
79 Cf. the courtier's taste for bucolic poetry or Marie-Antoinette's playing the milkmaid. The behavior of Euripides' Elektra is also revealing. Since her considerate peasant husband refused to "degrade" her sexually, she (masochistically) did *more* hard work than a slave. Again, I do not attribute to Euripides a knowledge of the psychodynamics of moral masochism; I simply point out the plausibility of his characterization of the deeply humiliated, because pathologically rank-conscious, Elektra.

Nurse: 320) which, as Phaidra's earlier remark indicates, is to be taken in a sexual sense; φίλος means here: an amorously loved person. Yet, it is quite striking that Phaidra shows no jealousy toward Theseus' lost love, Hippolyte. Hence, if despite a lack of textual support one feels that one must provide a *sexual* grievance for Phaidra, that offense can only be Theseus' seduction of Phaidra's sister, Ariadne. One could, on that basis, assume that she tries to get even with Theseus by seducing his bastard son—her own stepson. For a neurotic that would even the score.[80]

I conclude this section by stating once more that I do *not* consider the "sexual revenge" hypothesis credible, for the text does not even hint at it.

A further neurotic determinant of Phaidra's choice of a love object was already alluded to: Hippolytos' indifference, which exerts an irresistible attraction on Phaidra.

This fact obliges me to discuss at once—as an aside—a detail which those who—like Festugière—find in Phaidra's infatuation a proof of Hippolytos' merit could have (but apparently did not) exploited for the same purpose. In verses 1140ff. the Choros says: "by your exile the girls have lost their bridal rivalry for your bed." Schmid[81] feels that what is "hinted at" (*angedeutet*) here is that all the Troizenian girls are in love with Hippolytos. But this interpretation disregards the key word φυγᾶι = exile, for this rivalry *ceases* when Hippolytos *falls from* the exalted state of a privileged royal bastard. No girl offered to share his exile, nor would that fit Greek custom. Moreover, since Hippolytos strenuously avoided all women, the girls of Troizen were hardly sufficiently well informed to be able to appreciate his "moral excellence." For them, he was at best a remote and somewhat spectacular figure, of a kind likely to capture every little goose's imagination.

In fact, on closer scrutiny verse 1140 has curious overtones. The girls in question can only be the average, free-born girls of Troizen, and, in mythical Greece, even a royal bastard of some distinction was expected to marry a princess, instead of the daughter of one of his grandfather's vassals or free retainers. All this is so obvious that it is almost embarrassing to have to make this point.

Having made it, I can turn my attention to still another source of the

---

[80] On such "matched" pseudo-incests, cf. Devereux, *Ethnopsychoanalysis*, op. cit., chap. 7; overtones of a sexual rivalry between sisters are present also in the myth of Theseus' aunts, Philomela and Prokne. On the neurotic compulsion to "balance" things, cf. C. Odier, "Le Bilanisme et L'Horreur du Discontinu," *L'Evolution Psychiatrique* 9 (2): 35–80, 1939. The need to balance and "even up" things can even manifest itself in the form of motor behavior: touching *both* sides of an object, touching an object with *both* hands, etc. At a certain age many children so consistently display such behavior that it becomes a formal "game." Normal children outgrow this; neurotic ones do not.
[81] Op. cit., 1.3.382.5.

almost hypnotic effect Hippolytos has on Phaidra. The indifferent, self-contained narcissist's seductiveness is—at least for certain neurotics—once more a clinical commonplace. Since narcissism is a psychological defect, narcissists appeal only to those whose (complementary) psychological flaw requires that the object of their "love" should have the *particular* flaw which appeals to them.[82]

On the basis of clinical experience, I hold that Phaidra is almost hypnotically attracted by Hippolytos' principal psychological flaw: by his narcissism. His "glamour" is an enticing vacuum, which the neurotic Phaidra feels impelled to fill with her own excessive (and pseudo-incestuous) infatuation. And it is of some importance that she does *not* seek to fill it by attributing imaginary virtues to him; she left *that* task to Hippolytos' latter day eulogists.

In short, a neurotic woman's "love" proves only that the man she "loves" has a psychological flaw, which fits her neurotic needs.[83] Most neurotics are, by definition, unable either to love or to tolerate being loved and the one thing they dread most is the reciprocation of their "love."[84] If it is, they hasten to destroy it. The ideal of most neurotics is, therefore, the totally unattainable man or woman;[85] a hopeless love is safe, in that it does not put the "lover's" *claimed* ability to love to the crucial test of a real intimacy.[86] Unconsciously but intentionally self-abolishing or predictably doomed "loves" are almost the hallmark of the neurotic.[87]

---

[82] Nearly every discussion of love in Platon alludes, at least in passing, to the proneness of certain persons to become enamoured of "flawed" partners. The occurence of this tendency in Greece is therefore well documented. The only thing Platon did not realize is that *some* neurotics are attracted precisely *by the "flaw"* of the beloved. A trivial clinical manifestation of this is, e.g., gerontophilia.

[83] Masochistic women regularly fall in love with brutes; does this prove the brutes' moral excellence?

[84] Unless, of course, the partner's "love" is equally neurotic, in which case the relationship may turn into a complicated acting-out of complementary neurotic needs, as in a marriage between a masochist and a sadist. This, however, is not love, either in terms of ordinary commonsense or in terms of psychoanalytic theory.

[85] Cf. the ideal of courtly love in the Provence. Prince Jaufie Rudel set out to find his "princesse lointaine" and, very appropriately, managed to arrive just in time to die in her arms. If one recalls that boy-love in Greece was, by definition, a temporary relationship, it is possible to view courtly love as a pseudo-heterosexual variation on a Platonic theme.

[86] Schizoid persons—who are, by definition, incapable of real affection—often get along extremely well with babies and animals, because such relationships are safely asymmetrical. Hospitalized schizophrenics sometimes make "pets" out of severely deteriorated, stuporously vegetating fellow patients. Cf. H. Rowland, "Friendship Patterns in a State Mental Hospital," *Psychiatry* 2: 363–73, 1939; G. Devereux, "The Social Structure of a Schizophrenia Ward," *Journal of Clinical Psychopathology* 6: 231–65, 1944. A patient of mine claimed that he "adored" his mistress, but refused to say that he "loved" her. "I do not know what that word really means," he would reply when pressed for an explanation.

[87] I never fully understood the impression Helene made on the Trojan elders (Hom. *Il.* 3.154ff.) until I observed the hush that fell on some sixty guests at a party when in came a

Hippolytos, the sex-phobic and self-centered narcissist, is irresistible to the neurotic Phaidra, who dreads real love more than anything else while trying to persuade herself that she *is* able to love. The glamour of the narcissist is an enticing vacuum, which a neurotic like Phaidra would feel impelled to fill with imaginary charms. She would continue to be fascinated with him long after the hollowness of her pretenses had become apparent even to her. The narcissist's affectlessness incites others to compensate for it by an extreme (though warped) one-sided affectivity. The narcissist arouses in others the need to discover just what makes him (or her) "tick" and, if need be, the wish to *make* him (or her) "tick." This is the mainspring of the narcissist's great charisma.[88] Another source of the narcissist's glamour is that he seems to have achieved for himself a complete but infantile autarky, rooted in fantasies of omnipotence; he is the prototype of what the child lurking within every adult would like to be.[89] This is indirectly proven by the fact that a neurotic, infatuated with a narcissist, is little interested in the "object" of his or her "love" and is preoccupied almost entirely with his or her own feelings—as Phaidra so manifestly is.

Such pseudo-loves are, moreover, not in the service of Eros, but of self-destruction. The frustrations the neurotic accumulates in the course of such "affairs" make him (or her) a so-called "collector of injustices." This, in turn, causes the neurotic "lover" to become abnormally suspicious (paranoid) and self-destructive, since, if his (or her) "love" *is* reciprocated, he (or she) hastens to destroy it.[90] If it is *not* reciprocated, they destroy themselves. Thus, Phaidra's "love" is little more than a wayside station on her journey toward suicide.[91]

In short, Phaidra's love does not prove Hippolytos' moral excellence; it only proves that his neuroticism complemented hers. The one was as incapable of mature love as the other; in that respect at least they were

---

dazzlingly beautiful cover-girl, dripping with mink and diamonds. This dazzling beauty—a complete narcissist—was, for years, "madly in love" with a notorious homosexual. This enabled her to conceal from herself her own incapacity to love, which in turn permitted her to contract several short but extremely profitable marriages with millionaires as neurotic as herself.

[88] The politically charismatic leader, too, is incapable of real love or even of real friendship; cf. Alexander the Great, Napoleon, Hitler, Stalin, Mao, *e tutti quanti*.

[89] This is probably the best understood aspect of the narcissist and was admirably discussed in E. Fried, *The Ego in Love and Sexuality*, New York, 1960.

[90] Clinical examples in G. Devereux, "The Female Castration Complex," *American Imago* 17: 1–19, 1960.

[91] This is proven by her neurotic anorexia, resembling that of Demeter (Hom. *h. Cer.* 200f.): both are classical mourning reactions of a neurotic type, known to occur even in primitive society; cf. G. Devereux, *Mohave Ethnopsychiatry*^{2}, op. cit., pp. 82ff. and passim. I recall that starving oneself to death was a common form of suicide in ancient Greece (Solon, etc.). See also G. Devereux, *Dreams in Greek Tragedy*, op. cit., chap. 3 (ad A. *Ag.* 412f.).

perfectly matched. Much of this could have been said in a few paragraphs, had it not been necessary to disprove, point by point, the illusions so many commentators, both ancient and modern, have built up around their own preconceptions, instead of studying what the Euripides text actually says, time and again, directly and indirectly, from the first to the last line.

In summing up this section, I must stress once more that Phaidra has nothing good to say about Hippolytos. This shows that her irrational fascination survived whatever illusions she may once have had about his "excellence." She came very close to Catullus' "odi et amo," and, like Catullus, she despised herself for loving. The observable fact is that the affectlessness of the narcissist occasionally incites even mildly neurotic persons to compensate for it by an extreme (though warped) *onesided* outpouring of affect. In another sense, such Danaid-like attempts to pour water into a bottomless jar represent a last ditch attempt to find out what makes the narcissist tick—or even to bing him back to (affective) life. In short, a narcissist like Hippolytos has a *charisma* all his own and is at times able to exploit it to his advantage as effectively as Alexander the Great—a complete narcissist—exploited his.

Thus, Hippolytos was doubly inaccessible—as stepson and as narcissist—and *therefore* the perfect nail on which to hang all that is theatrical in the hysterical Phaidra's fantasies. How this psychodrama of neurotic "love" can be held to prove Hippolytos' moral excellence is a mystery I do not propose to solve here.

The only question remaining is whether Euripides was aware of all this, and, if so, on what level. The crux of my argument is that even primitive shamans have understood many aspects of such self-destrucive neurotic "loves" and have described them to me with insight and precision, long before I knew anything of psychoanalysis. I will cite only a Mohave shaman's meticulously detailed account of the life of the self-destructive lesbian witch Sahaykwisā, who, after being raped by the husband of a woman she had been trying to seduce, became (behaviorally) "heterosexual"—the better to maneuver her two lovers into murdering her.[92]

The manner in which the shaman Hivsū Tupōma told me this tale of woe left no doubt of his understanding of at least part of Sahaykwisā's neurotically self-destructive maneuverings. It can, thus, hardly be argued that Euripides was culturally or intellectually unable to match the insight of a Mohave shaman. Our sexually stupid culture may hamper our attempts to understand such behavior; Athenian culture did not so handicap either Euripides or Strepsiades. Hence, for me at least, the very failure of so many modern commentators to understand Phaidra's

---

[92] G. Devereux, *Mohave Ethnopsychiatry*[2], op. cit., 416–26.

neuroticism and Hippolytos' narcissism is proof positive that Euripides the Athenian *did* understand it. This does not mean that Euripides could have written the preceding pages, nor that he would have cared to write them.

4

Hippolytos' Diagnosis

Hippolytos' Grandiosity

Hippolytos' self-praise must not be appraised in terms of our own questionable value scale.[1] Plutarch knew that a healthy self-esteem can exert a good influence on one's conduct,[2] though overweening pride incites both men and gods to bring the boaster low. Moreover, absolute self-appreciation is less resented than is self-praise couched in invidious— comparative and superlative—terms. It is not really *hubris* for an Alexander to treat his name as a label of quality.[3] No one seems to have resented Pythia's remark to Lykourgos that she did not know whether to address him as god or as man (Plu. *V. Lyc.* 5.3) though her statement (in the superlative), that Sokrates was the wisest of men,[4] seems to have been resented.

The *degree* of the pathologicality of Hippolytos' arrogance must be appraised in sociological terms. His arrogance (an ethical-cultural term) transcends the boundaries of the normal; it does not betoken bad manners, but psychological disturbance.

I intend to examine first Hippolytos' claim that he possesses exceptional qualities and only then proceed to a scrutiny of his use of the superlative. One can lay claim to excellence without, by implication, casting aspersions on others. It is also one thing to say: "I am a scholar," and quite another thing to say: "I am pure." It is worse when—like Hippolytos—one says: "*I* am pure" in a manner which implies "*You* are impure." He further underlines the first person singular pronoun by claiming that: "*My* friends are pure" (997). Invidiousness is the salient characteristic of his self-praise: it begins with his saluting Aphrodite from afar, because *he* is pure (102), and ends with a Parthian shot aimed at Theseus: "May your legitimate children be as good as I am!" (1455).

What is in between is worse: the passages in which he declares himself to be unique and superlative are almost too numerous to list. Not only does he claim to be Artemis' *only* companion (84), but—as Aphrodite points out

---

[1] Goethe, "Nur der Lump is bescheiden," is an exception.
[2] Plu. *de vit. pud.* 528C, id., *de se ips. c. invid. laud.* 539A.
[3] E.g., "Were I not Alexander, I would wish to be Diogenes" (Plu. *Alex.* 332A).
[4] Pl. *Apol.* 21aff. On such invidiousness in general: Th. 2.35.

(16)—he pretends to associate not simply with one of the deities, but with the *greatest* of them all. He affirms his superiority over his father, by saying in effect that Theseus flatters himself if he thinks he can crush him (989). He is the most virtuous of all, may it not displease his father (1100);[5] the irony shows how little he thinks of Theseus. Being the most virtuous man in the world (993), he surpasses all others in virtue (1363); he is the worthiest of men (1242) . . . and so on, with only slight variations.

His grandiosity offends everyone. His slave warns him about it (98ff.); Aphrodite objects to it (19ff.); Phaidra mentions it (728); Theseus' usual good sense finds the right word for it: it is the cult of the self (1080) which is the starting point of "the cult of the personality" in dictatorships, right and left. Though the Nurse is less explicit—for she reproaches Phaidra, and not Hippolytos, for her reluctance to obey Aphrodite's commands (445ff.)— the manner in which she speaks of him and approaches him shows her awareness of Hippolytos' self-importance. This makes it unanimous . . . except for those who feel that a sex-phobia excuses every foible, and therefore try their utmost to whitewash—at times by deliberately toning down their translations—Hippolytos' arrogance and self-centeredness.

Two details show that his grandiosity and "purity" are neurotically (not psychotically) paranoid. He is unaware of his own grandiosity; he readily agrees with the slave that arrogance is odious (93ff.). The Prometheus myth shows that even Zeus had to learn moderation and Poseidon sternly states that even Zeus' prerogatives have limits (Hom. *Il.* 15.185ff.). A grandiosity so blind and so offensively expressed is—with the possible exception of that of Salmoneus—without parallel in Greek literature, and matched in modern times only by ideologically intoxicated dictators. Even the *hubris* of the Giants and Titans is nothing by comparison; though they thought that they could dethrone the gods, they realized that the fight would be hard.

Hippolytos' grandiosity is that of an almost paranoid character neurotic, who comes close to a break with reality and so isolates himself that he ends up by being almost all there is in the world. The paranoid element is highlighted also by the *exhibitionistic* character of his "virtuous behavior." He is condemned out of his own mouth, when he laments that the *hardships* he endured in performing his noble and pious actions *before men* were *in vain* (1367)[6] This exhibitionistic, approval-seeking sexual *askesis* disproves specious claims that he is so young and therefore still so sexless that he does not even repress his sexuality, but is simply unaware of it.[7]

Our monastic tradition makes critics all too ready to assume that the

---

[5] Méridier's translation, though not absolutely literal, catches well this ironic nuance.
[6] Cf. his lament that his mother's parturition was love's labor lost (1082).
[7] Thus Festugière (op. cit., pp. 13f.; id., *L'Enfant d'Agrigente*, 1950, chap. 1), who is simply more outspoken than other commentators. Yet Hippolytos must be at least eighteen.

basic purpose of asceticism is *always* a noble one. The history of religions teaches us otherwise. An evil demon, determined to overthrow the Hindu gods, tried to obtain the power needed for this *evil* enterprise, by subjecting himself to aeons of ascetic practices, thereby *automatically* accumulating the supernatural powers needed for his proposed sacrilege. Self-castigation is, thus, simply an investment that brings compound interest, *regardless* of the ethical quality of its ultimate purpose.[8] *Askesis*—a form of moral masochism—is simply a power maneuver, buttressed by a kind of emotional blackmail.[9]

A direct consequence of Hippolytos' grandiosity is his certainty that he alone is right and, what is almost "better," that everyone else is wrong. Nothing—be it argument, insult, the suffering of others or danger—can dent his conviction that he is the sole repository of truth and its sole judge. That his views are at variance with everyone's opinion and even with the most sober and realistic appraisal of one's social obligations, does not cause him the least concern.[10] So massive and crystallized a self assurance is clearly "borderline." It is often found in borderline paranoid schizophrenics, some of whom are brilliant men, endowed with *charisma*. Moreover, this certainty can only be achieved by an *almost* complete withdrawal from reality, lest one's rightness be tested in the crucible of facts,[11] and be proven wrong.

Extreme—and at times pathological—self-righteousness and near total *imperviousness* to reality and to reason must not be confused. Though the two often go together, their motivation is different. The capacity to resist even the persuasion of reality is pathognomonic, since sensible men learn to live with uncertainties and unanswered questions. The healthy Ego can tolerate a certain amount of uncertainty; the defective Ego usually *cannot*. Once it yields, be it but on a minor point, its subjective world-view disintegrates, as a "Venetian tear," held together only by vitreous surface tension, disintegrates into dust if it is so much as slightly chipped.[12]

---

8 I am indebted to Professor Weston La Barre for this example.
9 G. Devereux, *Reality and Dream*², 1969, esp. pp. 131f., 143f., and 483, cites some of the psychoanalytic literature. Id., *Basic Problems*, op. cit., chap. 12.
10 Such a detachment is by no means unheard of. Considerations which hardly stand in need of an explanation force me not to cite a public document—the verbatim account of a celebrated hearing—in which a person of great prominence and notoriety showed the same indifference to the opinions of his fellows and displayed the same autistic conviction of his own charismatic rightness.
11 Almost the only exception to this rule is the person who manages to maneuver himself into a position of absolute power . . . and even such persons are at times obliged to bend—or to lie—lest reality should shatter their power: one thinks of Orwell's "Newspeak," caricaturing the "party line."
12 Even Blaiklock (op. cit., pp. 43-44) speaks of "perverted animosity" and "fanaticism in self-defense," sensing, despite his partisanship, the paranoid element in the makeup of *his* admirably chaste Hippolytos.

It is precisely the *perfect* coherence and rigidity of such systems which proves them to be defensive maneuvers.

Two analogies may clarify this matter:

(1) Certain neurologically defective patients must obsessively over-organize their lives, their work, their personal possessions. Anything unforeseen—be it but the misplacing of a pencil—can trigger off a "catastrophic reaction" of great intensity, since they cannot cope with it.[13]

(2) Uneducated, stupid, or inarticulate persons,[14] subjected to pressure or to persuasion, often remain stubbornly silent, or oppose a massive "No" to everything. Being no match for their intellectually superior interlocutors and unable to foresee where even the slightest and most obvious admission *might lead*, they consider consistent negativism the only safe policy.[15]

The facts are, thus, quite simple: precisely because Hippolytos' views are untenable, they have a characteristically paranoid tight organization. They cannot be debated, let alone be modified, *in part*. They must be affirmed unconditionally and in their totality. Once a debate is engaged on any point, the delusional edifice collapses in its entirety. It is the old story of the oak and of the reed.

The Choros understands this *perfectly* and therefore condemns Hippolytos' extreme rigidity and dogmaticism (1115f.). By contrast, to judge by much of what is routinely written about Hippolytos, his pathology is still insufficiently recognized. What *formerly* prevented its proper evaluation was the automatic prestige enjoyed by fanatical puritans. *Today*, it is the "social prestige" of the more or less delusional, rigid, violent, and yet self-pitying fanatic, which obscures the extreme pathology of Hippolytos' character structure.[16]

The last point to be made is that Hippolytos' grandiosity is—like many other forms of grandiosity—a defense against depression (1078). In that sense, it is only *descriptively* paranoid. Functionally it wards off a

---

[13] K. Goldstein, *The Organism*, New York, 1939. For catastrophic reactions, without brain lesions, in groups subjected to extreme stress, cf. G. Devereux, "Catastrophic Reactions in Normals," *American Imago* 7: 343–49, 1950.

[14] I do not consider Hippolytos' "unaccustomed as I am to public speaking" (986ff.) relevant. It will be discussed in the proper place.

[15] Cf. *La Farce de Maître Patelin*, in which the shepherd plays the idiot. Reactions of this type (and even a blind lashing-out in response *to* Sokrates' maieutic technique) are fairly common. For reactions of this type in schizophrenics cf. G. Devereux, "The Nature of the Bizarre," *Journal of the Hillside Hospital* 8: 266–78, 1959. An obsessive, with a fragile Ego, preferred to find all answers by himself; he considered learning—be it but from a book—an interference with his identity, likely to obliterate it (G. Devereux, "Loss of Identity," op. cit.; id., "Renonciliation à l'Identité," op. cit.).

[16] The borderline psychosis of one such person was not recognized by the in-group until the erotomanic underpinnings of that subject's paranoid reactions could no longer be ignored.

desperate mourning over early childhood traumata: having lost his mother, the bastard Hippolytos is raised by his great-grandfather, Pittheus, for his father has taken a new wife, Medeia, and has legitimate children by her. I will have more to say about this in my appraisal of Hippolytos as a Euripidean "hero."

Other Diagnostic Signs

Other diagnostic signs also abound in Euripides' characterization of Hippolytos. Self-evident to the clinician, they are easily ignored by those who believe themselves safely sheltered behind the bastions of Greek culture (which, before Platon, contained nothing that would permit one to consider Hippolytos normal). They resemble a few self-proclaimed psychiatric anthropologists, hog-tied by naive cultural relativism and by an academically advantageous and encouraged incapacity to comprehend depth-psychology.

It seems simplest therefore to define in broad terms what standard cultural practices can be interpreted as genuine, clinically relevant symptoms. Since I have dealt with this matter in several papers,[17] it suffices to present here only a few paradigmatic examples.

There are two basic issues which vociferous advocates of diagnostic cultural relativism fail to grasp:

(1) *Vox populi, vox dei* is a psychiatrically unsound diagnostic principle. A hallucination *is* a symptom, whether it occurs spontaneously in a hospitalized psychotic or in response to social mandates in a Plains Indian who, by starving himself in an isolated spot, *tries* to hallucinate that he is being adopted by a supernatural being, believing that his success in life depends on such an adoption.[18] Hallucination is a serious symptom in the case of an Occidental businessman, since his culture does *not* encourage hallucinating; its forces support (in this respect) the rational Ego in its struggle against hallucinating. A hallucinating Occidental must be severely ill, if even the *combined* forces of his Ego and of his culture are unable to inhibit his capacity to hallucinate. By contrast, in the case of the Plains Indian, cultural pressures actually *weaken* the realistic Ego's capacity to ward off hallucinations.[19] Hence, a Plains Indian adolescent, who hallucinates *during* a ritual vision quest, is *less sick* than a spontaneously hallucinating Occidental businessman. But, even in the case of the former, hallucination *is* a symptom. Indeed *despite* cultural pressures, the Ego of *some* Plains Indians is so strong and

---

[17] *Basic Problems*, op. cit.
[18] R. Benedict, *The Guardian Spirit*, op. cit.; R. H. Lowie, *The Crow Indians*, New York, 1935, pp. 252ff. and passim.
[19] G. Devereux, *Basic Problems*, op. cit., passim.

rational that, much to their despair, they cannot hallucinate at all.[20]

(2) *Culture itself furnishes many ready-made symptoms* to the individual under stress. A Malay running *amok* not only knows how to behave "crazily" in the culturally expected and even "stylized" manner, but may even learn techniques permitting him to "go crazy" in the "proper" way and to dress "properly" for this great occasion. But even this does *not* mean that the initial stress was not pathogenic, nor that the *amok* runner is, despite his culturally stylized behavior, *not* psychotic.

This means that the olfactory aspect of Artemis' epiphany calls only for a very few methodological clarifications. In terms of Greek belief a wondrous sweet scent often announces a deity's epiphany. But it may— and indeed must—also be urged that the deity announces itself only to persons capable of having olfactory hallucinations. This view strictly parallels Leksy's finding[21] that the gods infuse divine courage only into men capable of being very brave on their own, as it parallels Dodds' repeatedly quoted "double causation" (i.e, Freud's "overdetermination").

Hence, as regards Hippolytos, one can accept all Lohmeyer has to say about the ritual role of "divine odor"[22]—and still assert that Hippolytos has olfactory hallucinations. Our chaotic contemporary world has taught us only too well that many social-cultural expectations can be met only by the mentally deranged, whom their "adaptive" defect then endows with much prestige in the eyes of the brainwashed and the unthinking.[23]

---

[20] F. Linderman, *American: The Life Story of a Great Indian*, New York, 1930. Linderman's data were used therapeutically in the psychotherapy of a Plains Indian (G. Devereux, *Reality and Dream*², 1969, pp. 139f., 402f., 428, 432). Like all psychiatric symptoms, hallucination is apparently an inherent human capacity. Experimental sensory deprivation causes even normal subjects to hallucinate after awhile (J. C. Lilly: "Mental Effects of Reduction of Ordinary Levels of Physical Stimulation on Intact, Healthy Persons," *American Psychiatric Association, Research Report* 5, 1956, pp. 1–28).

[21] A. Lesky, "Göttliche und menschliche Motivation im Homerischen Epos," *Sitzungsbericht Heidelberg, philologisch-historisch Klasse*, no. 4, 1961.

[22] E. Lohmeyer, "Vom göttlichen Wohlgeruch," *Sitzungsbericht Heidelberg, philologisch-historisch Klasse*, no. 9, 1919.

[23] Cf. Lesky, "Göttliche und menschliche Motivation," op. cit., on divine courage. Though nearly every primitive society "needs" real shamans, in most tribes only the severe neurotic and borderline psychotic is *capable* of behaving shamanistically: L. B. Boyer ("Notes on the Personality Structure of a North American Indian Shaman," *Journal of the Hillside Hospital* 10: 14–33, 1961; id., "Remarks on the Personality of Shamans," in W. Muensterberger (ed.), *The Psychoanalytic Study of Society*, New York, 1962, ii, pp. 233–54; id., "Further Remarks Concerning Shamans," *Israel Annals of Psychiatry* 2: 235–57, 1964) argues that the shamans of certain *very anomic* Apache tribes are *less* neurotic than their non-shaman fellows. This further confirms my basic view that some societies are so severely disturbed—consciously (according to Boyer himself) the Mescalero Apache—that the shaman, who has at least a *cultural model* of being neurotic to cling to, necessarily presents a *less* impoverished and disorganized personality profile than the average man, who has no such model to steady and pattern his psychic functioning (G. Devereux, *Basic Problems*, op. cit., passim).

Hence, one cannot give Hippolytos' hallucinations a "clean bill of health," anymore than one can give it to the S.S. sadist, who volunteered for *well rewarded* services in an extermination camp. Only a culture lacking a sound ethos—or about to lose it—blissfully hypnotizes itself into stupidity, by repeating the incantation: "Adjustment means normality!" Cultural relativism has no place in a genuine diagnostic science.

More significantly still, all of Hippolytos' psychiatric symptoms belong to the *same pattern*; they are pathognomonic of the same disease entity. Hence, only their *malignancy* need be evaluated, by determining whether or not these particular symptoms are, or are not, encouraged by his society and presented to him, ready made, by his cultural milieu.

Hallucinations resemble experiences ordinarily mediated to the senses by determinable external stimuli, but which, in the case of hallucinations, are *not* elicited by the external world.[24] At first Hippolytos only hears Artemis' voice (85); subsequently he both hears and smells her, but still does *not* see her (1391). No Greek (or other) *belief* in divine odors can turn an *experienced* hallucination into something normal. It is precisely the fact that only the "privileged" have such *experiences* that proves it to be an abnormal experience.

Auditory hallucinations are, generally speaking, the most common and (as a rule) the least malignant. As for the absence of visual hallucinations,[25] I indicate in another section that Hippolytos' sexual knowledge was derived from looking at (vase?) pictures and from hearing (obscene?) tales, and then I interpret the relevance of this fact. What matters here is Hippolytos' tendency to view even something simply "heard" as soilure (654) and to spit apotropaically (614). Psychologically, this represents an "expulsion" of the (intruding) "bad object."[26] The possibility that Hippolytos may

---

[24] An analogy will illustrate this. Until the age of 63 I had an exceptionally sharp hearing, particularly as regards very high-pitched sounds; I could hear even so-called "silent" dog whistles. Once, lecturing on hallucinations, I *thought* my ears were ringing, for I heard a very high-pitched whistling sound. This so disturbed me that I mentioned it to the class. When one student remarked that he, too, could hear it, we discovered that the sound emanated from the radiator: a trace of steam was escaping from a tiny crevice.
[25] As in the E. *IT* dream, one does not learn what the voice says; yet it is hardly a *divine* secret (G. Devereux, Dreams in Greek Tragedy, op. cit., chap. 8).
[26] Contrary to prevailing psychoanalytic views, a (neutral) object *becomes* bad *through* being expelled. (Saliva in the mouth is "good"; outside the mouth, "bad.") But bad objects do not become "good" by intruding and psychologically real "bad objects" are at first mostly intrusive ones, and, moreover, can usually be shown to have "come out" of someone else. The psychotic's fantasy of having been nursed with "bad" (poisoned) milk is typical; but this milk is no more "bad" while still *in* the maternal breast than snake-venom is poisonous *for* the snake. An important new dimension is added to this finding by the custom referred to in A. *fr.* 354 N². In a treacherous killing, the murderer must *first* put into his mouth and *then* spit out the victim's blood. This explains the monstrous character of so many apotropaic or purificatory (Heraclit. *fr.* 5, D.-K.) rites; one must increase the horror to maximum, in order to expel it effectively. Such rites also imply counter-intimidation: one out-monsters the

"listen to his own voice"[27] will be discussed below.

More disturbing even are Hippolytos' olfactory hallucinations, which are rare even in psychosis: they are almost invariably indications of malignance. If a seemingly neurotic patient suddenly begins to have olfactory hallucinations, he has either been misdiagnosed or a psychotic break is about to occur.

Hippolytos' olfactory hallucinations are, moreover prima facie evidence of a violent sexual *repression*—which is not the same as an (alleged) "natural" adolescent "lack of interest" in sex, postulated by Festugière (op. cit.). Odors (pheromones) play a decisive role in the sexual stimulation not only of mammals, but also—and especially—of insects.[28] Freud even connected man's erect posture with the atrophy of his olfactory capacities.[29]

This brings me to a paradox. Auditory hallucination is very often reproachful, for the "voice" is that of the Superego—in Hippolytos' case, obviously that of Artemis.[30] Though the voice Hippolytos "hears" is apparently *not* reproachful, it is assuredly the voice of the *virginal* mother figure, Artemis, whose eyes always observe his conduct.[31] He must be on his best behavior; hence, we find him lamenting the futility of the *arduous* piety he *displayed* before men! (1367ff.). By contrast, odors are—as noted—fundamentally sexual: the basic component of many perfumes is musk, the secretion of the glands of a certain male deer. The "göttliche Wohlgeruch" of Lohmeyer—and, of course, of his Greek and other ancient authorities—has, thus, very earthly antecedents, though this finding would no doubt shock Hippolytos quite as much as Lohmeyer.[32] The two hallucinations thus work at cross purposes: the auditory ones speak the language of the Superego, the olfactory ones the language of infantile oedipal sexuality.

---

monster; this is a form of identification with "the enemy." On this mechanism cf. Anna Freud, *The Ego and the Mechanisms of Defense*, New York, 1946, pp. 118ff., or, simply, O. Wilde, *The Canterville Ghost*, London, 1906.

[27] Norwood, op. cit., p. 209.

[28] V. B. Wigglesworth, *The Life of Insects*, Cleveland, 1964, pp. 208ff. and chap. 7.

[29] The quadruped's nose is level with the partner's genitals; bipedal man's nose is not. Cf. S. Freud, "On the Universal Tendency to Debasement in Love," *Standard Edition*, xi, 1957 (p. 189).

[30] The Superego is not to be confused with conscience, in the *ethical* sense, for it is archaic, brutal, stupid, and bribable. The mature conscience is its exact opposite.

[31] As he will "cynically" (Blaiklock, op. cit., p. 46) watch Phaidra's. This, too, is paranoid = persecutory (660).

[32] All groups are not equally inhibited in regard to this matter. Early Italian (Renaissance) poets waxed eloquent in praise of the "odor di femina." Modern man appreciates the smell of Roquefort cheese. The durian fruit's atrocious odor attracts both men and animals, for its taste is delicious. Cf. E. J. H. Corner, *The Life of Plants*, London, 1964, pp. 216ff. On smells and sex, Hor. *Epod.* 12 (esp. 4ff.), Petron. *Satir. fr.* 138 Ernout.

Touch Phobia

Hippolytos does not like to be touched; this may be related to his having seen erotic paintings. For him, as for many others of his kind, *all* touching has a sexual meaning. There is a "stimulus generalization." His lovely meadow—representing (as noted) Artemis' pubis—is intact (73); the Nurse may not even touch his clothes (606). His initial reaction, when the Nurse is still simply supplicating him and has, as yet, said nothing, is markedly impatient; he presumably feels uncomfortable when touched and tries to disengage himself. He promises silence so readily because it was probably the simplest way of making the Nurse let go of his hand. He threatens the slaves, who try to touch him on Theseus' orders (1086). When hurt, he asks the slaves *not* to touch him (1086), or to touch him lightly (1358). Though this makes sense medically,[33] his desire to be touched lightly is probably overdetermined. A touch phobia certainly fits Hippolytos, always afraid of "dirt." The fact that "handling" people was considered ill-bred in Greece—at least in the fourth to third century B.C.[34]—does not invalidate the basic diagnosis.[35] I therefore note, for what it is worth, that, unlike Theseus, Hippolytos does not seem to *wrestle*.

Etherealness—an epithet dear to Hippolytos encomiasts—is a schizoid trait closely related to touch phobias.[36] Everything Hippolytos praises is always "pure," "virginal," or "untouched" His song in praise of Artemis is "ethereal." This simply means that the *author* of that song, Euripides, had an "ear" not only for normal but also for abnormal speech.[37]

---

[33] J. de Romilly (*L'Evolution du Pathétique*, Paris, 1961, pp. 39-40) rightly compares S. *Trach.* 1007.
[34] Cf. Sokrates' rebuke to Kritias (X. *Mem.* 1.2.30), other indications in Thphr. *Char.* 5.1, etc.
[35] Notions of what is a "proper" distance between interlocutors vary from culture to culture and, within a culture, from person to person. An Arab wants to be close enough to be able to *smell* his interlocutor's breath. Cf. E. T. Hall, "A System for the Notation of Proxemic Behavior," *American Anthropologist* 65: 1003-26, 1963, with a good bibliography. Cf. also the literal and figurative meaning of "aloof."
[36] "Ethereal" responses to Rorschach and TAT-test cards are given almost exclusively by the schizoid.
[37] Etherealness and touch phobia are probably interrelated. An excellent clinician, the late Dr. F. Minkowska, found that schizophrenics, told to touch various objects, barely touch them with their fingertips, while their polar opposites, the epileptics, practically "massage" them (personal communication, 1946). I recall that organicists "cure" schizophrenics by administering convulsant drugs, or electroshock. I stress that no poet, musician, or artist of the first rank is *habitually* "ethereal" in his work. Mozart is earthly, of the earth.

The Schizoid Split

At one point (1078) Hippolytos says that if he could see himself (from the outside), he would cry over himself.[38] To a psychoanalyst, this "taking oneself as an object of interest" is neurotic narcissism[39]—and, possibly, even a schizoid splitting of the self-image.[40] His capacity to look at himself—*though not objectively*—from the outside is perhaps alluded to in his lament, that he cannot bear being *seen* as a bad person (1070)—and one cannot but recall that Hippolytos' virtue is highly exhibitionistic (1367ff.).

In my opinion the data cited so far are clinically more than just suggestive. One is on even safer ground when one passes to the auditory sphere, though much depends on the reading of verse 654. Norwood[41] suggests that, at this point, Hippolytos begins to listen to the sound of his *own* voice. I am unable to detect this nuance in the text, though it would be grist for my mill. I do not presume to contradict Norwood on this point, but neither can I interpret something I am unable to find in the text. However, certain other passages indicate that he actually hears Artemis' voice and thus provide indirect evidence of some splitting also in the auditory sphere. It is, of course, only Theseus who wishes (928ff.) that people had two voices: one for telling the truth, another for the rest. Now, it so happens that *some* neurotics do, in fact, have two such voices.[42] The fact that Theseus *wishes* Hippolytos had two voices, suggests, obviously, that he did *not* have them. Nonetheless, as a clinician I cannot help asking, why should Theseus make *this* remark à propos of Hippolytos? It seems logically uncalled-for, or at least unnecessary.[43] Its

---

[38] The explanations offered by Barrett, ad loc., are not persuasive. Méridier (ad loc.) comments platitudinously: "as Theseus sees him."

[39] This point, about self-inspection, was well made in S. Viderman, "Narcissisme et Relation d' Objet dans la Situation Analytique," *Revue Française de Psychanalyse* 32: 97–118, 1968.

[40] A sometimes insightful, though Jungian, study of the body image is A. Virel, *Histoire de Notre Image*, Geneva, 1965.

[41] Norwood, op. cit., p. 209. Barrett offers no comments.

[42] I myself analyzed one such patient; his "lying voice" was absolutely distinct from his normal voice. E. Jones ("The God Complex," *Essays in Applied Psycho-Analysis*, ii, 1951) describes a man having several voices. I knew personally an incredibly rigid and paranoid man, of considerable scientific stature, who had three perfectly distinct voices: a basso boom, a falsetto scream, and an aggressive whisper. Sometimes he used all three voices in uttering a single sentence. Now, having two or more voices reflects—among other things—an inner split. The literature on voice production mannerisms in neurosis is surprisingly small (cf. G. Devereux, *Basic Problems*, op. cit., chap. 4). By contrast, the literature on the voice as a symbol is considerable; cf. A. Grinstein, *An Index of Psychoanalytic Writings*, 3d series.

[43] This is as good a time as any to give an example showing how the psychoanalyst uses his—even to him puzzling—reactions, for scientific ends. As I write these lines, I suddenly remember once more the case of a psychoanalyst whose slips of the tongue showed that

connection with the *dissoi logoi* dear to the Greek is too remote to matter in this context.

Were Theseus on my psychoanalytic couch, I would neither believe nor disbelieve that Hippolytos has only one voice. I would simply conclude that *Theseus*—who, as Méridier rightly observes, is extraordinarily well informed about Hippolytos' ways and behavior (934ff.)—is aware of a deep contradiction in his son's makeup and *wishes* that it would manifest itself in some obvious way,[44] such as the possession of two voices. Next, I would wonder why Theseus chose *this* sign instead of—let us say—wishing that liars would blush to their ears, or be struck down on the spot by Zeus, guardian of Oaths.[45] I would conclude that Theseus—*unconsciously*—alludes to Artemis' "voice," which *his son* professes to hear. Thus, Hippolytos does "have" two voices, after all . . . and Artemis was, of course, played by a *male* actor.

This interpretation is more than somewhat probable. Those who find it too finespun can simply ignore it; it will not damage my case.[46]

A further slight indication of a split is that—at one time—Hippolytos had *looked* at sensual paintings and had *listened* to tales about sexuality—though ultimately with revulsion—the way he listened to the Nurse. There is also his usually overlooked remark to Theseus: "Phaidra's *body* was not the most beautiful in the world" (1009f.)[47] To know that, he must have looked. Who, then, is *his* standard of beauty? Not having seen Artemis, and not having courted girls, his yardstick can only be the phantasmatic vision of his "virgin mother." I hold that Theseus—as nearly always in Euripides—is right, when (966ff.) he tells Hippolytos

---

his unconscious understood his patient *better* than his (inarticulate) conscious did. Next, there comes to my mind a personal experience: In my entire psychoanalytic career, I used the "Centaur" image only twice in clinical interpretations. The second time I used it, I asked myself: "*Why* did I do so . . . what did these two patients have in common, to make *me* think of Centaurs?" This led me to realize that the two *did* have one unusual point in common, and that it was *this* which made me use the Centaur image, in both cases. This, in turn, made me understand that this seemingly minor similarity was actually an important part of their respective neuroses. Cf. Devereux, *From Anxiety to Method*, op. cit., for a formal analysis of the use the analyst makes of his own unconscious in his clinical work.

44 Cf. E. *Med.* 516; *The Veiled Hipp., fr.* 439; *Phoinix, frr.* 811, 812 N².
45 Once more I would like to highlight the way the analyst's mind operates: Only *after* writing this did I realize that my choice of those alternatives was not random. "Blush to their *ears*" is directly determined by the fact that I am speaking of voices. "Struck down by Zeus" anticipates what I propose to say further below on E. *Hipp.* 1191. The poet free-associates in much the same way, but for different ends.
46 If I am right in saying this, Norwood's hypothesis (that, at 654, Hippolytos listens to the sound of his own voice) may have been unconsciously inspired by what *Theseus* says about two voices. Even normal people, for example while lecturing, may "hear" their own voices "objectively," as if coming from outside.
47 Cf. Pasiphaë's depreciating remarks about the bull's "beauty" in E. *Cret. fr.* 11, vv. 11ff., in D. Page, *Greek Literary Papyri*³ (Loeb Library), 1950.

that he is unconvinced by the claims of young men to be truly chaste, in the sense of lacking interest in sex. Euripides—or Theseus (which in *this* passage is much the same)—realizes that the sex-hater is more obsessed with sex than the unabashed amorist.

Another split in Hippolytos' makeup is that this slaughterer of our dumb friends is a vegetarian. This scandalizes me as much as the report that the mountains of corpses in the first World War were *not eaten* is said to have outraged an African cannibal. Both he and I find aimless slaughter scandalous. Of course, the Pythagoreans were also vegetarians, while extolling military virtues, but the slaughter of one's fellow man has always enjoyed a position of honor in human culture. Besides, I am certainly not arguing that the Pythagoreans were sensible people: non-neurotic or non-schizoid;[48] in my frame of reference any resemblance between Hippolytos' behavior and that of the Pythagoreans only strengthens the argument that he was abnormal. This being said, Theseus' accusation that Hippolytos is an orphic requires detailed consideration.

I begin by noting that much depends on whose definition of orphism one accepts. Both I. M. Linforth[49] and Barrett (ad loc.) try to prove chiefly that Hippolytos is not a "real" orphic. In so doing, they disregard that it is still far from clear just *what* "real" orphism was. What matters is that the problem facing us at this point is not what real orphism was but what the public *imagined* orphism to be. Barrett (ad loc.) is assuredly over-optimistic in assuming that the public realized that Hippolytos is not a "real" orphic. The theater-goers may have known that mysticism and magic were essential features of orphism—but, if they knew *more* than this about orphism, they hardly expected secret matters to be shown or discussed on-stage. The fact that Hippolytos complains about Theseus' failure to consult diviners—i.e., a group dealing in hocus-pocus that proliferated during the Peloponnesian war and was thoroughly despised not only by Euripides but by all sensible men—does not, in itself, make Hippolytos a mystic. What does prove him to be one is his supposed personal intimacy with Artemis, which I discuss elsewhere (Chap. 1). I concede, of course, that there is no real nexus between Artemis and orphism; this matter need therefore not be labored further.

The charge of vegetarianism is more telling, for the orphics were—or were believed to be—vegetarians.[50] Now, it has been argued that a vegetarian could not be also an ardent hunter; Barrett (ad 952ff.) urges

---

[48] Here, too, I follow Dodds (*The Greeks*, op. cit., p. 167, n. 63), who urges that Pythagoras was a shaman—i.e., by definition a neurotic or a borderline psychotic. On Empedokles as shaman: J. Burnett, *Early Greek Philosophy*[4], London, 1930, chap. 7, p. 199.
[49] *The Arts of Orpheus*, 1941, pp. 50ff.
[50] Linforth, op. cit., p. 55.

that the vegetarian Pythagoreans avoided hunters and butchers as unclean (Eudoxos in *Vorsokratiker*, 14.9) but forgets that Hitler was a vegetarian. He also disregards two points I briefly made elsewhere:

(1) Euripides himself, in his *Cretans* (*fr.* 472 N²) speaks first of "omophagia" (verse 12) and then of "vegetarianism" (verse 19). Moreover, in another fragment of the *Cretans*, published by Page (*fr.* 11), Pasiphaë provocatively invites the "murderous" Minos to feed on her raw flesh (verse 34ff.).

(2) Linforth (op. cit., p. 58) and Barrett at verses 109f. seek to refute Theseus' charge of vegetarianism by claiming that the meal Hippolytos and his companions are about to eat is a "hunter's breakfast" consisting of freshly killed game. This supposition disregards the occurrence of the word σῖτος (109) in the text, though Linforth pointed out earlier (p. 52) that σῖτος means primarily grain or food derived from grain. Moreover, the wording of the text in question suggests that the table is already set. If this view is correct, it automatically excludes that game just killed was being served. Last but not least, I repeat a point made earlier but easy to "forget" (repress): nowadays game is "hung" for several days before it is cooked, but I do not know whether this was also a Greek practice. Lacking refrigeration the Greeks probably ate the liver and certain other inner parts of the cattle or game the very day of the kill (Hom. *Od.* 20.252). I observed the same practice amongst the Sedang, when they sacrificed water buffaloes.

All I assert here is that verses 109f. do not forbid one to view Hippolytos as a vegetarian hunter.

Theseus also accuses Hippolytos of being fond of the fume (verse 954, καπνούς) of *grimoires*. The orphics were, of course, much addicted to books allegedly written by Orpheus and Mousaios. Now, Euripides—said to have been the owner of a large personal library—hardly meant to criticize a man for being addicted to reading. The key to the nature of books Hippolytos is supposed to have read is provided by the word for smoke; Linforth (p. 52ff.) indicates that this term can designate also something insignificant and worthless, like the mystical trash circulating during the Peloponnesian war, scandalizing sober citizens.

But there may be more to it than a reference to the worthlessness of these books. Poseidonios (*fr.* 104) mentions the inhaling of the smoke of hemp, that is, of a hallucinogenic substance. I believe Euripides meant to indicate that Hippolytos' exalted, mystical behavior was inspired by such "grimoires" (Pl. *Rmp.* 364a).

Equally significant is the imputation of ecstatic raving to Hippolytos (βάκχευε, verse 954). This particular accusation *must* have had a basis in reality, for whereas one can conceal one's vegetarianism, mysticism, and perhaps even sexual abstinence, ecstatic seizures can hardly remain hidden. It would also be specious to object that the word for "raving" is related to Bakchos and not to Artemis. In the first place, that verb can be applied to almost any form of extreme affective behavior. In the second place, Artemis is a goddess notoriously capable of both sending and healing madness.[51]

One also notes that in the *Hippolytos* (verses 161ff.) Artemis and specifically Diktynna, the Cretan Artemis (at verse 146), are invoked by the Choros in connection with Phaidra's psychological (and secondarily somatic) disturbances.

In short, this part at least of Theseus characterization of Hippolytos must rest on known facts, such as Hippolytos' constant roamings, in a state resembling ecstasy, in the company of a hallucinated—or even "real"—Artemis. One should not forget that if the sight of Artemis' statue suffices to drive men mad,[52] her actual presence could hardly be soothing.

Thus, Barrett greatly understates the case when he asserts that Theseus' description of Hippolytos as an orphic is simply a jibe—that it only seeks to suggest that his impostor son resembles the notorious "orphic" arch-imposters of the fifth century B.C. The point at stake here is not orphic theology and ritual behavior, as Linforth and Barrett seem to think, but the occurrence of ecstatic seizures, on the one hand, and, on the other, an equivalence between Hippolytos' behavior, as described by Theseus, and the public image of the orphic impostor which scandalized sensible people in Athens.

The charge that Hippolytos is a corruptor of women (1068) is, by contrast, clearly false, but this does not mean that we should throw the baby out with the bath water. I state at once that I am not at all convinced by Linforth's allegation (p. 58) that Eugen Fehrle[53] errs in holding sexual abstinence to be orphic—and this, despite the fact that A. Dieterich[54] himself concurs with Fehrle. The point is that Dieterich cites precisely verses 943–57 of this play, which Kern reprints as *Testimonium* 213 in his *Orphicorum Fragmenta*. Linforth, who is determined to question *all* pre-Platonic references to orphism, chooses not to treat this passage as a description of orphism because it cannot be traced back to an "earlier" source. Such skepticism is self-serving; it reminds me of a song social work students at Smith College used to sing derisively in the 1930s: "but who psychoanalyzed Freud?" For the student of psychopathology, Hippolytos' fanatical sex phobia cannot be *purely* subjective; it must also have had a partly ideological (theological) basis.[55]

[51] Josef Mattes, *Der Wahnsinn im griechischen Mythos*, 1970, pp. 42f.
[52] Cf. the case of Astrabakos and Alopekos: Pausanias 3.16.7ff.
[53] "Die kultische Keuschheit im Altertum," *Religionsgeschichtlieche Versuche und Vorarbeiten*, VI, 1910.
[54] *Abraxas*, Leipzig, 1891.
[55] On sexual ideologies, cf. T. Nathan, *Sexualité Idéologique et Névrose*, Claix, 1977.

The point here, as noted before, is that peddlers of mysticism, such as the baser hangers-on of orphism, must have found it advantageous to *profess* to abstain from sex so as to gain easier access to the womenfolk, who are notoriously prone to be taken in by purveyors of cosmic slush. The well-known chastity of the early Christians was, to my mind, a powerful element of their success as proselytizers among women.

The last detail to be stressed is the notorious arrogance of mystics and ascetics—and, in this respect, Hippolytos' boundless arrogance is conclusive.

In summary, Hippolytos behaved the way the public believed orphics to behave or, if one prefers, the way they did, in fact, behave. Until proof to the contrary is forthcoming, I therefore concur with Méridier[56] that Theseus knew his son inside out. If Theseus describes Hippolytos as an orphic, his behavior must have resembled that of true orphics—or at least their public image. Theseus errs only in viewing his son as an impostor—an understandable mistake if one considers how great a proportion of mystics and mediums is made up of impostors, whom their followers continue to defend *even after their hypocrisy becomes public knowledge.*[57] At any rate, the claim that Theseus had called his son an orphic with nothing to substantiate the term in the eyes of the Athenian public seeks to present the image of a Theseus beside himself with rage, saying anything that pops into his head and that is likely to hurt his son. The rebuttal is simple. Euripides made more than one mentally deranged person speak onstage, and *not one* of them speaks the way Theseus does. The confused and foolish Theseus of some critics is an unpleasant fancy, whose purpose it is to salvage Hippolytos' chastity from seeming ridiculous.

In short, Hippolytos' orphism is, for Theseus, a sign of aberration (950ff.); the clinician concurs for the same reason that he finds contemporary cultist snake handlers abnormal.[58] I cannot go further into this matter, not wishing to get involved with the vexed problem of what orphism "really is." I take Theseus' description of Hippolytos' "orphic" behavior as my *sole* standard and state, as a clinician, that no sensible person behaves *that* way. If it be retorted that orphism was a cult, I will reply that adherence to it was as *optional* as enrollment in the S.S.; neurotics joined the orphics as sadists joined the S.S. It is as simple as that.

---

56 P. 20, n. 1, of his edition.
57 A brilliantly intelligent person, personally well-acquainted with a high ecclesiastical dignitary who died under scandalous circumstances, reacted rather strangely to my remark that this dignitary's conduct did not fit his ardent championship of ecclesiastical celibacy: "Ah, but he advocated only celibacy—*not chastity!* That is not the same!" It took me a minute to realize that this rebuttal of my criticism was to be taken seriously—that it was *not cynical.*
58 W. La Barre, *And They Shall Lift up Serpents*, Minneapolis, 1963.

Suicidalness

Suicidalness can be dealt with briefly. I already noted Hippolytos' provocative retort: "Had you (sc. Theseus) seduced my wife, I would kill you" (1044). This closely parallels Pasiphaë's (*Cret.* verses 35ff. P.) provocative invitation to Minos to kill and eat her. Nor can one overlook Hippolytos' asking Zeus to kill him *if* he is guilty, for Zeus *does* at least *allow* him to be killed. Despite the view that one god does not interfere with another (1328f.), this surely must have struck anyone who was properly pious—*eusebes, pistos,* and *hosios*—as significant. In short, the self-destructive Hippolytos literally asks twice to be killed and, as persons of his kind do, when he gets no cooperation he gets himself killed by causing "things" to happen. As noted, on the psychological level the real horse-panicker (*taraxippos*) was not the bull, but Hippolytos' own self-destructiveness.

I deliberately left to the last verses 986ff., in which Hippolytos declares himself to be a poor public speaker. It may well be little more than a pretense of youthful modesty—if one can imagine Hippolytos "modest" in any way. It is only his total lack of modesty which suggests that this utterance may be more than a dully polite "unaccustomed as I am to public speaking," and reflect some measure of inhibition. Further than that I cannot go.

The last word was said by Kitto: "an unbalanced mind or temperament like Hippolytos' is unsafe"[59] . . . to himself and to others.

Hippolytos the Theomachos

Hippolytos the Theomachos (god-fighter) marks an important turning point in Greek religious thought. The way Hippolytos fights Aphrodite is worlds apart from the way earlier *theomachoi* fought the gods or supernatural beings. Jacob wrestled with the angel. Herakles defied Apollon and wounded both Hera and Hades with his arrows. Diomedes wounded Aphrodite. Marsyas competed with Apollon and Thamyris with the Muses in musical contests. Arachne contended with Athene as a weaver. Others, misusing their royal powers, persecute the god and/or his followers (Lykourgos, Pentheus). Still others compete with the gods sexually (Ischys, Idas), usurp their rights (Salmoneus), divulge their secrets (Tantalos), deceive them (Prometheus), or even attempt to induce them to do monstrous deeds, like eating children (Lykaon, Tantalos).[60]

What matters in all these cases is that the struggle always takes place *outside* the *theomachos*; his behavior is, biologically, "alloplastic."

---

[59] Kitto, op. cit., p. 213.
[60] That several of these tales simply rationalize human sacrifices, etc., need not concern me here.

A transitional phenomenon in man's struggle against the gods *as they are* (or as they are traditionally imagined) is Aischylos' or Pindaros' attempt to change traditional conceptions of the gods—remolding them "nearer to the heart's desire." Thus, Euripides' Herakles cannot imagine the gods as evil (*HF* 1340ff.).[61]

Though attempts to re-shape the gods constitute (superficially) *alloplastic* behavior, in that moralizing poets do not profess to change themselves but the gods (or other people's conceptions of the gods), these undertakings are actually *autoplastic*, in that these poets try to imagine the gods otherwise than they had been *taught* to imagine them.

A further step—somewhat at an angle with the trail blazed by Aischylos and Pindaros—is taken by Sophokles: confident in his own strength, Aias (S. *Aj.* 766ff.) refuses Athene's proferred patronage, wishing to triumph without divine help. This is next door to atheism, which first manifests itself precisely at that period. The Sophoklean Aias heralds Diagoras' and Kritias' atheism,[62] which never really took roots.

Euripides' Hippolytos inaugurates an even newer approach to theomachy. He does not fight, remodel, or deny Aphrodite in the *external* world; his refusal to revere her is a deceptive side-issue. He proceeds "autoplastically." He makes—or tries to make—*himself* immune to her power. His approach is not that of Aias, enthusiastically devoted to Athene's warlike works, who simply wishes to claim all credit for his exploits for himself. Hippolytos *excludes himself internally* from the world of those who come under Aphrodite's sway.

In a sense, Phaidra also proceeds that way. She too struggles autoplastically against the goddess. As god-fighters, Phaidra and Hippolytos have, thus, much in common. The difference between them can only be expressed in psychoanalytic terms: Hippolytos *represses* his sexuality until it *ceases* to be conscious. Phaidra consciously *suppresses* and inhibits its manifestations.[63] Hippolytos is convinced that he never heard the call of Eros; Phaidra admits hearing it, but refuses to obey. So far as I am able to determine, both reactions are without precedent in Greek literature.[64]

---

[61] I agree with Festugière, *L'Enfant*, op. cit., pp. 3ff., that theomachies imply belief, but largely disagree with the rest of his interpretations.

[62] On Diagoras, cf. E. Zeller, *Die Philosophie der Griechen*, 1⁴, p. 864.1, Tübingen, 1844-52; Kritias *fr.* 25 D.-K.

[63] R. P. Winnington-Ingram, "Hippolytus: A Study in Causation," *Entretiens Hardt*, vi, Vandoeuvres-Genève, 1960, sensed this distinction, but obscured it, by saying erroneously that Phaidra *represses* while Hippolytos *suppresses* his sexual drive. His insight is correct; he simply inverted two technical terms.

[64] A. *Suppl.* is not a precedent. The Danaides do not profess to be neuters, nor do they resist a temptation. They are, at the most, oedipally fixated (Devereux, *Dreams in Greek Tragedy*, op. cit., chap. 9). Helene's reluctance to obey Aphrodite (Hom. *Il.* 3.399ff.) is *not* comparable.

The inner resemblance between the two is further accentuated by Phaidra's half-hallucinatory wish to roam the meadows, to hunt, and to race horses (208ff.)—like Hippolytos, with whom, as the Nurse fully realizes (212ff.), she identifies herself. In his usual blundering way even Hippolytos is aware of his kinship with Phaidra. At verses 1034ff. he calls her chaste *in her actions*; he calls himself chaste *in every way*, but elsewhere stresses only the purity of his body (1003).[65] In saying that she *showed* herself virtuous *without* being able to *be* virtuous, while he had simply made a poor use of his virtue (1034f.), he admits the same similarity.[66] What he fails to grasp is that Phaidra, who uses *suppression* (self-control), is the only one who is truly chaste; the pseudo-neuter who uses *repression* is not.

Hippolytos and Phaidra embody the two possible ways of struggling *autoplastically* against the goddess. They are the fountain-heads of a culture-historical and religious evolution, in which the scene of the struggle slowly shifts from the outside to the inside. This drama therefore marks a turning point in the history of man's conception of, and relationship with, the divine.[67]

The culture-historically crucial significance of this shift of the fight against a deity from the outside to the inside helps one to understand what the Empedoklean-Freudian Nurse means by her remark: "If there be anything greater than a god, it is Aphrodite" (359f.). Such a shift in the location of the conflict inevitably implies a change also in the conception of the deity.

That Aphrodite—when experienced in a certain way—is a personification of the sexual urge is plainly stated by Hekabe, in her *agon* with Helene:[68] it is Helene's own mind that *became* the Kyprian. This evolution in the conception of the gods becomes unavoidable once the struggle with the deity is *experienced* as internal; it even modifies the hierarchy of the gods. Hippolytos believes the "subhuman" (Kitto) Artemis—the force of repression—to be the greatest deity (16).

The Nurse urges, however, that it is Aphrodite—the instinctual life force (359f.)—and Helene, though professing to experience Aphrodite as

---

[65] The mind vs. body (= behavior) contrast is strong in the famous verse 612. His body is attacked in 1416ff.

[66] Méridier (ad loc.) is singularly insensitive when he suggests that Hippolytos means that, by her suicide, Phaidra simply *usurped* the appearances of chastity; contrast Dodds, "The αἰδώς of Phaidra," op. cit., p. 103.

[67] Even though, when one views her as a person, Phaidra simply dreads unchastity as an alcoholic mother's daughter dreads whiskey, this personal dread is culture-historically irrelevant.

[68] E. *Tr.* 988; Dodds ("The αἰδώς of Phaidra," op. cit., p. 101.5) also cites here E. *fr.* 1018 N². A. Lesky ("Psychologie bei Euripides," *Entretiens Hardt*, vi, Vandoeuvres-Genève, p. 131) concurs.

external to herself, says much the same: "Kypris has power even over Zeus" (E. *Tr.* 1010ff.). No theology has ever solved the problems that arise when a deity is *experienced* internally, but is *defined* as external. Yet the very possibility of a hierarchization of the gods[69] largely depends on whether the gods are experienced as external or as internal forces. The first Greek who appears to have apprehended this, at least intuitively, is Euripides.

I do not deviate from my topic in saying a few words about Euripides' conception of the gods. Regardless of whether he speaks of them as external or as internal, *he treats them exclusively as explanations (or as labels) of the inexplicable*. In Euripides, the gods appear to begin where his senses and theories end. He needs them because he inquires deeply into the lives of men, constantly coming up against insolvable riddles. In practice, it matters little whether logic defines what is beyond the reach of understanding as an (external) ultimate cause, or psychology defines it as the irrational substratum of the mind. In practice, and as experiences, the two are the same.[70]

Viewed as external, Euripides' gods are the types of psychopathic personalities who incite others to cause trouble, but carefully stay out of the fray themselves.[71] They are also Lévi-Strauss-ian[72] "bricoleurs"— dabblers who utilize whatever is handy—who bring (separately harmless) available elements together in a manner which insures an explosion: for example, Phaidra's bad heredity and Hippolytos' sex phobia.[73] At other times, they pile suitably chosen misfortunes on a person having *a certain character makeup*—for example, on a strong character, like Hekabe—until things reach what nuclear physicists call "a critical mass." They do not *create* such materials—they only see to it that they accumulate and explode.

Euripides' often criticized "divine prologues" may well be viewed as

---

[69] Phaidra's Nurse, Hippolytos, and Helene accept a divine hierarchy; Herakles rejects it (E. *HF* 1344) but, nonetheless, claims the right to be arrogant toward arrogant deities (E. *HF* 1243), just as Hippolytos wishes he could harm Aphrodite (E. *Hipp.* 1415) (cf. Achilleus Hom. *Il.* 22.20 and Plato's criticism [*Rmp.* 391a]). Both violate the rule that one should not be angry with the gods even in calamity: E. (?) *fr.* 1078 N^2. There is no way out of these difficulties, which constitute a vicious circle. Its central difficulty is whether or not the gods are superior to—and exist outside of—man.

[70] "Euripides uses his creations to bring on-stage a tragedy played behind the scenes" . . . "It is because Aphrodite is this (scil. 'a potentially disastrous element in our nature'), an internal not an external tyrant, that the *Hippolytus* is a tragedy" (Kitto, *Greek Tragedy*, op. cit., p. 214 and note).

[71] Clinical example: Devereux, *Therapeutic Education*, op. cit., p. 132; literary example: the trouble-making officer in H. Wouk's novel, *The Caine Mutiny*, New York, 1963. On the gods' mode of acting on men, H. Lloyd-Jones, *The Justice of Zeus*, Berkeley, 1971.

[72] C. Lévi-Strauss, *La Pensée Sauvage*, Paris, 1962, pp. 26–47.

[73] Chemical analogy: sugar *mixed* with permanganate of potassium is an explosive.

descriptions of projected "experiments" with human subjects, executed in the drama. That the prologues tell what will happen is obvious. What is even more important, though less obvious, is that, in primitive and archaic belief, very often only that which is prophesied, or has at least a supernatural precedent,[74] can happen. Students of primitive religions have pointed out often enough—though with little effect—this inevitable implication of any conception of an ordered universe. A prophecy insures that things will happen the way they are supposed to happen. The trick and irony is that the prophetic prologue is heard *only* by the audience; the actors must not hear it, since otherwise they *might* avoid disaster. It is hard to separate this dramatic device from Euripides' contempt for oracles: the oracles either lie or, if they do not, they speak the truth *so* that the interested cannot understand it.[75] This may even explain why Euripides apparently respects formal oracles less than he does *dream* revelations,[76] which reflect the inner truth about man's propensity for a tragic life. Man is by nature a *theomachos* and is tragic simply because he is what he is, for this enables the "bricoleur" gods—be they external or internal—to bring about his destruction.

This is nowhere more apparent than in the tragedy of the two *theomachoi* Hippolytos and Phaidra, the futility of whose similar and yet different attempts to resist Aphrodite—whoever and whatever she may be—are equally obvious. In this sense too, Euripides is, as Aristoteles well said, "the most tragic of poets,"[77] and his *Hippolytos* a prophetic landmark in the evolution of religious thought.

Appendix I

It is often alleged that several of Euripides' plays "break" in the middle; that there are, so to speak, two dramas.[78] That much depends on what one conceives the drama to be *about*, I have tried to indicate in connection with the E. *Hec.*[79] but things can also be envisaged in another way.

---

[74] G. Devereux, *Mohave Ethnopsychiatry*², op. cit., pp. xivff.

[75] O. Fenichel, "The Misapprehended Oracle," *The Collected Papers of O. Fenichel*, ii, 1954. G. Devereux, "Considérations Psychanalytiques sur la Divination, Particulièrement en Grèce," in A. Caquot and M. Leibovici (eds.), *La Divination*, ii, 1968.

[76] Cf. the great Delphic song of the Choros (*IT*. 1260ff.); Devereux, *Dreams in Greek Tragedy*, op cit., pp. xxviiif.

[77] To claim that Aristoteles meant only that most Euripidean plays do not have a happy ending does injustice to the philosopher quite as much as to the poet. In fact, man being what he is, it could be argued that the most tragic ending imaginable is "and they lived happily ever after," for this implies that only a static Nirvana represents a real escape from life's turmoil.

[78] This is also said of S. *Aias*; it may, perhaps, be said also of some other Sophoklean plays, such as the *Trachinian Women*.

[79] Devereux, *Dreams in Greek Tragedy*, op. cit., chap. 8.

In the incriminated dramas, the first part deals with those aspects of the personages' character which make their manipulation by the gods possible.[80] The real (inner) explosion takes place somewhere in the middle and continues through the second part. The final "explosion" is external only—it is little more than a Q.E.D.

This means that, in Euripidean tragedy, the *root* of the calamity is not primarily the character structure of the principal hero or heroine—as it conspicuously is in some Sophoklean dramas. Rather, it is the *conjunction of*—the *interaction between*—two *potentially* tragic characters. Antigone, Oedipous, Aias, etc., would find a way to end calamitously, no matter *in what situation* they found themselves, no matter *with whom* they interacted. By contrast, Phaidra and Hippolytos, Iason and Medeia, and several other paired Euripidean characters need a characterologically suitable foil to bring about a tragedy. In *this* respect Sophokles' *Philoktetes* (which ends happily) is almost Euripidean, while Aischylos' surviving plays never are. Euripides is the inventor of the tragedy of *human relationships*.[81]

All this has a direct bearing upon Kitto's claim[82] that Hippolytos and Phaidra are *not* complex characters It is a question of degree. Though neurotics and a fortiori psychotics are always less differentiated and less individualized than are normal, creative persons,[83] this does not mean that the *process* which *led* to their de-differentiation and de-individualization is less complex than any other psychological process. A seeming stupidity or limitation can have extremely complex determinants.[84]

One must, above all, differentiate between the complexity of character and the complexity of illness. Phaidra's and Hippolytos' neuroses are complex indeed and it is the complexity of their illnesses which leads to

---

[80] To use the previously given analogy, the first parts reveal that sugar, a pure carbohydrate, is highly combustible; also that permanganate of potassium can release the oxygen needed for rapid combustion. Predictably, their mixture can be made to explode in the *second* parts.

[81] Dodds, "The αἰδώς of Phaidra," op. cit., emphasizes the complementarity and interdependence of Phaidra and Hippolytos, and the interplay of these two personalities (p. 104). My conclusions generalize this.

[82] Kitto, op. cit., p. 212.

[83] G. Devereux, *Basic Problems*, op. cit., chap. 1.

[84] Case 1: A patient professed not to know how urine reached the bladder. Asked to enumerate the internal organs of the body, he mentioned even the Islands of Langerhans, omitting *only* the kidneys. His apparent (functional) "nescience" (omission) masked a complexly determined refusal to know.

Case 2: A patient displayed an incredibly bad taste in the choice of his clothing. Though he dressed drably enough, every color clashed violently with every other color. So *consistent* a bad taste represented a systematic repression of good taste, since he *never once* made the *"mistake"* of wearing matching colors. His analysis revealed that he dressed as he did partly exhibitionistically, but also to insure that girls would find him attractive only "for his own sake."

the impression of the *seeming* simplicity of their character structure.

Appendix II

The Troizenian Hair Sacrifice of girls about to be married, who dedicated their locks on the tomb of Hippolytos, is often misrepresented as being solely a devout homage to Hippolytos' nobility of character. Yet Artemis says plainly (1429ff.) that this rite *also* commemorates Phaidra's love. Moreover, this practice manifestly fuses mourning and funeral rites with marriage practices[85] (see below).

For the moment I will discuss only the fusion of funeral and wedding rites in this practice, though it also has an additional, far more important and systematically ignored, aspect. The peculiarity of an intermingling of funeral and nuptial rites is often simply disregarded. This only proves once again that, at critical times, our objective knowledge is available to us *only* if it does *not* clash with our preconception.[86]

My first task is to consider what the text itself says, quite plainly: Artemis regrets Hippolytos' death. *First* she promises to punish Aphrodite by killing *her* beloved, Adonis (1416ff.), with her "arrows" ($\tau \acute{o} \xi o \iota \varsigma$).... Both Méridier and Barrett think that Aphrodite's beloved is Adonis and both point out that he was slain not by Artemis' arrows, but by a boar. But Barrett at least stresses that this boar was sent by Artemis (Apollod. 3.14.4). One should perhaps reconsider the means and mechanisms of divine scourges in the light of Lloyd-Jones' analysis of *how* the gods act at a distance.[87] The notion that it is proper to punish A by attacking B, who is linked to A by bonds of kinship or love, is found already among Australian aborigines and is exemplified in Greece by the slaying of the arrogant Niobe's innocent children.

Only *after* settling the matter of retaliation does Artemis offer to compensate Hippolytos for his cruel death, by means of the Troizenian rite (1423ff.). This, too is conventional Greek reasoning. Those who died by violence (*biaiothanatoi*) are not kindly disposed toward the living. Achilleus in Hades bitterly envies those who are still alive (Hom. *Od.* 11.488ff.) and it is perhaps more than a coincidence that Achilleus was quite as self-satisfied, smug, and paranoid as Hippolytos.

It is, thus, best for the living to propitiate the dead Hippolytos, lest this sex-phobic "hero" should harm precisely brides about to engage in the lovely works of golden Aphrodite, which Hippolytos had renounced.

---

[85] Nilsson, *Geschichte*, op. cit.; Barrett, p. 4.
[86] Devereux, *From Anxiety to Method*, op. cit., indicates that I, myself, am no exception to this rule. Clinical practice shows that the patient's inability to use information which he possesses is, at times, matched by a comparable inability of the psychoanalyst—and, of course, also of the scholar.
[87] H. Lloyd-Jones, *The Justice of Zeus*, 1961.

Hippolytos' Diagnosis

The obvious parallel to this is A. *Eum.* 848 and, indeed, all of Athene's complicated negotiations with the Erinyes. Athene's main argument is if you refrain from doing harm, you will be honored and rewarded. And it is well worth noting that even after this "deal" is completed, the people of Athens still think it prudent to watch their words and not to rely too naively on the benevolence of the Erinyes:[88] "Hush, good words ye dwellers in the land" (1035), "Hush, good words all ye people" (1038).

The people of Troizen must, it seems, compensate Hippolytos, who feels ill rewarded for his ostentatious and strenuous sexual abstinence (1367ff.). The proper persons to offer him compensation are precisely girls about to be wedded—the very girls in whose arms he refused to render delightful homage to Aphrodite. For Hippolytos, every woman's joy in the arms of a man wiser and more fortunate than he was is a "provocation"; this entitles him to "compensation," not to mention blackmail.

But this sacrifice also has two other possible meanings. I indicated elsewhere that the shearing of the bride's hair in Sparta may imply, on the one hand, a "humbling" of a proud virgin, and, on the other hand, a facilitation of the groom's "sliding" from homosexuality to heterosexuality.[89] Should either or both of these interpretations fit also the Troizenian rite, that would *not* be to Hippolytos' credit. Be that as it may, nothing is more suitable in terms of religious psychology than to have to persuade a sex-phobic dead hero to let others enjoy a happy married life. After all, it is the mad berserker Ares one supplicates for peace of mind.[90] Like much primitive prayer and ritual, the Troizenian rite, too, is apotropaic.

It is almost embarrassing—five decades after Frazer's insightful study of such problems,[91] not to speak of subsequent research work—to have to make so obvious a point. Yet, to judge by the commentaries I consulted, the point has to be made, for the dead are, nearly everywhere, believed to resent the living;[92] they envy their aliveness. A few sophisticated dogmas profess to deny this, but the practices which subtend them prove the hollowness of the denial.

The same may be said of all deities and supernaturals, and not only in Greece.[93] Curiously enough, this attitude of the gods does not seem to

---

[88] G. Devereux, *Dreams in Greek Tragedy*, op. cit., chap. 4.
[89] Devereux, "Greek Pseudo-Homosexuality," op. cit. A *Venus Calva* connection is not impossible, but unlikely.
[90] Hom. *h. Mart.*, fin.
[91] Sir J. G. Frazer, *The Fear of the Dead*, 3 vols., London, 1933–36.
[92] Even the most generous of the extraordinarily generous Mohave Indians is held to become possessive and avaricious *the moment he dies*: his previously freely lent property must be cremated with him, lest he return to claim it (G. Devereux, *Mohave Ethnopsychiatry*², 1968, pp. 431ff.).
[93] E. R. Dodds (*The Greek and the Irrational*, 1951, p. 62, n. 108) is right in most respects on this point, which even S. Ranulf (*The Jealousy of the Gods*, 2 vols., London, 1937) did not really grasp.

be cited in support of the old hypothesis that they are the deified dead. *In words*, the gods profess to lead a more satisfying "life" than the living; *in practice*, they cannot get their fill of human favors and possessions.

Zeus (Hom. *Il.* 14.313ff.) makes it obvious that only the wearing of Aphrodite's girdle makes Hera *more* attractive than mortal women. Apollon's and Dionysos' sexual life seems limited to human women and to quasi-human nymphs and the like. Other examples of a divine preference for mortal persons and for choice human possessions (fine sacrificial animals, etc.) readily come to mind. But one must note chiefly that the immortals seem to prefer human sexual partners for the same reason that some neurotics prefer prostitutes to their wives and lovers,[94] for, like human cohabitation with prostitutes, divine coitus with human partners demands no affective or continuous involvement—a fact glaringly highlighted by Marpessa's preferring Idas to Apollo.[95] It is of some significance that the gods' only choice is between incest (with goddesses) and casual fornication with (sometimes unwilling: Kreusa, Kassandra) human women. This finding is psychologically significant, for Freud has shown that a preference for prostitutes is a defense against incestuous fantasies.[96]

In fact, in order to lead a prosperous and "civilized" life, the gods depend wholly on human "supplies." It is man who "domesticates" the gods. Without their worshippers they would not only lack the basic necessities of life,[97] but would behave like uncontrollable and capricious wild beasts—as, e.g., Artemis does whenever she is "forgotten" in a sacrifice (Hom. *Il.* 9.533ff., etc.). Theologically, this may seem an expression of righteous indignation; psychologically the "divine beast" is safe only when well fed. This is only to be expected: man's conception of the gods is modelled upon the child's image of the adult, who habitually behaves toward the child like an irascible psychopath.[98] All else is euphemistic self-reasurance, modelled upon the "transformation" of the Erinyes into Eumenides—*at a price*. Hippolytos is no exception to this rule. His cult proves him to be both dangerous and bribable; he is as envious and narcissistic in death as he was in life.

I can now present my last and strongest argument. In many parts of the Semitic Near East every woman had to prostitute herself at least once in her life, in a Semitic sex-goddess' temple; a custom also found in

---

[94] Freud, "On the Most Universal Degradation," op. cit.
[95] Hom. *Il.* 9.534; Apollod. 1.7.8; cf. for Koronis Pindaros *P.* 3.
[96] Freud, "On the Most Universal Degradation," op. cit.
[97] Zeus persuaded Demeter to let mankind survive only because mankind is *necessary to the gods* (Hom. *h. Cer.* 310ff.); cf. the blockading of the gods in Ar. *Aves.* 1230ff., 1515ff., etc.
[98] G. Devereux, "Charismatic Leadership and Crisis," in W. Muensterberger and S. Axelrod (eds.), *Psychoanalysis and the Social Sciences*, IV, 1955.

Hippolytos' Diagnosis

parts of Cyprus. What Herodotos (1.199) does *not* report is that, at Byblos, this ritual defloration could be replaced by a hair sacrifice[99]— i.e., by the equivalent of the Troizenian sacrifice to Hippolytos. This means that, at Troizen, this sex-phobic "hero" received a sacrifice which was the equivalent of the ritual defloration of girls doing for a while service as temple prostitutes, and which recalls (in part) Hippolytos' plan to have men buy children *in the temples* (618ff.). But the rite also fits the Greek notion that hair clipping is a humiliation—proud fillies, who refuse to be mounted by a jackass, had their manes clipped to make them humble[100]—and Hippolytos' contempt for women and his desire to humble them need hardly be recalled once more. This, in turn, can easily be linked with funereal hair clipping.[101]

Psychologically, the nexus between funereal hair-clipping and a humiliating hair clipping is quite obvious. Freud notwithstanding,[102] it is self evident that mourning, too, involves self-depreciation, as is shown by the ugliness of mourning costumes, etc.,[103] and by Kwakiutl Indian mourning reactions: a loss through death is equated with a public humiliation.[104] What subtends the variety of contexts in which hair is sacrificed is the infantile notion that sex is not only "impure" (as is death in Greek practice) and humiliating *to the woman*,[105] but may actually be compared to death.[106]

Summing up, the Troizenian hair sacrifice commemorates both Hippolytos' fate and Phaidra's love. Far from honoring the memory of his "virtuous chastity," it corresponds to the ritual defloration of temporary temple prostitutes. As a substitute for a divine *ius primae noctis*, it degrades the bride-to-be and compensates Hippolytos for the pleasures of love which he renounced in life.

How students of this drama failed to see this is something best passed under silence. For it is a fact that "in each case"[107] Hippolytos' precinct contained a temple of Aphrodite—and not, as one "might"

---

[99] G. A. Barton, *A Sketch of Semitic Origins*, London, 1902, p. 83.
[100] S. *fr*. 659P = Ael. *NA* 11.18, 2.10; Apul. *Metamorph*. 11, etc.
[101] Hom. *Il*. 23.250f.; A. *Choe*. 116; E. *Alc*. 75f.; cf. 428 and A. M. Dale, ad loc. For clipping hair from the head of a sacrificial animal, cf. Hom. *Il*. 19.254.
[102] S. Freud, "Mourning and Melancholia," *Standard Edition*, xiv, 1957.
[103] G. Devereux, *Dreams in Greek Tragedy*, op. cit., chap. 3.
[104] R. Benedict, *Patterns of Culture*, Boston, 1934.
[105] This is clearly a latently homosexual *male* fantasy (G. Devereux, *Ethnopsychoanalysis*, 1977, chap. 7).
[106] Alexander the Great felt that coitus reminded him of his mortality (Plu. V. *Alex*. 22.4). Two promiscuous and totally frigid young women said that during coitus they felt "devoured" by the partner from within. Cf. tribes in which "to eat" is either a euphemism or a vulgar, slang word for: "to copulate." Certain women's fear of orgasm is furthermore rooted in the belief that orgasm = death or madness.
[107] Barrett, op. cit., p. 5.

expect, a temple of Artemis. I suggest that, since it would be absurd to find a temple of Zeus in Salmoneus' or in Ixion's precinct, or of Aphrodite in the precinct of Diomedes, or simply a heroon of Paris in Achilleus', of Lykomedes in Theseus', of Deianeira in Herakles' precinct, it would be "absurd" to find a temple of Aphrodite in the precinct of her "victim" Hippolytos. I would therefore not in the least be surprised were new *evidence* to show that Hippolytos was, originally, a ritual deflowerer—or, as some suspect, a hero linked originally with Aphrodite rather than with Artemis, though Euripides' drama makes no allusion to such antecedents.

I note, in fine, that the other known hair sacrifices of brides, as listed by Barrett (op. cit., p. 4, n. 3), are, without exception, offered to *female* personages: to the virginal heroine Iphinoe, (daugher of Alkathoos; Paus. 1.43.4), who has vague connections with Artemis, but of whom nothing else is known; to Hera, protectress of marriages (*gamostolos*); to the Moirai (who give each person his, or her, "portions" in life); to Athene, the virginal champion of male supremacy; and, finally, to Artemis who, like Athene, was a virgin but, unlike her, not well-disposed to the male of the species. How a (half-)male like Hippolytos ended up by receiving the hair sacrifices of brides can, I think, be explained only as I explained it above. For though religion is seldom truly logical, it always makes "sense," in terms of the peculiar "logic" of the unconscious and of the emotions. Unless my analysis of the "suitableness" of the hair sacrifice of brides to a personage like Hippolytos is accepted, I doubt that any other rationale for that offering can be formulated.

5

Epilogue: Character, Action, Fantasy

According to Aristoteles' *Poetics* (1450a15ff., etc.), tragedy is about action rather than character. If this view is accepted, the complaints of some critics that in S. *Trach.*, as well as in E. *HF*, Herakles turns up late in the play, while Deianeira in S. *Trach.* and Phaidra in E. *Hipp.* disappear early, are futile. It is primarily the *action* that must have a configuration (*Gestalt*)—a fact sensed by those who argue that both the *Iliad* and the *Odyssey* "originally" ended sooner than do the versions we possess. Whether the reasoning of these critics is persuasive is another matter and does not concern me here.

The Aristotelian view appears to require the play to have a high degree of temporal integration (*Gestalt* of the plot), but *not necessarily* also a high "spatial" integration, in terms of complex *and* fully interlocking characterizations.

In reality a complex characterization is nearly always present, though Zürcher, blinded to facts by Aristoteles' dictum,[1] could not see it.

In Greek tragedy personages are integrated in terms of "to do" or "to have" rather than in terms of "to be." Given the importance of the plot as against that of character *in drama*, this is—in terms of Aristotelian perspectives—as "natural" as that, *in life*, character should outweigh action. In Greek drama, the plot reveals—i.e., "creates"—character; in life, character creates the life-"plot." The great dramatist's art seeks to persuade his audience that a given incident—in which some aspect of a particular personage first becomes perceptible—simply *reveals* something that was "there" *all along*. A failure to perceive this skill of the Greek tragedians led both the younger Wilamowitz[2] and Zürcher to the absurd conclusion that there is not true psychological characterization either in Sophokles or in Euripides. Needless to say, the errors of these critics are due largely to their *total* unawareness of what real psychology—as distinct from "literary psychologizing"—really is.[3] Yet it is precisely the capacity of Greek tragedy to reveal *new* aspects of character

---

[1] W. Zürcher, *Die Darstellung des Menschen im Drama des Euripides*, Basel, 1947.
[2] T. v. Wilamowitz-Moellendorff, *Die dramatische Technik des Sophokles*, Berlin, 1917.
[3] G. Devereux, *Dreams in Greek Tragedy*, op. cit., General Introduction.

through the plot *while* persuading one that these—just now revealed—aspects of the character had been "there" all along, that differentiates it from plot-less modern "character" plays.

Now, man can and must be integrated in both "time" and "space." One can be integrated in time by changing oneself to fit events following their logic, but also by remaining "stationary"—i.e. "oneself," following one's own "logic." In the same sense one can contrast archaic "to be" or "to have" statues with post-classical "to do" statues. Hence, an author belonging to a period of rapid, bludgeoning change, will delineate characters which resist change either by not changing at all (like the enduring *"Dulder"* Herakles) or else by an extreme and shrewd habitual pliancy (like Odysseus of the many wiles). But one must view matters differently if the author (or his personages) belong to a polysegmented (Durkheimian) "caste" or even "class" society, in which any "social mobility" entails an inner split, which accepts external change *through* Ego-threatening adaptive actions. Thus, though Euripides' enslaved Andromache (E. *Androm.* 56) is still called "princess" by some, she replies with: "Dear fellow-slave" (verse 64).

The only way the poet can insure the inner coherence of his personages, in a play whose "hero" is the action rather than any particular personage, is to depict, by *temporal* means ("plot"), the personages as being "integrated" and stable in an internal "space" : "character." This approach fits a kind of fatalism—that in which, regardless of the past, a total freedom of choice is *not* possible at *every* moment; where the subject's freedom is "diminished" by oaths, by the counsel (will) of Zeus or by the "portion" allotted to him by the Moirai and their like. But this "constriction" of an *incoherent*, weathervane-like "freedom" becomes the very essence of free will where there is an emphasis on *structured* (*non*-anecdotal) action. An action endowed with *Gestalt*—and capable of giving structural coherence to those through whom the action manifests itself—marks creative periods that have not only discovered causality (the "because-therefore" sequence)[4] but, being fascinated by it, can exploit it in the "temporal" arts. This also fits the discovery of genuine personal responsibility (e.g., by Solon), as "responsibility" is defined by Adkins.[5]

Character-drama, *stricto sensu*, belongs to a very different universe of discourse. It fits sin, accursedness and impurity more than "crime" or "guilt." It calls for "coping" rather than for "growing" and ties in with the absence of a *social* recognition of individuality.[6]

In Aischylean drama in particular one *is* a Hero—one is *not* the hero

---

[4] A. L. Kroeber ("Seven Mohave Myths," *University of California, Anthropological Records*, 11.1, 1948 [p. 65, note 137]) observes that this sequence is made explicit only in a single detail of one of the many Mohave myths he had collected.

[5] A. W. H. Adkins, *Merit and Responsibility*, Oxford, 1960.

[6] G. Devereux, "Social Structure and the Economy of Affective Bonds," *Psychoanalytic Review* 29: 303–14, 1942.

of a tragedy. Aischylean tragedy is mainly a tragedy of the Hero. The Hero is at most in (but not "of") the tragedy, whose real hero (in the modern sense) is action: Time, as an ordered sequence of events.[7]

Thus, Zürcher is, in one sense, *almost right*, though in the *wrong way*, for one can still ask *legitimately*: How did Hippolytos or Orestes get to be "*that* way"—how did they become what they are? Once "formed" by myths or by the poet, the Hero is stable and his actions can be studied in terms of his (supposed) *past* and of his discernible, continuously stable (but not simple, let alone simplistic), *self*. This does not permit one to confuse an *intricate* stability with a kaleidoscopic characterological hopscotch. I hope I made this stability and coherence of the personality evident not only with respect to the central figure of drama, but also with regard to the other personages on whom the "shape" of the hero's fate depends.

In a far from figurative sense, the crux of this network of relationships between the "hero" and those whose actions maneuver him into his position of "central figure," somewhat resembles the problems that arise when one studies the many, and at times "contradictory," meanings a word may have. For the key problem is not the multiplicity and diversity of meanings a word may possess, but the discovery of the hidden pattern which the *totality* of these variegated meanings presupposes. In other words, the problem is not that of splitting up the word "gift" two ways: a "present" (in English), a "poison" (in German); or of showing that δέχομαι can mean a welcome and a hostile ambush;[8] or of dissecting the meaning of μῆτις into countless slices. One's task is to reveal the latent, unifying pattern which brings out the *total* meaning of such a many-faceted word as, e.g., Detienne and Vernant[9] brought out that of the word μῆτις. For the *basic* meaning of that word is precisely its *capacity* to mean many things, so that each of its specific meanings can be used to shed light upon its (*present*) total meaning. Similarly, the central meaning, which the word "hand" possesses *today* includes the many non-anatomical meanings (e.g., "hands of the clock") that this originally anatomical term picked up in the course of time. Also, even though the watch both "runs" (in English) or "goes" (*marche*, in French), its "needles" (French) are called in English: "hands," *not* "feet" (legs). The choice of the term "hands" underlines, I think, the *precision* of their motion and their *pointing* rather than their movement ("run") per se.

There are things of this kind to discover also in tragedy—most notably the fact that *one* dramatic personage *can* clearly be viewed as the *fantasy-projection of another*. Orestes is assuredly what he "is"—but an important part of what he "is," is his capacity (and obligation) to be also

---

[7] Devereux, *Ethnopsychoanalysis*, op. cit., chap. 11.
[8] G. Devereux, *Tragédie et Poésie Grecques*, Paris, 1975, chap. 8.
[9] M. Detienne and J. P. Vernant: *Les Ruses de l'Intelligence*, Paris, 1974.

what Elektra desperately *fantasizes* him to be—for only if he is *just that* can he gratify *her* needs. Still, he manages to remain "himself," simply by *making* Elektra's needs his own: he *is* the one who *assents* to being his sister's fantasy, the avenger of *her* wrongs, which he *agrees* to view as their *joint* wrongs.

As regards Hippolytos, matters are more complex. It is at times advantageous to view difficult matters from an unusual angle, even if this perspective momentarily leads to a maximal distortion of most features of the object *so viewed*. In accordance with this heuristic finding, I propose here to view briefly both Phaidra and Theseus as *projections* of Hippolytos' fantasies—even though, in so doing, I momentarily seem to substitute Hippolytos for Euripides as the "author" of the play—so as to find out if this approach *can* teach one anything new and useful.

Phaidra and her agony can be viewed as projections of Hippolytos' needs and fantasies. Hippolytos concedes that Phaidra struggled hard against her infatuation (verses 1034f.); Artemis, too, admits as much (1300ff.). One learns that her struggles against temptation made Phaidra weak and anorexic and changed her appearance. They caused her to isolate herself, to feel that her limbs are broken and her head-band tight. She is also thirsty (dehydrated) and feels the need to rest outdoors. She longs to hunt and to drive horses. Her reason is twisted (παρακόπτει φρένας), she is a mad victim of ἄτη. She blushes in retrospect from shame and sheds tears. She suffers, longs for death, and expects nothing from the future; she is (allegedly) silent—though in reality she is loquacious enough, except as regards the *cause* of her wretched state. She looks so starved and ravaged that her face would betray her secret, were Theseus there to see it (280).

The obstinate clinging to sexual abstinence, the rigid if narcissistic self-control which Hippolytos has perfected for himself in the course of the years during which apparently no one "tempted" him, have no meaning or purpose *unless* they are viewed as preparations for an almost incredibly extreme "test" or temptation of a highly specific (sexual) kind. His long training would be of no use were Hippolytos confronted with a *different kind* of temptation. In the same sense, the harsh, lifelong training of the Spartans for military exploits only—their acquiring an extreme contempt for death, a perfect military discipline, etc.—did *not* enable them, after the Peloponnesian war, to cope also with the temptations of wealth. The stern, dour, ascetic soldiers of Sparta became highly corruptible officials in conquered foreign cities. Their long training for one kind of situation of stress did not give rise to a "transfer of learning." Having never *imagined* themselves confronted with the temptations of wealth in the absence of immediate supervision, they lacked (*even in imagination*) a "preparatory stance,"[10] anticipating *that* temptation.

Hippolytos prepared himself all his life for extreme sexual temptation and, therefore, quite unconsciously but also quite inevitably, for an *oedipal* kind of sexual temptation. That temptation *had* to be multivalent if it was to be a quintessence—a concentrate—of *all* that could revive his many subjective problems: his bastardy, the early loss of his mother, his resentment of both his mother and his father, his being raised far from his father, and so forth. Needless to say, he was "set for" that struggle, but also "set for" the punishment (pain, distress) *of* those responsible for his predicament, and, last but not least, for his ultimate "moral" triumph over those "responsible" for his "bad luck." But since these "persecutors" were *also* his own kin, no "victory" over them could be unaccompanied by guilt. Hippolytos *had* to vanquish and, in vanquishing, he *had* to die, so as to expiate his oedipal "victory."

It is therefore easy to suppose that Phaidra's distress fits well the fantasies a bastard—and especially one as sensitive about his bastardy as Hippolytos—would have *about his mother*. It matters little whether Hippolytos *imagined* that Phaidra struggled, as *his* mother had struggled (in vain!), against her love for Theseus, or whether Hippolytos bitterly compared Phaidra's gallant struggle to his mother's *failure* to resist temptation. *In either case* Phaidra's state would correspond to something Hippolytos did fantasize, in connection *with his own mother*—which would, of course, make *his* plight that much more acute. Under these circumstances, the Amazon's "sin," which made Hippolytos a bastard (and, by a ricochet, his mother a "slut"), parallels Phaidra's incestuous desires (and seductiveness) and, of course, also her self-exonerating lies, which—by making Hippolytos into the kind of rapist he *imagines* his father to have been—destroy him in the end. For, *unlike* the average bastard, Hippolytos blames his father less than *his mother*. This alone explains his misogyny. In the same sense, Theseus, too, can be viewed as a projection of Hippolytos' fantasy world: the father—himself a bastard—is the amorist his bastard son *refuses to be*; he is a lover of tempting women and also the king his bastard cannot hope to be. He is, in fine, the warrior whose exploits Hippolytos can only approximate through routine hunting and the like.

Actually, the affinity between Hippolytos' sex-phobia and his father's uninhibited career as an amorist is even closer than I have indicated so far. It is manifest even in Hippolytos' ultimate disaster. Indeed, the destruction of Hipplytos—whom Phaidra's lie *makes out* to be the kind of rapist Hippolytos *imagines* his father *to have been* with respect to his mother—is, in a sense, the *kind* of punishment Theseus *should have*

---

[10] O. H. Mowrer, "Preparatory Stance (Expectancy): Some Methods of Measurement," *Psychological Monographs*, vol. 52, n. 2, 1940.

suffered for his (imaginary) rape of Hippolyte. The irony—expressed in the form of hidden symmetries—is further increased by the self-evident fact that the sexually phobic Hippolytos is punished for a rape he did *not* commit in fact—though, as indicated elsewhere in this study, he did probably commit it in an unconscious fantasy—and he is punished precisely by his sexually uninhibited father, Theseus. In short, this father, whom Hippolytos *imagines* to have *genuinely* raped Hippolyte, is the one who punishes Hippolytos for a rape he did *not* commit *in fact*.

Theseus is much more than Hippolytos' counter-ideal. He is everything his Oedipus-complex-ridden bastard son does not even dare to approximate. This forces Hippolytos to glory in his *renunciation* of all he *dares not* undertake, or be.

Though this experimentation with an unusual way of looking at facts must not be carried too far, I stress that the above findings are far from unique. In Euripides' *Herakles the Madman*, Theseus is once again the *projection* of the central personage's—of the crushed Herakles'—a "rescue fantasy," which happens to fit the "real" Theseus of the myth. And it is of some importance that, in Euripides' *Children of Herakles*, Iolaos' final actions are bewildering,[11] chiefly because Iolaos *cannot* accept either Demophoon or Hyllos as incarnated rescue-fantasies. As a typical "rheumatoid arthritis personality," he must *pretend* to be *his own rescuer*.

It is, I think, mainly because Phaidra is a projection of Hippolytos' fantasy that Euripides' play is called *Hippolytos* and *not* (like Sophokles', Seneca's, and Racine's plays): *Phaidra*. For Euripides' *Andromache* could have been called *Hermione*, as his *Elektra* could have been called *Orestes*, if only the importance of their respective *actions* mattered. This point also explains, I think, why the Sophoklean Oidipous of *King Oidipous* is so different from the one of *Oidipous at Kolonos*. In each of these plays Oidipous, *as a personage*, is a *different* person's fantasy projection. In S. *OT* he is chiefly the Choros' fantasy; in S. *OC*, he is, first and last, Antigone's fantasy.

It goes, of course, without saying that, in great drama, the fantasies of *each* personage can be held to shape the characters of *all* the other personages. These fantasies regularly form a structured whole. It is this projected *fantasy source* of Greek dramatic characters which is responsible for the "*illusion*" of their seeming "immobility,"[12] for it is clearly *not* the Hero but *only* the theater-goer who experiences a *katharsis*. And it stands to reason that John Doe's *image* of Richard Roe *necessarily* changes *more slowly* than Richard Roe will *actually* change.[13]

---

[11] G. Devereux, *Tragédie et Poésie Grecques*, op. cit., chap. 6.
[12] L. H. G. Greenwood, *Aspects of Euripidean Tragedy*, 1953, is particularly insensitive to this fact.
[13] A satirical hit song, of around 1960, makes the wife of a newly psychoanalyzed man

One may even assume that, in some respects, people's fantasies *about others* are *more realistic* than are their (character shaping) *fantasies of themselves*. Hippolytos does at least *threaten* to break his oath (verse 612), but cannot grasp *in time*, that, in view of his threat, Phaidra had *some* justification for *actually* lying about him. Only much later does he manage to concede that Phaidra had at least *tried* to be virtuous (1034f.). But, even so, he never quite manages to see how *utterly* devoid of grace and humanity he himself remains to the bitter end. He probably understands in the end why Phaidra lied even beyond the grave, but never realizes that his own silence was *not* actuated by his fatuous virtue, but by an unconscious awareness of his (fantasied) oedipal guilt.

Phaidra's fantasy of Theseus is relatively realistic and also socioculturally well anchored. She is manifestly a young woman burdened with the heritage of a sexually twisted and even perverted feminine family. Her mother cohabited with Poseidon's bull and bore the half-human Minotauros. Her sister loved Theseus at a time when the latter was still Minos' tribute-slave,[14] and she, in one tradition, already the bride of Dionysos. Also, she betrayed for Theseus' sake not only her half-brother, the Minotaur, but also Minos and, possibly, Dionysos as well. In Greek myths such girls[15] are regularly killed by the men for whose sake they betrayed their fathers. Furthermore, in another version, Ariadne was claimed later on by Dionysos—i.e., she presumably became a dissolute Mainad[16]—and was killed for her wrongdoings by Artemis. Also, Phaidra was married to an amorist almost old enough to be her father—for Hippolytos cannot have been much younger than she was. In her fantasy this paternal husband was apparently both a seductive and stern oedipal parent, whose cuckolding (which she both craves and dreads to actualize) is, in some ways, patterned on the betrayal of other fathers by amorous daughters, such as Komaitho, Skylla, Ariadne, etc. In other words, in accordance with the mythical models just cited, Phaidra's suicide is indirectly, but also quite manifestly, caused by the man for whose sake she wished to betray her (fatherly) husband. I must therefore note, at least in passing, that Hippolytos' admirers systematically minimize *his* responsibility for Phaidra's suicide. In this drama Phaidra obviously visualises Theseus *only* as her lawful husband and not also as her passionate lover—which his mourning *shows him to be*.

---

say to him: "I cannot adjust to you, who got adjusted to me." This may explain why divorces after psychoanalysis are perhaps more common than are job-changes, because jobs are of necessity "functionally specific," whereas the pre-analytic marriage may *not* have been functionally *sufficiently* diffuse (T. Parsons' terminology, but my interpretation).

14 Cf. Freud, "On the Most Universal Degradation," op. cit.

15 Komaitho, Apollod. 2.4.7, etc.; Skylla, ibid., 3.15.5f.—the latter myth is linked with that of Minos and may have been some overtones of castration (Tzetz. *Lvc.* 650).

16 G. Devereux, "Trance and Orgasm in Euripides' *Bakchai*," in A. Angoff and D. Barth (eds.), *Parapsychology and Anthropology*, New York, 1974.

This, as well as the age difference, makes it possible for her to maneuver, in fantasy, Theseus into the role of the betrayed father and herself into that of the daughter enamoured of her father's arch-foe, who finally "punishes" her for her betrayal of family ties.

There is no need, in this context, to go into details about the Nurse. It is almost certain that, in the second (surviving) *Hippolytos*, she does *for* Phaidra—but also *against* Phaidra's conscious will—that which, in the lost first *Hippolytos*, Phaidra did *for herself*. The Nurse is, thus, not Phaidra's fantasy, but merely an instrumental exteriorization of the selfsame wishes which, in her own person (and psyche), Phaidra suppresses and asserts to be Ego alien (= detrimental to her fame). In a sense, the Nurse is a naive and homey equivalent of the Procuress' dreamed voice in Aischylos' *Prometheus Bound*.[17] In the surviving *Hippolytos*, Phaidra can have the αἰδώς, so admirably discussed by Dodds,[18] simply because the earthy Nurse *permits* her to treat, if *not* her *desire*, then at least her *wish* to have her desire *gratified*, as Ego alien. This does *not* decrease the realism of Euripides' characterization of the Nurse; it implies only that, in this drama, the Nurse is no one's fantasy projection and also that, like Theseus, she, too, is a practical realist strayed into a world where sensible and simple solutions—operative and efficacious in the world of sane people—become vicious circles undistinguishable from booby traps. In that specific sense the Nurse is akin to Hippolytos' sober servant, who is the spokesman of reason and measure—and, in a way, even similar to Theseus—at least as I see him.

As for Theseus, he fantasizes very little: in the midst of fantasy-haunted persons he trustingly clings to *reality*—or at least to the *appearances* of reality. His fault—if fault it be—is to approach two lunatics—unaware that, having already gone "through the looking-glass," they live in a fantasmatic world of their own making. Theseus' initial approach to his son is that of a decent if disappointed (and angry) father—to Phaidra, that of a sane and trusting husband. He is unable to distinguish fantasies (very real for those who evolve them) from reality—and at times even from lies. No one in the play is a projection of *his* fantasy. He is doomed as, in our day and age, a sane man is doomed when caught in the riptide of the lunatic ideologies of fanatics. He perfectly exemplifies La Rochefoucauld's maxim that it is mad indeed to try to be sane all by oneself. In that sense, at least, the tragedy of Theseus is a timeless one. He is the perennial sanely realistic visitor to the topsy-turvy lunatic asylum described by Edgar Allen Poe in "The Method of Dr. Tarr and Professor Fether."

And yet, the hope of the world rests on the small band of such naive

---

[17] G. Devereux, *Dreams in Greek Tragedy*, op. cit., chap. 2.
[18] E. R. Dodds, "The αἰδώς of Phaidra," *Classical Review* 29: 102-4, 1929.

realists, who, even in the act of *mistaking* the delusions of others for realities, implicitly reaffirm the primacy of reality over delusions—and therefore of poetry over the coquetries of madness.

I am aware, of course, that my appraisal of Theseus will displease many. But I wonder how any one of my potential critics would react if, returning from an—apparently ritual—voyage, he found that his wife had just hanged herself, leaving a letter in which she accuses her peculiar, sex-phobic stepson of rape—especially since Hippolytos' ostentatious prudishness tends to make the accusation *credible* not only to the criminal psychologist but even to the good novelist.[19] Hence, I suppose that, under comparable conditions, Theseus' critics would also blow their tops, especially if they had fathered a rabidly sex-phobic and somewhat peculiar eccentric.

The blame Artemis heaps on Theseus for Hippolytos' death (1285–1325) is also held to confirm Theseus' violence, irascibility, and lack of good sense. But this "subhuman goddess" (Kitto) is not an objective character witness. She takes pleasure in Theseus' grief, she almost claims that conclusive evidence was lacking—a view with which no trial lawyer would agree. She blames Theseus for not consulting diviners, whom Euripides notoriously distrusted. Yet, a few verses later, Artemis concedes that verbal evidence—emerging from a confrontation of Hippolytos with Phaidra—was not available (1336f.). Moreover, by verse 1404, even Artemis is obliged to admit that Theseus and Phaidra, too, were Aphrodite's victims. But, by verse 1420, her divine savagery once more gets the upper hand: she plans to get even with Aphrodite by killing an (innocent) man, dear to the love-goddess.

On the whole, Artemis as a character witness is simply not credible. Her partisanship and violence are as flagrant as her unscrupulous vindictiveness. She is completely unable to discard her prejudices and preferences. The only one of her opinions of Theseus that carries weight is her admission that the misleading appearances were *completely* persuasive and that Theseus had no means of testing their validity by forensic means.

I hold that, under the same circumstances, anyone else would also have found Hippolytos guilty of a deed he did *not* commit. Hence, Theseus is not a violent fool, nor does his judicial error sanctify Hippolytos—it only causes him to deserve compassion.

This being said, I concede that Theseus was an absentee father for Hippolytos—as were most Athenian fathers of that period (Pl. *La.*, init.).

---

[19] In Stephen Becker's *A Covenant with Death*, New York, 1964, it is not the both dissolute and cuckolded husband, but an inhibited puritan neighbor who murders the town's provocative belle. Any textbook of criminology will confirm that the rapist is, as a rule, a sexually inhibited person.

The charge that he was an absentee husband is unprovable. That he felt guilt toward Hippolytos, for having neglected him, is possible, and if he did feel guilt, he probably resented the son for whom he proved so inadequate a father.[20] Unfortunately nothing in the play directly confirms these plausible suppositions.

There remains the crucial problem of whether Theseus understood his son or failed to understand him. Méridier holds that Theseus knew his son inside out,[21] a view with which I concur. There is no shred of evidence *in* the play that could serve to invalidate Theseus' characterization of his son. The praise he lavishes on him later—after his innocence is revealed by Artemis—is relief over not having to carry the burden of ritual soilure and a measure of atonement for the injustice he had unwittingly perpetrated.

In short, I find it hard to doubt Theseus' angry characterization of his son and accept as the Gospel his contrite praise for the dying young man.

Appendix: The Tanais Story

Introduction

It is proposed to discuss here the Tanais "myth"—inspired primarily, though not exclusively, by the Hippolytos myth—as a sample of late and syncretistic pseudo-mythopoiesis, which raises a number of important substantive and methodological problems.

The Tanais "myth" is known chiefly through Pseudo-Plutarch's *de fluviis* 14.1. Other allusions to it do not suffice to prove that this story was believed to be an authentic myth.

According to Ps.-Plutarch, Tanais was the son of Berossos and of the Amazon Lysippe.[22] He worshipped only Ares and hated women. This so angered Aphrodite that she made him fall in love with his own mother. Tanais sought to escape his anxiety-arousing and uncontrollable passion by drowning himself in the Amazonias river, which thereafter became known as the Tanais river.

After his suicide, he was accorded divine honors by the Massagetai (Max. Tyr. 2.8).

Some scholars assume that the Aphrodite who punished Tanais was called Aphrodite Tanais. Others deny that the relevant text[23] implies this. They hold that, in *this* context, Tannais is a corruption of Anais = Anahitis.[24]

---

[20] I owe these suggestions to Professor Segal.
[21] In his edition, p. 20, note.
[22] Hyg. *fab.* (*excerpta . . . genealogica* 6, p. 2 [Rose]) makes him the son of Okeanos and Thetys.
[23] Iamblichos Dram. 9 (Photios, *bibl.* c. 94 p. 756 = Parthenios 42 Passow).
[24] For such corruptions of the name of that non-Greek goddess, see Strabon 11.8.4; also Eustathios, *ad Dionys. Perieget* 846; and *ad Hom. Il.* 987.11.

Epilogue: Character, Action, Fantasy 151

The Connections

Geography: The Tanais myth is set in Amazon country; Hippolytos mother was an Amazon.

Genealogy:
(1) *Father*:
  (a)*Berossos*: no comparison with Theseus is possible; data are lacking.
  (b)*Okeanos*: Theseus' father was the *sea-god* Poseidon (and/or Aigeus, King of Athens).
(2) *Mother*
  (a) *The Amazon Lysippe*, whose name is the symmetrical equivalent of that of Hippolyte, mother of Hippolytos.
  (b)*Thetys*: only a remote nexus, via Okeanos and Poseidon.

The fact that Hyginus gave sea deity parents to Tanais may be related to Tanais' death by drowning, rather than to some aspect of the Hippolytos myth.

The Exclusive Worship of Ares, chief deity and even father of the Amazons, corresponds to Hippolytos' exclusive dedication to Artemis, who was an important goddess of the Amazons (D.S. 4.16); they even had a special cult of Artemis Tauropolos (D.S. 2.46). There will be more anon about this Artemis of the bulls.

Tanais' hatred of women, though obviously patterned on the misogyny of Hippolytos, may *perhaps* be correlated also with the eunuchoidism (?) of the (androgynous?) Skythian 'Ενάρεες (*Hdt.* 4.67; Hp. *Aër.* 22). This hypothesis is the more tenable as the two impious and war-loving persons of Greek myth who worshipped *only* their *own* spears were:

(1) Parthenopaios (Maiden Face?), son of the Amazon-like Atalante (A. *Sept.* 529ff.).

(2) Kaineus, who had originally been a woman.[25] Thus, Skythian effeminacy would accord well with an obsessive, incestuous fixation on the mother.[26]

Incest: In the Hippolytos myth it is Phaidra who is haunted by an incestuous love; in the Tanais story it is the young man. The Tanais story also "upgrades" the amorous stepmother, making her the young man's own mother. This "upgrading" of the stepmother to the rank of mother confirms my view that, for Hippolytos, love for Phaidra would be genuinely and totally incestuous. The incest theme's (literary) "intensification"

[25] Ant. Lib. 17; sch. AR 1.57; etc. Cf. G. Devereux, "The Awarding of a Penis as Compensation for Rape," *International Journal of Psycho-Analysis* 38: 398-401, 957; id., *Femme et Mythe*, Paris, 1982.
[26] Although it is in many respects quite fanciful and factually slipshod, the first chapter of H. Deutsch, *A Psychoanalytic Study of the Myth of Dionysus and Apollo*, New York, 1969, brings out well the effeminate Dionysos' mother fixation.

simply replaces the stepmother with the real mother, whom she unconsciously represents even in the Hippolytos myth.

Moral Quandry: In the Hippolytos myth, as in Sophokles' *Oidipous the King* (980ff.), the "son's" anxieties are minimized by the mother equivalent. In fact, Euripides' Phaidra, though painfully aware of *her own* moral predicament, seems unaware of the moral problem incest would represent *for Hippolytos*. By contrast, the Phaidras of Ovidius and of Seneca *are*, as noted, aware of Hippolytos' *moral* resistances. The short Tanais story mentions *only* the anguish of the son, who apparently makes no advances to his mother.

The incest is completed in the case of Oidipous; the incestuous goal is not attained in the case of Hippolytos and of Tanais.

Suicide: Oidipous only blinded himself, but Hyginus (*fab.* 242) considers that, by this means he actually killed himself. That Hippolytos' "accident" was a suicide in disguise was made evident above. Tanais' death is, by contrast, a genuine suicide, described as such.

Water and Death: Water plays no role in Oidipous' self-aggression. In the Hyppolytos myth, the immediate cause of the fatal chariot accident is a monstrous bull emerging *from* the *sea*. In the Tanais story the young man leaps *into* the *Amazonias* river, to drown himself.

The Drowning Symbolism: Biologists have noted that coitus, especially at the moment of orgasm, involves respiratory anomalies related to suffocation,[27] i.e., to drowning.

The Amazon-son's leap *into* the *Amazonias* river obviously symbolizes incest. In some simple organisms "coitus" consists in the male's piercing of—and total and permanent disappearance into—the female;[28] "coitus" consists in the *total* penetration of the male into the body of the female, whose body then "absorbs" his body entirely; this extreme situation corresponds to Ferenczi's view that, in fantasy, coitus represents a partly successful return to the womb.[29] In other instances (praying mantis, etc.), the female devours the male during copulation.[30] In still another instance, fertilization takes place only after the male is already in the process of being digested.[31] And, as Caillois notes (p. 36), in some insects the structure of the female's *mouth* is very similar to that of her *genital tract*.[32]

The Amazon-son Tanais' fatal leap into the Amazonias river is, thus,

---

[27] R. Caillois, *Le Mythe et l'Homme*[2], Paris, 1972, p. 78.
[28] V. Dröscher, *Ils Se Déchirent et Ils S'Aiment*, Paris, 1975, p. 28; cf. Caillois, op. cit., p. 62: myth (Eskimo) equivalent.
[29] S. Ferenczi, *Thalassa*, Albany, NY, 1938, p. 18.
[30] Caillois, op. cit., chap. 2.
[31] V. Dröscher, op. cit.
[32] Caillois cites W. Wesché, "The Genitalia of Both Sexes in the Diptera, and their Relation to the Armature of the Mouth," *Transactions of the Linnean Society*, 2d series, Zoology IX, 1906.

a fatal *symbolic approximation* of the incest his suicide sought to prevent or to avoid.

But this leap also has specific "Skythian" equivalents, at least in Greek belief. A young Skythian stallion, deceived into covering his disguised dam, committed suicide by leaping into the sea.[33]

Rites: The Masagetai accorded divine honors to Tanais (Max. Tyr. 2.8), though we do not know whether these rites corresponded in any way to the Troizenian hair sacrifices.

Aphrodite plays the same role in the Hippolytos myth and in the Tanais story. Now, there was in Troizen a special temple for Aphrodite Κατασκοπία (Paus. 2.32.3). This may explain psychologically the already mentioned corruption of Anais into an (Aphrodite) Tanais. That corruption was no doubt inspired by the existence of a special (Hippolytos-and-Phaidra linked) temple, for an Aphrodite having a suitable special epithet.

It is, by contrast, somewhat odd that the clearly sexual goddess Anais (= Anahita) should have been linked, in one place at least, with Artemis. Her priests in Erez (in Akilisene)—exploiting the name of a nearby mountain, called Tauros (= bull)—claimed that their temple was the Taurian Artemis' temple, from which (in E. *IT*) Orestes stole the sacred statue of *Artemis*.[34] Yet, quite apart from priestly rapacity and thirst for prestige, the fusing of the two polarly opposite female deities *of the Hippolytos myth* into one (of Anais [Anahita] = Aphrodite "Tanais," with Anahita = Taurian Artemis) is neither mythologically nor psychologically as farfetched as it may seem.

It could, in principle, be argued that, in the admittedly sketchy Tanais story, Ares is no *fully* equivalent substitute for the important Artemis of Euripides' *Hippolytos* and that this called for a partial fusion of Artemis with her Euripidean opponent, Aphrodite. But I do not propose so to argue, for the Aphrodite Anahita (of Erez) = Artemis of the Taurian chain of equivalences was correlated by Anahita's priests (in Erez) *not* with *Tanais, but* with *Orestes* the matricide.

The real point of this linkage is that the Asian "Artemis," like her pre-Hellenic prototype, was not an asexual goddess.[35]

The "Artemis" (the Ταυρική θεὰ) of the priests of Anahita (in Erez)

---

[33] Arist. *H.A.* 9.47f.; Plin. *H.N.* 8.156; Varro *R.R.* 2.7.9; Ael *NA* 4.7. The fact that this tale is objectively rooted in the scarceness of purebred "Kolaxian" horses in Western Skythian lands (G. Devereux, "The Kolaxian Horse of Alkman's *Partheneion*," *Classical Quarterly* 15: 176-84, 1965) does not attenuate the symbolic mythical import of this theme.

[34] Claim recorded by Prokopios, *de bello Goth.* 4.5.

[35] On the sexual aspects of the "original" Artemis, highlighted by W. K. C. Guthrie, see my discussion of the myth of Hera's *alleged* revirgination (*Femme et Mythe*, Paris, 1982). I hold, with Guthrie, that the "original" Artemis was not "virginal" but simply "unmarried," that being the *original* meaning of παρθένος.

was obviously the highly sexual polymastic (or perhaps nipple-less polyscrotal; cf. H. P. Duerr, *Sedna*, Frankfurt am Main, 1984) Asian Artemis of Ephesos, the sacking of whose temple is said to have caused the appearance of androgynous, impotent ’Ενάρεες amongst the Skythian. This makes good sense, for only a fertility and sex goddess could and would punish those who sacrilegiously plundered her temple by a withdrawal of her sexual gifts—by impotency.

These considerations do *not* imply that I believe that there is no lapsus in Strabon (11.14.16) and that there actually existed an Aphrodite Tanais. I simply hold that each lapsus has, as Freud has shown,[36] a discernible cause and that the cause of this lapsus is indirectly revealed by the equating of Anahita in Erez with the Taurian Artemis who, unlike the classical Greek Artemis, was a goddess of fertility.

In short, though the incest theme is a generally human one, and though a tale of this type may well have existed amongst the Massagetai, complete with divine honors for the dead son,[37] there is little doubt that the (abridged) Tanais story was transmitted in a form heavily influenced by the Hippolytos myth. But the elements borrowed from the Hippolytos myth appear in the Tanais story far more explicitly than in the Hippolytos myth: in the hands of a literary botcher they underwent the kind of intensification that differentiates, e.g., an explicit love story from mere pornography or a tale of heroism from one of blood and gore.

Though deplorable as art, these gross explicitations are useful for the analysis of Euripides' far more allusive drama. The transformation of the stepmother into the mother—who, like Hippolytos' mother, was an Amazon (named Lysippe)—proves the validity of my equating Phaidra with Hippolyte and of viewing her love as strictly incestuous. In the same way, my interpretation of Hippolytos' chariot "accident" as disguised suicide is confirmed by Tanais' outright suicide.

What clinches this argument is that I discovered the Tanais story purely by accident, while looking up in Roscher's *Lexicon* another entry—and this at a time when my *entire* text concerning Euripides' drama had just been typed in final form. In other words, my discovery of the Tanais story was a serendipity, pure and simple, which confirmed the key interpretations of an already completed text—the *belated* discovery of this story being thus a second, methodological serendipity, validating the method of interpretation I used.

[36] S. Freud, "The Psychopathology of Everyday Life," *Standard Edition*, vi, 1960.
[37] One can mention, side by side with the Troizenian hair sacrifice for Hippolytos, also the shrine of Oidipous at Kolonos, etc.

Appendix I: Seneca

Though Seneca's *Phaedra* imitates mostly Euripides' (lost) *Veiled Hippolytos*, that author was certainly familiar also with Euripides' surviving *Crowned Hippolytos*. Hence, his *Phaedra* should also provide clues to certain nuances of the *Crowned Hippolytos*, for even a Roman rhetorician's imitation of a Greek model can sometimes clarify a few details of the latter. Two short examples may be cited:

Riding: According to Barrett, verse 1133 (unemended) seems to say that Hippolytos was riding a horse—which is altogether unusual in both epic and tragedy. However, in Sen. *Ph.* 809 the hero straddled a horse, so that verse 1133 (unemended) might hint at his riding horseback, if not then and there, then on some other occasion. Ar. *Thesm.* 153 makes this a near certainty.

Amazonian Traits of Hippolytos: Some moderns incomprehensibly suggested that Hippolytos lacked Amazonian traits. However, Seneca refers nearly every one of Hippolytos' major traits back to his Amazon ancestry. Though it is possible that Hippolytos' Amazon ancestry was made more obvious in the lost *Hippolytos* than in the surviving one, Seneca must have been aware also of the *second* Hippolytos' Amazonian character. After all, Euripides' characterizations always take into account the—hereditary and/or educational—antecedents of his personages. In this respect, the difference between E. *Hipp.* and Sen. *Ph.* is only that between allusive poetry and flatfooted rhetoric. Euripides hints at Hippolytos' Amazon-like traits; Seneca talks this matter into the ground. This exemplifies the essential differences between great poetry and versified rhetoric.

Appendix II: *Phaëthon*

Most students of Euripides' *Phaëthon* seem to have devoted more attention to the speculative reconstruction of the play's plot and to the identification of Phaëthon's bride-to-be than to the elucidation of this play's actual remains. Thus, Reckford[1] compares Phaëthon to Hippolytos and to Ion, constructing a romance about a virginal youth who dreads mature sexuality, though one fragment (772), not necessarily uttered by Phaëthon, mentions only the drawbacks of *unequal* marriages. In this conversation with his mother Klymene, Phaëthon shows no reluctance to marry, nor does he speak like the "chaste" Hippolytos. The only fragment at all reminiscent of the *Hippolytos* is *fr.* 782, which expresses hostility to athletic pursuits.

A far more plausible analysis would be one that links this play with the *Bakchai*. Like Semele's tomb, the treasure room of the palace is smoking continually (781). Smoke comes through the joints of the door and though there is no flame, the room is full of ashes (781ff.). The catastrophe reminds the Choros of the flaming bolts of Zeus' lightning which, of course, smote Semele.

Now, like Semele, Phaëthon, a mortal—though son of the god Helios (the Sun)—is about to contract a divine marriage which, we learn, will make him "the only son-in-law of the Immortals." In my estimate this rules out the hypothesis that he is to marry Aphrodite herself, who is Zeus' daughter in Homer only. Zeus' traditional son-in-law is Menelaos. Neither Hephaistos nor Ares—let alone Tithonos—are so designated. He is the husband of Helen, whose divinity is by no means of the same order as that of Aphrodite.

Another consideration must, however, also be advanced. Already Alkman warned men against *hubris*: "Let no man fly to the sky, nor try to marry Aphrodite the Queen . . . or any daughter of Porkos, etc."[2] Now, Phaëthon did try to "fly to the sky" in a sense: he presumed to drive his father's sun-chariot and crashed.

---

[1] K. J. Reckford, "Phaëthon, Hippolytus and Aphrodite," *Transactions of the American Philological Association* 103: 405–32, 1972.
[2] Alcm. *fr.* 1, verses 17ff.

What is striking is the linking of a man's ascent to the Sky with the daughters of Porkos or with the Muses living with Zeus. This erotic element both separates and links Phaëthon and Hippolytos. The first seems to aspire to a hypergamous marriage with a divine partner, the second refuses a hypergamous (father's wife) affair, but claims a uniquely close connection with the traditionally celibate Artemis.

While these affinities between the two young men are not negligible, they are not substantial enough to justify Reckford's speculations.

INDEX

Abnormality in Greek tragedy, 10–11
Achilles, 94
Achilleus, 15–16, 29, 51, 136
Admetos, 14, 51
Adultery and incestuous desires, 96–114
Aelius Aristedes, 40
Agamemnon, 16, 21, 40, 44, 60, 89
Agave, 16, 54
Aias, 61, 63, 79, 131
Aias Telamonides, 29
Aigeus, 34
Aischylos, 31, 38, 76, 90, 131, 142, 148
Alkmene, 61
Amazons, chastity, 26–28; style of horsemanship, 24–28, 145, 156
Anchises, 105
Andromache, 3, 6, 92, 97, 142, 146
Antigone, 60, 146
Antisthenes, 103
Aphrodite, 30, 45, 51, 78, 149–50, 153–54; contempt for Hippolytos, 62, 79, 86–88, 93–95, 105; hostility of Hippolytos, 28, 30, 115; neutralization of, 6; Phaidra, influence over, 1, 16; sexual rites, 22
Apollo, 39, 105, 138
Apollon, 51, 89, 130, 138
Arachne, 130
Ariadne, 54, 98, 102, 106, 110, 147
Aristophanes, 25, 94
Aristoteles, 76, 146
Arnott, P. D., 82
Artemis, 11, 16–17, 21, 33, 42, 144, 147, 149, 151, 153; Amazons and horsemanship, 27; devotion of Hippolytos to huntress, 20–21, 23–25, 115, 120–23, 125–28, 132, 136, 138–40; merits of Hippolytos, 85–87, 89, 91, 93–95; mother image held by Hippolytos, 43–53, 62–64, 67, 71, 80–81, 122; Phaidra relationship, 53–57
Asklepios, 51, 91

Atalante, 21, 54
Athena, 36, 85
Athene, 21, 45, 51, 89, 130–31, 137, 140
Augustine, St., 35
Autolykos, 89

Bastardy, Hippolytos and utopian and infantile birth theories, 33–43, 145
Bellerophontes, 3, 30–31, 65, 89
Berossos, 150–51
Burkert, W., 22

Caillois, C., 152
Character neurotic, 8–10, 14
Chastity, 3; Amazons, 26–28; devotion of Hippolytos to Artemis, 20–21, 23–24; masculinity of Hippolytos and gender identity, 19–28
Cult of the self, 115–19

Danaides, 90
Deianeira, 8–9, 23, 141
Demophoon, 146
Detienne, M. and J. P. Vernant, 143
Diagoras, 131
Dieterich, A., 79, 128
Diktynna, 53, 94, 128
Diomedes, 130
Dionysos, 14, 30, 36, 97, 102, 106, 138, 147
Dodds, E. R., 1, 72, 84, 120, 148
Dover, Kenneth, 68
Duerr, H. P., 46, 154

Elektra, 3, 14, 16, 59, 144
Empousa, 36
Empson, William, 6
Eteokles, 14, 30
Eurystheus, 61

Familial curse, 95–96
Fantasy, Hippolytos, masculinity and gender identity, 19–32, 68; identifications and appersonations, 13; virginal mother, 40–43
Fehrle, Eugen, 79, 128

Ferenczi, S., 152
Festugière, A. J., 7, 96, 98, 110, 122
Frazer, J. G., 137
Freud, Sigmund, 24, 90, 92, 96, 107-9, 120, 122, 138-39

Glenn, J., 11
Grene, D., 67, 74
Guthrie, W. K. C., 79

Hallucination, 119-22
Harrison, J. E., 101
Hegel, G. W. F., 3
Hekabe, 60, 132-33
Hekate, 44
Hektor, 51, 89, 97
Helene, 14-16, 65, 109, 132
Hephaistos, 39
Hera, 4, 29, 39, 130, 138, 140
Herakles, 19-23, 63, 65, 89-90, 99, 130-31, 141-42, 146
Herodotus, 28, 139
Hestia, 4, 94
Hippolytos, accusations, trial and judgment of, 77-83; and Amazons, 26-28, 145, 156; Aphrodite's hostilities, 28, 30, 62, 79, 86-88, 93, 95, 105, 115; arrogant purity, 93-94, 115-19, 128; bastardy affecting utopian and infantile birth theories, 33-43, 145; character of, 85-86; condemnation by Theseus, 60-77, 86-88; devotion to Artemis, 20-21, 23-25, 115, 120-23, 125-28, 132, 136, 138-40; enjoying misfortune of others, 95; familial curse, 95-96; father and son male models, 20, 36, 64-76, 115-16, 146; god-fighter, 130-34; homosexuality, 67-68, 74-75; horsemanship and gender identity, 19-28, 53, 156; insight lacking, 86; irascibility, 95; male virginity, 90-93; masculinity, 19-32, 68, derided by father, 64-76; merits of, 86-89, 96-114; narcissism, 1, 3-10, 14, 17, 59-77, 86-88, 111-14, 124-29, 144; needs and fantasies, 144-50; neurosis, 5, 8, 86; orphism, 126-29; personal relations, 59-64, 87, 115-16, 130-33, 136, 138-40; Phaidra's love, 96-114, 116, 131-34, 136-40; piety, 94-95, 122; primal scene, 32-33; repression of sexual drive and narcissistic character, 1, 3-10, 14, 15; reproach of forebears, 14; resenting Theseus for his bastardy, 33-43, 145; schizoid split, 124-29; self-praise, 115-19; sexual asceticism, 86, 89-90, 122, 144; sexual identity and Phaidra, 28-32, 53, 60-61, 63, 71, 74; suicidalness, 130; touch phobia, 123; utopian and infantile birth theories, 33-43; vegetarianism, 126-27; virginal mother image of Artemis, 40-53, 62, 64, 67, 71, 80-81, 83, 122
Homeros, 35, 97
Homosexuality, 67-68, 74-75
Horsemanship, Hippolytos and gender identity, 19-28, 53, 156
Hunting, devotion of Hippolytos to Artemis, 20-21, 23-24
Hyginus, 151-52
Hyllos, 63, 99, 146

Idas, 130, 138
Impotency, Hippolytos and Amazons, 26-28
Incestuous desires, 96-114, 156, and adultery, 96-114
Interaction, awareness of opinion of others, 13; Hippolytos and personal relations, 59-64
Iolaos, 19, 63, 99, 146
Iole, 63, 99
Ion, 14-15, 34
Iphigeneia, 14-16, 23, 44
Ischys, 130

Kadmos, 16, 60
Kaineus, 151
Kallisto, 19, 21
Kamerbeek, J. C., 30
Kassandra, 89, 138
Klymene, 157
Klytaimestra, 15-16, 89
Knox, B. M. W., 11
Kreon, 60
Kreusa, 39, 105, 138
Kritias, 131
Kypris, 133
Kyrene, 21, 23, 34

Lesky, A., 72, 120
Linforth, I. M., 78-79, 126-28

Index

Lloyd-Jones, H., 136
Lohmeyer, E., 120, 122
Longo (Longus), 56
Love and sex, destructive love, 16; valuation of, 3, 5–6
Lucian, 22, 36, 52
Lykaon, 130
Lykourgos, 93, 115, 130
Lysippe, 150–51

Marpessa, 105, 138
Marsyas, 130
Masculinity, Hippolytos and gender identity, 19–32, 68; Theseus deriding Hippolytos' characteristics, 64–76
Mead, George Herbert, 13
Megara, 63, 99
Meleagros, 19, 23
Menelaos, 92
Méridier, L., 30, 45, 66, 77, 106, 125, 129, 136, 150
Mother image, Hippolytos and Artemis, 40–53, 62, 64, 67, 71, 80–81, 83, 122
Mousaios, 127
Murray, Gilbert, 59, 69
Myrtilla, 22

Narcissism, 1, 3–10, 14, 17; personal relations of Hippolytos, 59–77, 86–88, 111–14, 124–29, 144; repression of sexual drive, 1, 3–10, 14, 15
Neurotic sex-phobia, 5, 8, 86
Nireus, 97

Odysseus, 21, 24, 52, 97, 142
Oedipal fixation and conflicts, 63, 72–73, 76, 122; son-father rivalries, 42–43
Oidipous, 60, 152
Okeanos, 151
Orestes, 3, 21–22, 59, 143, 153
Orpheus, 91, 127
Ovidius, 100, 102, 152

Parthenopaios, 151
Pasiphaë, 98–99, 127, 130
Peleus, 3
Pentheus, 14, 16, 60, 130
Perikles, 62
Phaidra, 11, 41–42, 53; Artemis relationship, 53–57; contempt for Hippolytos, 61–74; day-dreaming of Hippolytos, 25; destructive love, 17; familial curse, 95–96; fantasies, 12; fantasmic projection, 13; god-fighter, 131–32; influence of Aphrodite, 1, 16; love for Hippolytos, 96–114, 116, 131–34, 136–40; sexual identity of Hippolytos, 28–32, 53, 60–61, 63–66, 71, 74; suicide and accusation of rape, 65; tragedy, character, action, fantasy, 141–54
Philoketes, 60
Phoinix, 63
Piety, 94–95, 122
Pindaros, 40, 136
Pittheus, 20, 39, 74, 89, 119
Platon, 51, 75, 76, 79, 108, 119
Plautus, 82
Plutarchos, 65, 93, 115
Poe, Edgar Allen, 148
Polymestor, 60
Polyneikes, 14
Poseidon, 87, 98, 116, 151
Prokris, 21, 54
Prometheus, 130
Purity, Hippolytos and arrogant purity, 93–94, 115–19, 128
Pylades, 59
Pythia, 115

Racine, 146
Rankin, A. V., 11
Reckford, K. J., 157–58
Russell, Bertrand, 86

Salmoneus, 116, 130
Sarpedon, 51
Schmid, W., 10, 15, 110
Segal, C. P., 14, 20, 25, 52, 68, 71–72
Self-discipline, sexual abstinence, 86, 89–90
Self-praise, 115–19
Seneca, 65, 146, 152; *Phaedra* compared, 156
Sex, Hippolytos, masculinity and gender identity, 19–28; love and sex, 3, 5–6, 16; neurotic sex-phobia, 5, 8, 86; primal scene and child, 32–33; repression of sex drive, narcissist characteristic, 1, 3–10, 14–15; sexual aberations, 96–114; sexual asceticism, 86, 89–90, 122, 144; sexual purity, 17;

sexual rites, 22; utopian and infantile birth theories, 33–43
Sokrates, 81, 93, 108, 115
Sophokles, 61, 63, 67, 69–70, 76, 131, 141, 146, 152
Suetonius, 35

Tanais myth compared, 150–54
Tantalos, 130
Taygete, 21
Teiresias, 16
Telemon, 40, 74
Teukros, 40, 63, 74, 79
Thamyris, 130
Theognis, 35
Theophrastos, 38
Theseus, 85–88, 93–95; condemnation of Hippolytos, 60–77, 86–88; father-son male models, 20, 31, 64–76, 115–16, 146; Hippolytos' resentment of his bastardy, 33–43; interaction with Hippolytos, 59–64; tragedy, character, action, fantasy, 141–54; trial and judgment of Hippolytos, 77–83
Thespios, 89–90
Thetis, 89, 151
Tragedy, character, action, fantasy, 141–54; structure of Euripidean tragedy, 134–36
Transference, repressed childhood experiences, 13
Troizenian Hair Sacrifice, 136–40, 153
Trophonios, 89

Vernant, J. P. and M. Detienne, 143
Vespasian, 35

Wilamowitz-Moellendorff, T.v., 141
Wilamowitz-Moellendorff, U.v., 70
Winnicott, D. W., 87
Winnington-Ingram, R. P., 2

Xenophon, 28, 43
Xuthos, 34, 39

Zürcher, W., 141, 143

Southern Methodist Univ.
PA 3973.H7D48 1985   br
The character of the Euripidean Hippolyt

3 2177 00975 4548